# TWENTIETH CENTURY VIEWS

The aim of this series is to present the best in contemporary critical opinion on major authors, providing a twentieth century perspective on their changing status in an era of profound revaluation.

Maynard Mack, *Series Editor*
Yale University

# THE BRONTËS

# THE BRONTËS

## A COLLECTION OF CRITICAL ESSAYS

Edited by

*Ian Gregor*

Prentice-Hall, Inc.  *Englewood Cliffs, N. J.*

A SPECTRUM BOOK

# Contents

# THE BRONTËS

# Introduction

## by Ian Gregor

Criticism of the Brontës is voluminous and (not surprisingly) uneven in quality. To read it at length is to become aware that two basic questions recur again and again, in a variety of ways and under a number of guises. The first question is concerned with the relationship of the artist to his material; the second with the latitude of interpretation any particular work can stand. In introducing briefly a number of essays on the Brontës it seems useful to isolate these questions and look at them in turn.

At the heart of the question about the highly distinctive relationship of the Brontës to their work is the status of the imagination present in their novels. At times self-indulgent and privately enclosed, at other times finely disciplined and impersonal, the imagination revealed by *Jane Eyre* and *Wuthering Heights* has attracted commentary as much as it has eluded definition. These novels cast an interesting light on Eliot's famous dictum that "the more perfect the artist, the more completely separate in him will be the man who suffers and the mind which creates." Anyone trying to account for the power of Charlotte Brontë's fiction, particularly *Jane Eyre,* must feel uneasy about the truth of that dictum. It is not simply that we feel the presence of biographical detail in the fiction, but rather that, in the creation of her central characters, there is, in Matthew Arnold's phrase, "the dialogue of the mind with itself," which makes us feel that the fictional world is tensely defining itself in the face of autobiographical pressures that its creation has released. And so it is not surprising that when we come to talk about such fiction, we find our commentary reaching its sharpest definition as we move towards pondering "the character of Jane Eyre," or "the character of Lucy Snowe," particularly when those characters are seen as existing in a series of subtle shifting relationships to their creator. "Where does the author stand in relation to . . . ?" is the question, above all others, that seems to provide the drift of the final paragraphs of criticism on *Jane Eyre* and *Villette*. It is a question prompted not by biographical speculation, but by trying to formulate inclusive accounts of the novels. It is part of their structure, it is in the texture of the prose, it determines the distinctive idiom in which they speak to us.

This circumstance has given a peculiar stamp to the criticism that Charlotte Brontë's novels have received. Broadly speaking, we find little disagreement about interpretation, but the assessment of the interpretation has led to strikingly different estimates. And one of the principal reasons for this is the way in which we are involved with a particular temperament—a temperament which we feel either as majestically controlled or incoherently intense.[1] While it must be remembered that this is a temperament that is there for us only because it has been created by the fiction—it is not a simple biographical projection—nevertheless, it is a kind of creation which elicits markedly different responses on the part of the reader. The importance of analysis is not minimized by saying that, in the case of Charlotte Brontë, we have to acknowledge "taste" as a very special influence.

When we turn to Emily Brontë the position is different. Here indeed Eliot's dictum seems irresistibly right. It is not merely that we have no Mrs. Gaskell to give us Emily's life as she gave us Charlotte's; rather the only life of Emily's that now seems to matter is in the novel *Wuthering Heights*. That would certainly seem to be part of what critics have meant by describing the anonymity of the novel, its relationship to the world of the ballads. Here we do not find the question, "How does the author stand in relation to . . . ?" forming, however remotely, in our minds. We would find extreme difficulty in completing such a phrase. Relation to what? There seems no single focal point in *Wuthering Heights*, certainly no focal point that can be expressed in terms of "character." Constantly, critics have talked of "the world" of *Wuthering Heights*, and the multifariousness of that term is an index to the reason why the novel has been open to an astonishing variety of interpretations.

Behind the critical attention that has been given to *Jane Eyre* and *Wuthering Heights* would seem to lie two very different emphases— emphases intimately connected with the impression each novel gives of its relationship to the author. With *Jane Eyre*, there is little disagreement about interpretation; there is extreme diversity of view about the nature of its success. With *Wuthering Heights*, there is little disagreement about its success; there is extreme diversity of view about its interpretation. From this point of view criticism can become as illuminating in its scope as in its detail, reminding us that in *Wuthering Heights* and *Jane Eyre* we are dealing with novels strikingly different in their structure and in their effects, however much the circumstances of familial history may have brought them together.

---

[1] Or politically subversive. "We do not hesitate to say that the tone of mind and thought which has overthrown authority and violated every code human and divine abroad, and fostered Chartism and rebellion at home, is the same which has also written *Jane Eyre*." *The Quarterly Review*, CLXVII (1848), 174.

In each case, the difference can to some extent be described by seeing a different relationship between "the person who suffered" and "the mind which created." There was, we feel, in the case of Charlotte Brontë, a minimum of dislocation between the pressures of her existence as a governess, an elder sister, or an Englishwoman from the remote north of England encountering the cosmopolitan world of Brussels, and the pressures of shaping that existence into art. Emily's life, we feel, had been transmuted in the labyrinthine ways of her response to literature and in the long inhabiting of the world of Gondal, so that when finally she came to write her single novel, it came as something so distilled from her common experience that her sister was awestruck by it and its first reviewers could find in this novel by the daughter of the parsonage something "too abominably pagan to be palatable even to the most vitiated class of English readers." [2]

From its initial adverse reception to its present acceptance as a classic, *Wuthering Heights* has provided the center of Brontë criticism. But it is a center that has been seen in a multitude of ways. In the development of literary criticism on both sides of the Atlantic during the last few decades, *Wuthering Heights* has been considered so frequently that to read through the various critiques is to have the sense of a continuing debate, though at times, admittedly, the debate has become needlessly repetitive. Time has now afforded a perspective on twentieth-century views of the novel, and we can see that key essays in initiating, and to some extent characterizing, the nature of the debate were, in England, David Cecil's essay in *Early Victorian Novelists* (1934), and in America, Richard Chase's centennial essay published in *The Kenyon Review* (1947).[3] It is obviously difficult to point to any single essay as a source for certain ideas. However, it could be said with some confidence that Cecil's essay, in emphasizing the dialectical structure of the novel between the values of "The Grange" and those of "The Heights," and Chase's, in relating the novel to the world of myth rather than to the world of social circumstance, established something like a latitude and longitude from which subsequent critics have constantly taken their bearings, if only to modify or in some cases to reject them.

To read through the criticism that the novel has received is an instructive exercise in the difficulties that attend upon novel criticism in general. We have those critics who feel that the heart of the novel lies in the relationship between Cathy and Heathcliff and consequently are driven on to give some account of what that relationship *means,* when looked at in more conceptual terms than the novelist

[2] *The Quarterly Review,* CLXVII (1848), 175.
[3] Richard Chase's essay is reprinted in the present volume, pp. 19–33.

employs. And out of this arises the celebrated concern with "the metaphysic" of the novel, a dimension that, these critics would argue, seems encouraged by Emily Brontë herself, both structurally, in her calculated contrasts between the Heights and the Grange, and the first generation and the second, and psychologically, in the famous "definitions" offered by Cathy to Nelly of her love for Edgar Linton and her love for Heathcliff.

Reactions against this emphasis on what might loosely be called "the metaphysical dimension" would seem to have taken two sharply distinctive forms. One has been to emphasize the local rootedness and sociological density of the novel—northern England in the early nineteenth century, the clash between the new kind of landlord and dying eighteenth-century tenantry. This note is caught sharply in Arnold Kettle's remark that we have to remember that "Heathcliff was born not in the pages of Byron, but in a Liverpool slum." [4] The other reaction to a metaphysical reading of the novel casts a cold eye on the product of the Liverpool slums and sees in Heathcliff not some inscrutable energy that we can hardly dare to name, but—in adverse accounts—a yielding of Emily Brontë to her Gothic fantasies, or—in favorable accounts—a careful placing and gradual taming of that ferocity as it is driven to come to terms with the changing social norms of the generation represented by Catherine and Hareton.

Behind these two accounts lies a common wish to give emphasis to the book's extraordinary detail [5] and circumstantial solidity, and to see in its second part a dramatic counterpoint that effectively comments upon, if it does not reverse, the drift of the first part, where a "romantic" or "metaphysical" reading receives more sanction. The necessity of bringing the two parts intimately together and seeing the work as a whole would seem to be encouraged by the sophistication of its structure, revealed in its complex use of narrators and its skilled control of time-shifts. Granted that the presence of these elements need not argue a Jamesian self-awareness, they do encourage accounts of the novel that seek to bring its heterogeneous parts into a calculated unity. But just here difficulties arise. The more resolutely an inclusive account is pursued, the less convincing it seems to become. This is not because criticism stiffens into a thesis—though obviously this is a danger with this as with any other novel—but rather because the story has genuinely recalcitrant elements of undeniable power which it seems difficult to bring into focus. In this respect at least, criticism of *Wuthering Heights* shares some of the features of criticism of *Hamlet*.

[4] *Introduction to the English Novel* (London: Hutchinson, 1951), I:130.
[5] The kind of detail that C. P. Sanger's essay reveals; see pp. 7–18 of this volume.

Some of these difficulties are illustrated by the most recent extended criticism of the novel in an essay by Mrs. Q. D. Leavis, subtitled "A Fresh Approach to Wuthering Heights." [6] She begins her account of it by explicitly recognising its heterogeneous nature: "it certainly isn't a seamless 'work of art' and candour obliges us to admit ultimately that some things in the novel are incompatible with the rest, so much so that one seems at times to find oneself in really different novels." This admission, together with the firm conviction that the novel is a masterpiece, seems an admirable beginning for a fresh essay on *Wuthering Heights*. And indeed, in the account that follows, Mrs. Leavis has some new and striking things to say. But they remain matters of detail and the new perspective promised by the opening pages never really emerges. She is so anxious to ensure that we read *Wuthering Heights* as "a fully human novel," and to describe that quality in terms that belittle examinations of its thematic antecedents ("variants of the demon-lover motif") or its internal structuring ("lock and key imagery"), that the genuinely mysterious elements are virtually removed and Nelly Dean's commentary becomes our own.

However seriously we take Nelly and the general function she is required to perform in the novel, her limitations are clear, and it is difficult to see how we can think of the intensities of Cathy's speeches to her about Heathcliff in Chapter IX ("If all else perished and *he* remained . . .") as "not very impressive rhetoric" without lessening considerably the impact the novel is concerned to make. I quote Mrs. Leavis' remarks partly because they come from the most recent comprehensive account of *Wuthering Heights*, but chiefly because they provide an instance of someone setting face against many of "the twentieth-century views" of the novel and, in trying to redress the balance, producing a critical account that seems too normative and too assured in its social and psychological convictions to catch the disturbing force of this strange masterpiece. That force seems to lie in the intensity of its conception rather than in the structuring of its constituent parts. Trying to convey this in critical terms certainly seems to involve us in considering the novel itself as a form that is constantly in process rather than stasis. And yet here we have of course an abiding difficulty attendant upon novel criticism in general. The emphasis of criticism, almost inevitably we might say, is static—whether it analyzes dialogue, scene, or even the interplay of character —whereas a good deal of the power of *Wuthering Heights* lies in that unmistakable mood that links event to event and person to person so that implausibility and disparateness of intention become

[6] *Lectures in America* (London: Chatto & Windus, 1969), pp. 85–152.

subsumed within its atmosphere. Definition within brief compass is difficult, but I think we can find in Wordsworth some analogy with this mood, particularly in the *Lucy* poems, where, no matter how subtle and flexible our analysis, their generally agreed impressiveness eludes our critical categories. They are, we feel, the work of a mind of astonishing imaginative transparency; the complete obverse of the well-wrought urn. And so for all its structural complexity is *Wuthering Heights.*

It goes without saying that there have been very distinguished accounts of the novel and indeed of Brontë criticism in general. But to read that criticism at length, particularly insofar as it affects *Wuthering Heights,* is to be made sharply aware that the kind of imagination the Brontës reveal defines the boundaries of good criticism with uncommon clarity. Yet if warning bells sound out loud and clear, the incitements are no less plain—and as I hope the pages that follow will show—the rewards also.

# The Structure of
# *Wuthering Heights*

## *by C. P. Sanger*

By common consent *Wuthering Heights* is a remarkable book. I do not propose to discuss its literary merits, but to confine myself to the humbler task of investigating its structure, which presents certain peculiarities. Whether this is worth doing I do not know, but I found that it added to my interest in the book and made the tale much more vivid for me.

The main theme is how a sort of human cuckoo, called Heathcliff, sets out with success to acquire all the property of two families, the Earnshaws and the Lintons. The tale is a fairly complicated one, and the incidents extend over a period of more than thirty years. Stated as baldly and shortly as I can, the plot is as follows: Mr. and Mrs. Earnshaw live at Wuthering Heights, a farmhouse on a Yorkshire moor. They have two children, a son called Hindley and a daughter Cathcrinc. Onc day Mr. Earnshaw, who has been to Liverpool on business, brings home a waif he has picked up there. This waif, Heathcliff, is brought up at Wuthering Heights. Not long after, Mrs. Earnshaw dies. Heathcliff is Mr. Earnshaw's favourite; he is also great friends with Catherine, but Hindley, who is older, bullies him. At last, Hindley is sent off to college. When Mr. Earnshaw dies, Hindley returns for the funeral, bringing with him a young wife. He takes possession, ill-treats Heathcliff, thrusts him into the position of a mere servant, and allows him no more education. But Catherine and Heathcliff have remained great friends, and one Sunday they go for a walk, and out of curiosity look at Thrushcross Grange, a gentleman's house in a park four miles off where Mr. and Mrs. Linton live. Catherine and Heathcliff peep in through the drawing-room window and see the two Linton children— Edgar and Isabella. The Lintons, hearing Heathcliff and Catherine and taking them for robbers, let the bulldog loose on them; the dog seizes Catherine and hurts her ankle badly. She is taken in and looked

"The Structure of *Wuthering Heights*," by C. P Sanger. From *Hogarth Essays*, XIX (1926), 193–208. Reprinted by permission of Miss Daphne Sanger and The Hogarth Press, Ltd.

after at Thrushcross Grange for five weeks, and returns to Wuthering
Heights elegantly dressed. Heathcliff, who is very dirty and untidy, is
ashamed. The next day the two Lintons come to dinner; Heathcliff
behaves ill and is punished by Hindley. The next year Hindley's wife
gives birth to a son—Hareton. She, however, is consumptive and does
not survive long. In despair at her death Hindley takes to drink. When
Catherine is fifteen Edgar Linton proposes to her. She accepts him,
feeling all the time that she is doing wrong because she loves Heathcliff. She tells Hareton's nurse, Ellen Dean, about it; Heathcliff over-
hears part of the conversation, runs off and vanishes. Catherine is
distracted by this, gets fever, and when convalescent goes to stay at
Thrushcross Grange. Her host and hostess, Mr. and Mrs. Linton, both
catch the fever and die. This may be considered the end of the first
stage of the story. The elder generation are all dead. The next generation are all alive—Hindley and Catherine at Wuthering Heights,
Edgar and Isabella at Thrushcross Grange. Hindley's wife is dead, but
his son Hareton—the only representative of the third generation—
is alive. Heathcliff has disappeared. His passion for Catherine and his
revenge is the main theme of the root of the story.

Catherine in due course marries Edgar and goes to live at Thrushcross Grange. After six months of happiness, Heathcliff, who has mean-
while mysteriously got some education and money, reappears. He sets
himself to ruin Hindley, who gambles and drinks. He also finds that
Isabella is in love with him, and decides to marry her to get her money.
One day, after a violent scene between Heathcliff and Edgar, Catherine
goes on hunger strike and gets brain fever. Isabella elopes with Heathcliff, who treats her abominably, and finally brings her back to Wuthering Heights. One Sunday while Edgar is at church, Heathcliff comes to
see Catherine. There is a passionate scene. That night Catherine gives
birth to a daughter and dies. On the night after the funeral, Hindley
tries to kill Heathcliff but is nearly killed by him. Isabella escapes from
Wuthering Heights and goes to the South of England, where she
gives birth to a sickly child named Linton Heathcliff. Soon after this
Hindley dies of drink, and Heathcliff is left in possession of Wuthering Heights with Hareton, whom, out of revenge for the way he was
treated as a boy, he brings up as a mere brute. At this stage there is a
long gap in the story. Edgar's daughter, who is also called Catherine,
lives with him at Thrushcross Grange; Isabella's son, Linton, lives in
the South of England with her. Catherine is kept in ignorance of both
her cousins Linton and Hareton.

Edgar hears that Isabella is dying and goes to see her. Catherine in
his absence goes to Penistone Crags, and in doing so has to pass Wuthering Heights, where she sees Hareton. On Isabella's death, Edgar comes
home with Linton, but Heathcliff claims him, and he is taken to

Wuthering Heights. Catherine is not allowed by Edgar, her father, to go there. One day, after some time, Catherine on a walk meets Heathcliff and Hareton and goes to Wuthering Heights, where she sees her cousin, Linton. Catherine and Linton correspond secretly. The correspondence is detected and stopped. Catherine's father, Edgar, becomes ill. Heathcliff meets Catherine and tells her that Linton is seriously ill. She goes to see him, and many times visits him secretly. One day, just before her father dies, she is kidnapped by Heathcliff and forced to marry Linton. Soon after Linton dies, having made a will leaving all his personal property to his father, Heathcliff. Heathcliff takes possession of Thrushcross Grange, and lets it to Mr. Lockwood, who tells the story. But Heathcliff dies soon after, and Hareton and Catherine marry.

How is a long story like this to be told? How is the reader's interest to be excited? How is the tale to be kept together? How are we to be made to feel the lapse of time without being pestered by dates? How far did the authoress accurately visualize the ages of the characters in the different incidents, the topography, and so on? And how did Heathcliff succeed in getting the property? These are the questions I attempt to answer.

The most obvious thing about the structure of the story which deals with three generations is the symmetry of the pedigree. Mr. and Mrs. Earnshaw at Wuthering Heights and Mr. and Mrs. Linton at Thrushcross Grange each have one son and one daughter. Mr. Linton's son marries Mr. Earnshaw's daughter, and their only child Catherine marries successively her two cousins—Mr. Linton's grandson and Mr. Earnshaw's grandson. See the pedigree [below].

In actual life I have never come across a pedigree of such absolute symmetry. I shall have to refer to this pedigree again later. It is a remarkable piece of symmetry in a tempestuous book.

The method adopted to arouse the reader's interest and to give vividness and reality to the tale is one which has been used with great success by Joseph Conrad. But it requires great skill.

After Edgar Linton's death, Mr. Lockwood, the narrator, takes Thrushcross Grange for a year. He goes to call on his landlord, Heathcliff, at Wuthering Heights, and is puzzled to find there a *farouche* young woman and an awkward boor. At first he supposes Catherine to be Heathcliff's wife; when told she is his daughter-in-law, he then supposes that Hareton is Heathcliff's son, and has again to be corrected. He, and the reader, are naturally puzzled at this strange trio. Lockwood calls again, and is forced to spend the night because of a heavy fall of snow. In his room he finds some books with the name Catherine Earnshaw and Catherine Linton, and a sort of diary of Catherine's in a childish hand which gives a vivid picture of the situation just after

| MR. EARNSHAW | m. | MRS. EARNSHAW | | MR. LINTON | m. | MRS. LINTON |
|---|---|---|---|---|---|---|
| d. Oct. 1777. | | d. Spring 1773. | | d. Autumn 1780. | | d. Autumn 1780. |

| HINDLEY | m. | Frances | CATHERINE | m. | EDGAR | Heathcliff | m. | ISABELLA |
|---|---|---|---|---|---|---|---|---|
| b. Summer 1757. | 1777. | b. d. late 1778 | b. Summer 1765. | April 1783. | b. 1762. d. Sept. 1801. | b. 1764. d. May 1802. | Jan. 1784. | b. late 1765. d. June 1797. |
| d. Sept. 1784. | | | d. Mar. 20, 1784. | | | | | |

| HARETON | m. Jan. 1, 1803. | CATHERINE | m. Aug. 1801. | LINTON |
|---|---|---|---|---|
| b. June 1778. | | b. Mar. 20, 1784. | | b. Sept. 1784. d. Oct. 1801. |

her father's death. Mr. Lockwood has a nightmare in which Catherine's spirit comes to the window, and he also witnesses a strange scene of Heathcliff imploring Catherine's spirit. Our interest cannot fail now to be excited. What is this strange man and this strange ménage? Who was this Catherine who died years before? What were her relations with Heathcliff? Naturally, Lockwood is much intrigued. On his way back next day he catchest a chill and becomes ill. To pass the time he asks Ellen Dean, the housekeeper at Thrushcross Grange, what she knows about the family at Wuthering Heights. She, who was first Hareton's nurse and then the younger Catherine's, tells him the story of the past thirty years in considerable detail. So that during the major part of the book Mr. Lockwood is telling us what Ellen Dean told him, but sometimes, also, what Ellen Dean told him that someone else—for instance, Isabella—had told her. Only a small part, perhaps one-tenth of the book, consists of direct narrative by Lockwood from his own knowledge. But such a scheme may be confusing, and it is easy to muddle the time. Did Emily Brontë realize and let us know the dates when each event happened? She did, but not by giving them directly. Look again at the pedigree. The dates there have all been derived from the book, yet only one is directly stated. What first brought me to study the book more closely was when I noticed that the first word in the book was a date—1801. I thought this must have some significance. Similarly, the first word of Chapter XXXII is 1802. Apart from this, only one other date is given directly. In the last sentence of Chapter VII, Ellen Dean says, "I will be content to pass on to the next summer —the summer of 1778, that is, nearly twenty-three years ago." This gives no further information, as 1801 is twenty-three years after 1778, but in the first sentence of the next chapter she tells us that Hareton was born in June. This is how I get June 1778 for Hareton's birth in the pedigree. But what about the rest of the dates, not only those in the pedigree but of all the incidents in the story? There are a considerable number (perhaps nearly a hundred) indications of various kinds to help us—intervals of time, ages of characters, the months, the harvest moon, the last grouse, and so forth, and we learn, incidentally, that the younger Catherine's birthday was on 20th March. Sometimes, too, we know the day of the week—thus Ellen Dean will remember something which happened on a Sunday, or on a Christmas Eve. Taking all these indications, it is, I think, possible to ascertain the year, and, in most cases, the month of the year in which every event takes place—also the ages of the various characters, except, naturally, there is a slight doubt as to Heathcliff, because no one knows his exact age when he was found by Mr. Earnshaw. But one has to go warily and consider all the indications together, for there is a curious subtlety that sometimes the characters are described as *looking* some ages which are not exact. Thus Lockwood when he first describes them says that Healthcliff was about forty and Catherine did not look seventeen. In fact, Catherine was seventeen and three-quarters and Heathcliff cannot have been more than thirty-eight. It would be too tedious to state the process by which I have discovered each date. . . . But I will give one or two illustrations. We already know that Hareton was born in June 1778; we are told that he was nearly five when Catherine Earnshaw married Edgar Linton, so that the marriage was before June 1783. But Heathcliff returned in September after they had been happily married for six months. Thus the marriage was in April 1783. We are told that the scene that led to Catherine's death was a Sunday in the March after Heathcliff's return, and that her daughter, Catherine, was born about midnight, and the mother died two hours later. Later on we learn that Catherine's birthday was the 20th (and that this was also treated as the day of her mother's death). Hence Catherine died at 2 A.M. on Monday, 20th March 1784.

I will give only one other instance. Lockwood begins his account in 1801; it is snowy weather, which might be in January or February or in November or December. But he returns in 1802 before his year's tenancy is out. Hence the story begins at the end of 1801. A Michaelmas tenancy begins on the 10th October—not on 29th September—because when the calendar was reformed eleven days were left out. Therefore, the story begins after 10th October 1801. Now after Lockwood has been ill three weeks Heathcliff sends him some grouse, the last of the season. Since the Game Act, 1831, grouse may not be shot after 10th December, so we may take this as about the date for the last grouse. Thus the story begins about the middle of November, and this fits pretty well with the later indications. That is sufficient to illustrate the process. Sometimes it is only by fitting together several indications, each rather vague, that one can find the month. There is, however, one curious fact. We can ascertain Hindley's age. Now Ellen Dean was of the same age. She was his foster sister, and the doctor also refers to her as being of the same age as Hindley. Yet she makes two mistakes about her own age. Middle-aged people do, of course, make mistakes about their age, and these slips may have been intentional on the part of Emily Brontë, but, if so, it seems to me a little over-subtle.

The topography is equally precise. On going from Thrushcross Grange to the village of Gimmerton a highway branches off to the moor on the left. There is a stone pillar there. Thrushcross Grange lies to the south-west, Gimmerton to the east, and Wuthering Heights to the north. The distance from Thrushcross Grange to Wuthering Heights is four miles, and Penistone Crags lie a mile and a half farther on. It was half an hour from Gimmerton to Thrushcross Grange.

The botany is sure to be correct. Emily Brontë loved the country. I was a little surprised to find an ash tree in bud as early as 20th March, but then I realized that it was not on the moor but in the park at Thrushcross Grange, which lay low and was no doubt sheltered.

I now come to the final problem. Heathcliff schemed to get all the property of both the Earnshaws and the Lintons. How did he do it? Emily Brontë clearly had a considerable knowledge of the law. We know the source of George Eliot's use of a base fee for the plot of Felix Holt. We do not know the source of Jane Austen's unerring grasp of the law of real property; but she lived among people who had settled estates and could easily have obtained it. But how Emily Brontë acquired her knowledge I cannot guess. There is also this difficulty. *Wuthering Heigths* was written in the eighteen-forties. It was published in 1847. But the period of the tale is from 1771 to 1803. The Inheritance Act of 1834, the Wills Act of 1837, and, I think, the Game Act of 1831, had changed the law. Did Emily Brontë apply the law at the time she wrote or that at the period of the tale? In one case, as we shall see, she used the earlier law.

Novelists sometimes make their plots depend on the law and use legal terms. But they frequently make mistakes and sometimes are absurd as Trollope is in *Orley Farm*. What is remarkable about *Wuthering Heights* is that the ten or twelve legal references are, I think, sufficient to enable us to ascertain the various legal processes by which Heathcliff obtained the property. It is not a simple matter. There was a fundamental difference between the law of land (real property) and that of money and goods (personal property).

Let us begin with Wuthering Heights. The Earnshaws were farmers and not likely to have their estate settled. The property had been in their family since 1500. We may take it then that Mr. Earnshaw was owner in fee-simple, that is in effect absolute owner, of Wuthering Heights, and was not likely to have possessed any investments. It is

more likely that there was a mortgage on the house and farm. On
Mr. Earnshaw's death the land descended to Hindley as his heir-at-law.
There is no mention of a will. The personal property, which, probably,
was only the farming stock and the furniture, would go equally to his
children, Hindley and Catherine, subject to the payment of his debts
out of it. On Catherine's marriage Edgar would have become entitled
to her personal property. Now Hindley drinks and gambles away all
he has, and at his death the property is mortgaged up to the hilt.
Heathcliff we find is the mortgagee. The personal property would also
be liable to the debts. So that Heathcliff is mortgagee in possession and,
for practical purposes, owner of all the Earnshaw property except any
personalty that had gone to Catherine. This is all fairly simple; but
it is more difficult when we come to the Linton property. They were
landed gentry; they had a park, they had tenants. Mr. Linton, and
Edgar after him, was a magistrate. Such people, generally, had a settlement of their land, and we find, in fact, that Mr. Linton had settled it
by his will. To understand what happens it is necessary to go into the
intricacies of real property law and to look at the pedigree.

I must explain very shortly the law of entails. What is called an
estate tail is an estate which descends according to the following rules:
(1) Males are preferred to females; (2) males take in order according
to seniority of birth, but females take equally; (3) descendants represent
their ancestor. In case of a conflict between them, rule (3) prevails. A
tenant in tail of full age in possession could by means of a fictitious
action (for which a deed was substituted by the Fines and Recoveries
Act, 1833) bar the entail and obtain the fee-simple, which practically
amounts to absolute ownership. By his will a testator could settle his
land on living persons for life, but could not give life estates to the
children of such persons who were not alive at the testator's death.
Consequently, if he wanted to tie up his estate as long as possible, he
gave life estates to such of his descendants as were living at his death,
followed by estates tail to their children.

Now the settlement made by Mr. Linton's will must have been as
follows: The estate was devised to Edgar, his only son, for life, then to
Edgar's sons in tail; Edgar's daughters were passed over in favour of
Mr. Linton's daughter, Isabella, who, presumably, had a life interest
with remainder to her sons in tail. This is the usual form. Thus on
Edgar Linton's death, Linton Heathcliff became tenant in tail in
possession during the few weeks he survived his uncle. As a minor he
could not bar the entail. It is most improbable that he had an estate
in fee-simple; that would have been too unusual. Isabella might have
had an estate tail instead of a life interest. This is most improbable,
but if she did, her son, Linton Heathcliff, would have become tenant
in tail by descent, so the result is the same. Heathcliff claims the

property—by what right? Ellen Dean says that he claimed and kept the Thrushcross Grange estate in his wife's right and in his son's also. She adds: "I suppose, legally at any rate, Catherine, destitute of cash and friends, cannot disturb his possession." She is quite right in her suspicions. Even if Isabella had had an estate tail, or even an estate in fee-simple, Heathcliff would not have had any right as husband to an estate for life—the estate known as an estate by courtesy—because Isabella was never in possession. And even if, which to my mind is not possible, Linton Heathcliff had had an estate in fee-simple, his father would not have been his heir before the Inheritance Act, 1833, because it was considered unnatural that an inheritance should ascend directly; and, as Ellen Dean knows and states, Linton Heathcliff as a minor could not dispose of his land by will. There is no difficulty as to the personal property. Whatever Isabella had Heathcliff got by marrying her. There was no Married Women's Property Act in these days. They eloped, so there was no question of a marriage-settlement. Edgar Linton had saved out of his rents to make a provision for his daughter, Catherine. When dying he decides, in order to prevent Heathcliff getting at them, to alter his will so as to settle them on Catherine for life and then for her children. The attorney for whom he sends is, however, kept from going by Heathcliff, and Edgar dies before his will is altered, so the money passes to Catherine and then to her husband, Linton. He, though a minor, could (before the year 1838) make a will of personalty. He is induced or forced to do so, and leaves it all to Heathcliff.

Thus, at Heathcliff's death, the position seems to be that he has acquired all the personal property of both families: he is mortgagee in possession of Wuthering Heights, and is, though wrongfully, in possession of Thrushcross Grange, which he has let to Lockwood. He thinks of making a will but does not do so. What then happens on his death? He has no relations, so that his real property will escheat, and his personal property will go to the Crown as *bona vacantia*. What then becomes of Hareton and Catherine who, when the tale ends, are to be happily married on New Year's Day, 1803? At one time I thought this was the climax of the tragedy. These young people, ill-educated and incompetent, were to be left destitute. But that would be going too far. Catherine, as you will see from the pedigree, is the sole living descendant of Mr. Linton. In some way or other, I need not go through the various alternatives, she must have become entitled to Thrushcross Grange, which is plainly by far the most valuable property. Heathcliff had been mortgagee in possession of Wuthering Heights for eighteen years, but this was not long enough to obtain an absolute title by adverse possession. Hareton, as Hindley's heir, would be entitled to the equity of redemption. Now if Heathcliff, who managed well, properly accounted for his profits during the eighteen years as he could be made to do, it may well be that they were sufficient, if he was charged a proper occupation rent, to pay off the mortgage. So that Hareton would get the house and land unencumbered or, at any rate, only slightly burdened. The personal property was comparatively unimportant, and we can only hope that the Crown did not insist on its rights, if it knew of them, or that if it did insist, the happy couple could buy out the Crown's claim out of the rent which Lockwood, as we know, paid.

There is, so far as I know, no other novel in the world which it is possible to subject to an analysis of the kind I have tried to make. This in itself makes the book very unusual. Did the authoress carry all the dates in her head, or did she work with a calendar? Was 20th March 1784, for example, on a Monday? According to my calculations it was not, it was a Saturday, but I should like to have this confirmed by some competent chronologist; for if I am right, it shows that Emily Brontë did not use a calendar, and that nothing will be gained by finding out, for instance, the date of Easter in 1803.

However dull and technical the above details may be, they do, I believe, throw a light on the character of Emily Brontë and her book. German romances can hardly have been the source of her knowledge of English law. A great critic has spoken of the passionate chastity of the book; but the extreme care in realizing the ages of the characters at the time of each incident which is described seems to me a more unusual characteristic of a novel. It demonstrates the vividness of the author's imagination.

## CHRONOLOGY OF WUTHERING HEIGHTS

CHAP.

| | | |
|---|---|---|
| | 1757, before September | Hindley Earnshaw born. |
| | 1762, " | Edgar Linton born. |
| | 1764, " | Heathcliff born. |
| | 1765, summer | Catherine Earnshaw born. |
| | " late | Isabella Linton born. |
| IV. | 1771, summer, beginning of harvest | Heathcliff brought to Wuthering Heights. |
| | 1773, spring or early summer | Mrs. Earnshaw dies. |
| V. | 1774, October | Hindley sent to college. |
| | 1777, | Hindley marries. |
| | " " | Mr. Earnshaw dies. |
| VI. | " " | Hindley returns with his wife. |
| III. | " October or November | The scene described by Catherine. |

| | | | |
|---|---|---|---|
| VI. | " | November, third week, Sunday | Catherine and Heathcliff go to Thrushcross Grange. |
| VII. | 1777, | Christmas Eve | Catherine returns to W. H. |
| | " | Christmas Day | The Lintons visit W. H. |
| VIII. | 1778, | June | Hareton Earnshaw born. |
| | " | late | Frances Earnshaw dies. |
| | 1780, | summer | Edgar Linton calls at W. H. and proposes to Catherine. |
| IX. | " | " | Hindley returns drunk. |
| | " | " | Catherine tells Ellen about Edgar. |
| | " | " | Heathcliff goes off. |
| | " | " | Catherine gets wet through and catches fever. |
| | " | autumn | Catherine, convalescent, goes to Thrushcross Grange. Mr. and Mrs. Linton catch the fever and die. |
| | 1783, | April | Edgar marries Catherine. |
| X. | " | September | Heathcliff returns and sees Catherine. |
| | " | autumn | Isabella falls in love with Heathcliff, who visits Thrushcross Grange from time to time. |
| XI. | " | December | Ellen Dean sees Hareton. Heathcliff kisses Isabella. |
| | 1784, | January 6, Monday | Violent scene at Thrushcross Grange. Heathcliff is turned out and Catherine goes on hunger strike. |
| XII. | " | January 10, Friday | Catherine delirious. |
| | " | " " 2 A.M. | Isabella elopes with Heathcliff. |
| XIII. | " | March 13, Monday | The Heathcliffs return to W. H. |
| XIV. | " | March 15, Wednesday | Ellen Dean goes to W. H. |
| XV. | " | March 19, Sunday | Heathcliff sees Catherine: violent scene. |
| XVI. | " | " midnight | Catherine Linton born. |
| | " | March 20, Monday, 2 A.M. | Catherine (the elder) dies. |
| | " | March 21, Tuesday | Heathcliff puts a lock of hair in Catherine's locket. |
| | " | March 24, Friday | Catherine's funeral. |

CHAP.

| | | |
|---|---|---|
| XVII. | 1784, same day, midnight | Heathcliff nearly kills Hindley, who tried to kill him. |
| " | March 25, Saturday | Isabella runs off. |
| " | September | Linton Heathcliff born. |
| " | September or October | Hindley Earnshaw dies. All his property is mortgaged to Heathcliff. |
| XVIII. | 1797, early June | Catherine goes to Penistone Crags and meets Hareton. |
| XIX. | " June | Isabella dies. Edgar brings back Linton Heathcliff. |
| XX. | " " | Linton Heathcliff is taken to live at Wuthering Heights. |
| XXI. | 1800, March 20 | Catherine and Ellen meet Hareton, and go to Wuthering Heights where they see Linton. |
| " | March or April | Catherine and Linton correspond. |
| XXII. | " late October or November | Catherine sees Heathcliff, who says that Linton is seriously ill. |
| XXIII. | " late October or November | Catherine and Ellen go to see Linton. Ellen catches cold and is ill for three weeks. |
| XXIV. | " November | During Ellen's illness Catherine visits Linton secretly. |
| XXV. | 1801, March 20 | Edgar too ill to visit his wife's grave. |
| " | June | Edgar declining. |
| XXVI. | " August | Ellen and Catherine go to meet Linton. |
| " | August, Thursday, a week later | They are kidnapped. |
| " | Monday? | Catherine and Linton marry. |
| XXVII. | " August or September | Ellen is let out. |
| " | next Tuesday | Edgar is dying; he sends for Mr. Green, the lawyer, who does not come. |
| | harvest moon | Catherine escapes and comes to Thrushcross Grange. |
| XXVIII. | " Wednesday, 3 A.M., | Edgar Linton dies. |

CHAP.

| | | | |
|---|---|---|---|
| XXIX. | 1801, | September, evening after the funeral | Heathcliff comes to the Grange and takes off Catherine. |
| XXX. | " | October | Linton Heathcliff dies. Hareton tries to please Catherine. |
| I. | " | late November | Lockwood calls at W. H. |
| II. | " | next day | He calls again and has to stay the night. He finds Catherine's diary and sees Heathcliff's outburst. |
| | " | next day | Leaves at eight. Catches cold. |
| IV. | " | " | Ellen Dean begins her story. |
| X. | " | three weeks later | Heathcliff sends grouse. |
| | " | one week later | Heathcliff calls. |
| XV. | 1802, | January, one week later | Lockwood continues his account. |
| XXXI. | " | January, 2nd week | Lockwood calls at W. H. |
| XXXII. | " | beginning of February | Ellen goes to live at W. H. |
| | " | March | Hareton has an accident. |
| | " | Easter Monday | Catherine is nice to Hareton. |
| XXXIII. | " | Easter Tuesday | Scene about altering garden. |
| | " | (after March 18) | Heathcliff getting odd. |
| XXXIV. | " | April | Heathcliff goes on hunger strike. |
| | " | May | Heathcliff dies. |
| | " | September | Lockwood visits Thrushcross Grange and Wuthering Heights. |
| XXXIV. | 1803, | January 1 | Catherine and Hareton marry. |

# The Brontës: A Centennial Observance

## by Richard Chase

When *Jane Eyre* and *Wuthering Heights* appeared in 1847, they were widely denounced as coarse, immoral, and subversive. Later Mrs. Humphrey Ward and the Brontë Society came to cherish the Brontës —"these dear women," one member called them—as Romantic rebels against repressive conventions and as writers who had made "passion" a part of the novelistic tradition: the Society was safe in this attitude, for neither Jane Eyre nor Catherine Earnshaw had violated the marriage law—and Wordsworth had after all spoken of passion. The nineteenth-century critical vocabulary, which depended so heavily on words like "rebellion," "passion," and "imagination," was often inaccurate; and Victorian criticism of the Brontës remains nebulous— nebulously rhapsodic as in Swinburne's *A Note on Charlotte Brontë* or nebulously ethical as, say, in the writing of A. C. Benson, from whom the following passage is taken:

> Charlotte Brontë's new philosophy of love . . . was not a revolt against tame and formal conventions so much as a new sense of right and dignity, a manifesto, so to speak, of the equality of noble love. Compare the conception of love, from the woman's standpoint, in the novels of Dickens and Thackeray, with Charlotte Brontë's conception. In Dickens and Thackeray love is at best a reward, a privilege, graciously tendered and rapturously accepted; and the highest conception of wifely love is one of fidelity and patience and unselfish tendance gently rendered by a domestic angel, whose glory is self-repression, and whose highest praise is to afford an uncritical haven of repose to an undisputed master.

The truth of these sentences is superficial. The reader of *Jane Eyre* has every reason to feel that the coy badinage of the closing pages none too subtly transforms Jane into the "domestic angel" herself. The reader even finds himself with the same doubts about Jane that he has about Richardson's Pamela: maybe she planned it that way. The new century brought the Brontës into better perspective, and

"The Brontës: A Centennial Observance," by Richard Chase. From *The Kenyon Review*, IX, no. 4 (Autumn, 1947), 487–506. Copyright © 1947 by Kenyon College. Reprinted by permission of *The Kenyon Review* and the Estate of Richard V. Chase.

in such an attack as Rosamond Langbridge's *Charlotte Brontë: A Psychological Study* we see Charlotte pictured as a kind of scribbling Florence Nightingale, an intensely neurotic woman whose early family life had filled her with unquenchable urges to succeed, and, if not to succeed, then to expire under the burden of a masochistic "duty." I call this a better perspective because it makes us think of the Brontës as true-blue Victorians rather than as Romantic rebels. The purpose of the present criticism is to proceed from that point. Why do *Jane Eyre* and *Wuthering Heights* now seem the most exciting of Victorian novels? Because, I think, these novels translated the social customs of the time into the forms of mythical art, whereas many other Victorian novels were translated by the social customs into more or less tiresome canting.

## II

The familiar stories about the Brontës' home life may or may not be true in detail. But there is no doubt that it was harrowing. The horrendous Puritanism of the Reverend Patrick Brontë, who catechized his children on the differences between the male and female bodies and on the advisability of preparing for Eternity, pervaded the isolated Yorkshire parsonage. Mr. Brontë may or may not have fired pistols out of the back door, burnt up the pretty new shoes of his small daughters, and torn to bits the only silk dress of his wife as she lay dying of cancer after bearing her sixth child in seven years. But there is no doubt that Haworth Parsonage was a man's society, brooded over by the usually invisible poetry-scribbling patriarch who lived in his room, as one writer says, "in a fiery and impotent seclusion." He was the living symbol of the nineteenth-century patriarch: the Romantic Man of Mystery, alternately maudlin and fanatical, his brilliant eye bespeaking the libidinal potential of Sex and War, his gloomy brow displaying the emblems of ancient guilt, his stern jaw advertizing the tenacity of his self-repression. And if this scribbling patriarch began to lose his lustre as the sisters grew older, there was their theatrical brother Branwell to admire when he soliloquized or painted pictures or to behold with awe when, dying of alcohol and opium, he sank down among the multitudinous tombstones of Haworth churchyard, armed with a kitchen knife in case he should meet the Devil. Small wonder that Emily Brontë should have burned herself with a red-hot iron and beaten her dog Keeper into insensibility or that Charlotte developed an agonizing sense of inferiority which she never overcame. The wonder is that Emily should have written a first-rate novel about the violent forces of human nature and that Charlotte produced, as Rebecca West says, the subtle and complete analysis of inferiority which constitutes her novels.

Swinburne, whose soul was full of Great Mothers, thought it an "insoluble riddle" that Charlotte Brontë "came first to conceive and finally to fashion that perfect study of noble and faultful and suffering manhood," Edward Rochester. Our debunking Freudian, Miss Langbridge, finds no riddle: All the Brontë men characters "have the pettifogging tyranny of the Victorian father, and the Victorian only son. As Mr. Rochester is transcendental Branwell, with his 'coarse' bygone amours and theatrical remorses, his Olympian damns and virile thunderings, so St. John Rivers in his tyrannical evangelism, his cold, harsh dominance, his torpid Christian love-making is Mr. Brontë *père*." It is all too simple, but again we have been put on the right track.

"If he were a *clever* man and loved me, the whole world weighed in the balance against his slightest wish should be light as air," writes Charlotte to a friend. This indicates what, in their intellectual parsonage, the sisters came to admire and fear most: sexual and intellectual energy. In *Jane Eyre* and *Wuthering Heights* the universe is conceived as the embodiment of this energy or *élan*. In *Jane Eyre* the wondrous Helen Burns, as she is dying, places her faith in "the impalpable principle of life and thought, pure as when it left the Creator to inspire the creature: whence it came it will return; perhaps again to be communicated to some being higher than man—perhaps to pass through gradations of glory, from the pale human soul to brighten to the seraph! Surely it will never, on the contrary, be suffered to degenerate from man to fiend?" The "principle" of life and thought in the Brontë novels is sexual Energy; the universe is the stone and flesh which make the Energy palpable; it is a masculine universe. Art is the representation of the "principle" as the Brontë heroines perceived it embodied in nature, in man, in seraph, and in fiend.

Charlotte, always given to imagining concrete situations, pictures herself in her poems as the wife of Pilate, who "sought my presence dyed in blood," who exercised a "cold and crushing sway," who crushed "my mind, and did my freedom slay." Or she imagines "Gilbert," who gloats over the abjectness of the wife to whom he had descended "like a God." Or she pictures the enslavement of a woman with an "endowed and youthful frame" by a tyrannical husband who finally kills himself with an axe. Or she feels a "perfect energy" within her and when this energy burns in harmony with her lover's soul, she achieves "identity" in a newly meaningful universe which was once "dumb/ Stone-deaf, and blank, and wholly blind," "dark—imageless—a living tomb." "Point not to thy Madonna, Priest—/ Thy sightless saint of stone," she writes in another poem; rather will she worship the burning image of her lover lord.

Emily writes of a daughter who longs to be with her father in "the eternal home":

> From suffering and corruption free,
> Restored into the Deity.

Elsewhere she speaks of "selfish-hearted men" but her first impulse is always away from the concrete situation and toward the symbolization of principles. Whereas Charlotte seeks "identity," Emily longs to sleep in an eternal ocean of mild light "without identity." In the fine poem which begins "Ah! why because the dazzling sun," after a night-long peaceful watch, the "glorious eyes" of the stars "gazing down in mine" with "one sweet influence," the sun bounds over the hills—"Blood-red, he rose, and arrow-straight/ His fierce beams struck my brow." She buries her face in her pillow to escape the intolerable force, but

> It would not do—the pillow glowed,
> And glowed both roof and floor;
> And birds sang loudly in the wood,
> And fresh winds shook the door.

The energy, when it kindles the universe, is intolerable to the sensibility which revolts against its own identity, since identity implies being part of the palpable universe and thus being subject to the agony of the intense illumination. The world is moved to exquisite vibrancy:

> The curtains waved, the wakened flies
> Were murmuring round my room,
> Imprisoned there, till I should rise,
> And give them leave to roam.

And the poem ends with a prayer that the poet may "sleep through" the "blinding reign" of the hostile light and awake among the gentle stars.

Sometimes Emily Brontë says that the illuminating energy is the only reason for bearing the burden of existence and that she wishes for death because the illumination will not come. Addressing "that spirit," she writes

> Had I but seen his glorious eye
> *Once* light the clouds that wilder me,
> I ne'er had raised this coward cry. . . .

Again, and this is the typical note, she speaks of death as a return to the Light she once knew in Eternity. In "The Prisoner" she has left one of the most striking and exact records of the withdrawal and return of the spirit. A "messenger of Hope" comes to her:

> He comes with western winds, with evening's wandering airs,
> With that clear dusk of heaven that brings the thickest stars.
> Winds take a pensive tone, and stars a tender fire,
> And visions rise, and change, that kill me with desire.
>
> Desire for nothing known in my maturer years,
> When Joy grew mad with awe, at counting future tears.
> When, if my spirit's sky was full of flashes warm,
> I knew not whence they came, from sun or thunderstorm.
>
> But, first, a hush of peace—a soundless calm descends;
> The struggle of distress, and fierce impatience ends;
> Mute music soothes my breast—unuttered harmony,
> That I could never dream, till Earth was lost to me.
>
> Then dawns the Invisible; the Unseen its truth reveals,
> My outward sense is gone, my inward essence feels:
> Its wings are almost free—its home, its harbor found,
> Measuring the gulf, it stoops and dares the final bound.
>
> Oh! dreadful is the check—intense the agony—
> When the ear begins to hear, and the eye begins to see;
> When the pulse begins to throb, the brain to think again;
> The soul to feel the flesh, and the flesh to feel the chain.
>
> Yet I would lose no sting, would wish no torture less;
> The more that anguish racks, the earlier it will bless;
> And robed in fires of hell, or bright with heavenly shine,
> If it but herald death, the vision is divine!

She says that the winds grow "pensive" and that the stars take on a "tender fire" at the beginning of the mystic experience; we do not comprehend all of Emily Brontë's meaning if we repeat that the universal *élan* is the energy of sex and intellect; but this concept seems indispensable here as elsewhere in reading the Brontës.

In that somewhat fantastic Gothical-Byronic character Edward Rochester we have Charlotte Brontë's symbolic embodiment of the masculine *élan*. Jane Eyre's feelings toward Rochester are, as Freud would say, "ambivalent." He draws her to him with a strange fascination; yet she is repelled by his animalism and his demonism. She wishes to submit herself to him; yet she cannot. She is nearly enthralled by the "tenderness and passion in every lineament" of his "kindled" face; yet she shrinks from the flashing of his "falcon eye" and from the glamor of his self-proclaimed guilt and his many exploits among women of other countries (in France, Céline; in Italy, Giacinta; in Germany, Clara—"these poor girls" Jane calls them). She cannot permit the proffered intimacies of this man who keeps a mad wife locked up in his attic. And if her moral scruples would allow his embrace, still she could not endure the intensity of his passion. The noble, free companionship of man and woman does not present itself to her as a possibility. She sees only two possible modes of behavior: meek submission or a flirtatious, gently sadistic skirmishing designed to keep her lover at bay. Finally her sense of "duty" compels Jane to run away. The inevitable parting of the lovers had been forecast when the lightning, summoned from the sky by their first declaration of love, had split the garden chestnut tree asunder.

The splitting of the tree, however, symbolizes also two alternate images of Jane Eyre's soul, two possible extremes which, as she believes, her behavior may take. At one extreme is Bertha, Rochester's mad wife; at the other is St. John Rivers, the clergyman cousin whom Jane meets after she flees Rochester and who wants to marry her. Before the story can end, Jane must look into her Narcissus' mirror and purge these false images of herself. Bertha represents the woman who has given herself blindly and uncompromisingly to the principle of sex and intellect. As Fanny E. Ratchford (the expert in the voluminous juvenile romances written by the Brontës) has shown, the character of Bertha was evolved from a certain Lady Zenobia Ellrington, a heroine of Charlotte Brontë's childish fantasy-kingdom of Angria. Miss Ratchford describes Lady Zenobia thus: She was a "noble woman of strong mind and lofty thought. On the other hand, she is given to fits of rage in which she shrieks like a wild beast and falls upon her victim hand and foot. On one occasion she kicked Lord Charles [a juvenile version of Rochester] down the stairs. Always she is depicted as tall of stature and strong of body. Lord Charles once declared that she could spar on equal terms with her husband, "one of the best boxers on record." She was, furthermore, a learned and intellectual woman, a blue-stocking in fact. Like Bertha, she was a Creole and she came from a family notorious for mad crimes and passions. May not Bertha, Jane seems to ask herself, be a living example of what happens to a woman who gives herself to the Romantic Hero, who in her insane suffragettism tries herself to play the Hero, to be the fleshly vessel of the *élan?*

We may think that fear drives Jane away from Rochester; *she,* however, says that it is "duty." In St. John Rivers she meets duty incarnate. In a poem Charlotte Brontë had imagined herself as a missionary to the pagans. No "coward love of life," she says, has made "me shrink from the righteous strife." Rivers has given up Rosamond Oliver, a charming and life-loving girl, and wants to marry Jane and take her to India, where he plans to devote himself to missionary work. Plainly, it would be a sexless marriage. Rivers wants a wife to "influence." He is cold, selfish, fanatical—a narrow bigot, who shakes Jane's confidence in "duty." She cannot marry Rivers; she must purge her soul to the image of "duty" as she has of the image of Bertha.

How to resolve the plot? It must be done as Charlotte, the leader of her sisters in all practical matters, was accustomed to do things: by positive action. The universe conspiring against Jane Eyre, like the circumstances which so often conspired against the sisters, must be chastened by an assertion of will, catastrophic if necessary. And so she sends Rochester's house up in flames and makes him lose his eyesight and his left hand in a vain attempt to save Bertha. Rochester's injuries are, I should think, a symbolic castration. The faculty of vision, the analysts have shown, is often identified in the unconscious with the energy of sex. When Rochester had tried to make love to Jane, she had felt a "fiery hand grasp at her vitals;" the hand, then, must be cut off. The universe, not previously amenable to supernatural communication between the parted lovers, now allows them to hear each other though they are leagues apart. Jane Eyre now comes into her own. She returns to Rochester. She baits him coyly about her relations with Rivers; he exhibits manly jealousy. They settle down to a mild married life; they have a child; Rochester partly, but only partly, regains his eyesight. The tempo and energy of the universe can be quelled, we see, by a patient, practical woman.

In the fantasy of Jane Eyre she is able to answer Rochester's question whether she is entirely his by saying, "to the finest fibre of my nature, sir." In *Wuthering Heights,* we remember Cathy's passionate declaration of oneness with her lover: "I *am* Heathcliff." Heathcliff is Emily Brontë's symbol of "the impalpable principle of life and thought." He is the very spirit of the wild Yorkshire moors, an "unreclaimed creature," as Cathy knows, but the only creature who can "reconcile her to God and Humanity." Like Rochester, he is flamboyant, mysterious, morose, and sadistic. Cathy *is* Heathcliff, yet even as she admits this she rejects him for reasons which she herself cannot enunciate and takes Edgar Linton, who, though a good gentleman, disgusts her with his effeteness. She is, apparently, afraid of Heathcliff. And unlike Rochester, he can never be domesticated. He is less human and more of the essence of the universal *élan.* We realize that with a few readjustments of the plot he need not have entered the story as a human being at all. His part might have been played by Fate or Nature or God or the Devil. He is sheer dazzling sexual and intellectual force. As Heathcliff expires at the end of the book, we feel, not so much that a man is dying, as that an intolerable energy is flagging. And we see that Heathcliff without energy cannot possibly survive in human form. His "termination" is "absurd," as he himself says. The titan is now reduced to a buffoon who tries clumsily to leap out of the flesh into the spirit, to beat down invisible walls; he is a tumbler trying to transfigure himself into the Other World; he is, as he says, a "sport" of "intolerable torture." Heathcliff and Cathy die without making a fact of the oneness they both feel is theirs. To Emily Brontë, their marriage is unthinkable. It can happen only as a distant parody: the marriage of Hareton Earnshaw and Cathy the younger at the end of the book. Hareton is watered-down Heathcliff; Cathy is a pale, though still vivacious, replica of her mother. The two novels end similarly: a relatively mild and ordinary marriage is made after the spirit of the masculine universe is controlled or extinguished.

## III

We have so far maintained that the Brontë novels are concerned with the neuroses of women in a man's society. But surely this theme alone cannot account for the wonder and interest we feel in *Jane Eyre* and *Wuthering Heights*. The personalist theme involves a societal theme; the sexual involves the utopian. What is the large moral upshot of the relation between Jane and Cathy and their lovers? What is the ultimate significance of these heroines? Well, obviously *Jane Eyre* is a feminist tract, an argument for the social betterment of governesses and equal rights for women. But we have to see this propaganda and other explicit elements of the Brontë novels in comprehensive mythical images before we can begin to understand their full significance.

A serving woman sings these disheartening verses to little Jane:

My feet they are sore, and my limbs they are weary;
  Long is the way, and the mountains are wild;
Soon will the twilight close moonless and dreary
  Over the path of the poor orphan child.
Why did they send me so far and so lonely,
  Up where the moors spread and the grey rocks are piled?
Men are hard-hearted, and kind angels only
  Watch'd o'er the steps of a poor orphan child.

This poor orphan child with a mission in a hostile world is like Cinderella certainly. Also she is like Joan of Arc and, as Chesterton observes, the solitary virgin of the folktales who goes to the castle of the ogre. I suggest that to the Brontës this pilgrim virgin is a culture heroine. The culture heroes of mythology are those figures who, like

Hercules, Prometheus, or the animal deities of the American Indians, slay the monsters or overcome natural or human obstacles or bring intelligence to men so that civilization can be born out of savagery and chaos—"transformers," the anthropologists call these culture heroes. It was the Victorian period which supposed that the primeval social order consisted of a murderous old man and his company of females and weaker males and which bequeathed the idea to Freud. We may almost say that the Brontë household *was* this primeval social order. The purpose of the Brontë culture heroine as a mythical being is to transform primeval society into a humane and noble order of civilization. But this idea requires another excursus.

There are many methods of describing the transformation of primitive society into civilization. But the method most applicable to the problem as creative writers conceive it in novels and poems is that of A. J. Toynbee (*A Study of History*, 1933–38). Briefly, Toynbee's method is mythological: primitive society is a stasis presided over by a once creative Father-God, Whose perfection is also a stasis. God must be forced into the motion of further creativity by a wager flung to Him by the Devil. The human protagonist of the cultural tragedy (Toynbee follows the theme of Goethe's *Faust*) must perform a dynamic act, which will set God and the Devil at war. In the path of the culture hero there stands an Obstacle. The dynamic act of the hero hurls him against the Obstacle—if he is overcome by it, the Devil has won the wager and society fails to advance along the path of civilization; but if he overcomes it, God has won; the Devil, who sought to perpetuate the death-like stasis, is routed; and God, the creative *Élan* or "the impalpable principle of life and thought," as Helen Burns calls Him, reasserts Himself in the soul of man. Our Brontë culture heroine, then, is the human protagonist of the cosmic drama. Rochester and Heathcliff are portrayed as being at once God-like and Satanic. In them the universal enemies may be set at war by a culture heroine who performs the decisive dynamic act. Then, if the Devil is overcome, a higher state of society will have been achieved. The tyrannical Father-God will have been displaced. The stasis will have been smashed by the creative *élan* of sex and intelligence. The Brontë heroines fail in their mission; they refuse to venture so much; they will not accept the challenge of the God-Devil, for fear the Devil should win. Yet when we understand these heroines in some such terms as the foregoing, they acquire a new significance: it had not occurred to us that the stakes were so great.

Charlotte Brontë, whose many practical predicaments, as we have noted, forced her to solve problems by forthright acts of will, made the plot of *Jane Eyre* proceed in a rhythm of stasis and activity. Thus we find Jane on a hillside near Rochester's estate after she has been hired as governess but before she has met Rochester. She has forced herself out of her inert existence at Lowood School, having a great desire for "liberty" and adventure. As yet she has not found the driving force of the new life for which she hopes. The universe is frozen in the cold of winter; the world is silent, in "leafless repose." The pale moon presides over the scene. Then suddenly the stasis is shattered by a vigorous animal invasion; Rochester with horse and dog comes upon the scene. Not knowing it to be her "master," Jane returns to the house reluctantly: "To pass its threshold was to return to stagnation . . . to slip again over my faculties the viewless fetters of an uniform and too still existence." But she is soon in love with her master. He "eclipses God." As the time comes for the abortive wedding (interrupted by the announcement that Rochester has a lunatic wife), Jane Eyre is "an ardent, expectant woman." Apparently, she is on the point of rescuing herself definitively from the "leafless repose." But when the wedding fails to come off, she is again "desolate" in a frozen world; her "blooming and glowing" wishes are "stark, dull, livid corpses." She flees Rochester and turns to St. John Rivers. If in the soul of Rochester the Devil might meaningfully fight with God, there can be no such struggle in the soul of Rivers. "God" has become, not the creative principle, but a prim, puritanical taskmaster, and there is no doubt that the Devil will easily defeat Him. "If I were to marry you," says Jane, "you would kill me. You are killing me now." She has now renounced two men; an obviously Devilish man and a possibly Devilish man. Disgusted with Rivers, she sets out to find Rochester. She does not yet know that his wife has died and that he has been maimed. Have her spiritual adventures now prepared her to give herself unequivocally to Rochester? Charlotte Brontë leaves the question unanswered and we can only discuss what Jane actually does. Yet there is a hint that the culture heroine was prepared for her noble mission: "It was *my* time to assume ascendancy. *My* powers were in play, and in force."

The aesthetic procedure of Charlotte Brontë makes her novel a series of set pieces, *tableaux,* or great scenes which periodically resolve themselves out of the interspersed areas of formless activity (like the charades staged by Rochester and Blanche Ingram for his aristocratic guests). Emily Brontë's work lacks this differentiation and consequently is harder to discuss, which is why most discussions of *Wuthering Heights* take refuge in such superlatives as "passion," "purity," and "powerful." Charlotte constantly lays violent hands on the progress of her story. Emily simply stands in the midst of things and records what goes on. There is "an amazing quality of innocence" in the Brontës, especially in Emily, writes Herbert Read. And it is true that they do not always seem to be fully aware of what is implied in their own novels. In *Jane Eyre* this produces some remarkably naive and inapposite dialogue. Emily Brontë's "innocence," however, is akin to what Keats called "negative capability"—the ability of the tragic writer to retain an unbaffled, even unenquiring, perception of elementals in the midst of awful and confusing events. Charlotte perpetually inquires, analyses, and moralizes; Emily watches the terrific interplay of events with no comment except that they are terrifying or beautiful. She does not moralize: in a poem she recalls how she had once raged at fools and fiercely defended "truth, right, liberty," but she has learned that

> however I frown,
> The same world will go rolling on.

"The world is going," she exclaims elsewhere, and we realize that her detachment is not only a moral one. It is an immediate sense impression of being set apart from the material world, a truly frightening homelessness.

> The very grey rocks, looking on,
> Asked, "What do you do here?"

Herbert Read cannot be right to say that Emily Brontë "is forever perplexed by the problem of evil." She does not allow herself to be perplexed; if she did she would no longer be "innocent" and she would no longer be a tragic writer, if we are to stick to Keats's stringent prescription. She has not even the grandly humane moral sense of Sophocles; she is Aeschylean. Heathcliff is a creature whose beginning and end remain, in the purely mundane moral sense, meaningless. He does not, like Oedipus, finally recognize himself as a man whose hidden deeds have bound him up with certain inescapable moral consequences. There is no such recognition of the hero's own complex humanity anywhere in *Wuthering Heights*.

But though Emily Brontë cannot be said to be "perplexed" by evil, there is a central moral assertion in *Wuthering Heights*. This we come upon in the scene where both Heathcliff and Cathy realize the appalling consequences of Cathy's failure to fulfill her mission; which was, clearly, to marry Heathcliff. The terrible recriminations which pass between the two lovers are the anguished utterances of human beings who are finally, because of the moral failure of Cathy, being dragged down into the flux of the dehumanized universe. Cathy dissolves into pure matter and force almost before our eyes (as Heathcliff is to do later) and while she still retains enough of sensibility to make the experience articulate. Yet though this is the single moral assertion, the whole action of the book depends upon it.

As in *Jane Eyre*, the culture heroine of *Wuthering Heights* fails. Heathcliff relentlessly charges her with her failure: "You teach me now

how cruel you've been—cruel and false. *Why* did you despise me? *Why*
did you betray your own heart, Cathy? I have not one word of comfort.
You deserve this. You have killed yourself. Yes, you may kiss me, and
cry; and wring out my kisses and tears; they'll blight you—they'll
damn you. You loved me—then what *right* had you to leave me? What
right—answer me—for the poor fancy you felt for Linton? Because
misery and degradation, and death, and nothing that God or Satan
could inflict would have parted us, *you*, of your own free will did it."
Like Jane Eyre, Cathy has refused the act which would have set Satan
at war with God in the soul of Heathcliff. The penalty for not daring
to throw herself into the agony of the spiritual struggle and birth is
certainly unequivocal: she must die. This spiritual agony Emily Brontë
pictures in a poem:

> So stood I, in Heaven's glorious sun
> And in the glare of Hell
> My spirit drank a mingled tone
> Of seraph's song and demon's moan—
> What my soul bore my soul alone
> Within its self may tell.

If, then, we are to call *Wuthering Heights* a tragedy, we must leave
room in our definition of the word for the following circumstances: a
heroine comes to understand the significance of her spiritual mission
too late; the hero degenerates into "absurdity" and dies, since the God-
Devil figure is absurd without the human protagonist on whom he
depends.

Emily Brontë's "innocence" or "negative capability" is partly due
to her almost absolute devotion to death. Surely no first-rate writer
has ever been more of the Other World. She was

> Weaned from life and torn away
> In the morning of [her] day.

She is also, as one would expect, devoted to her own childhood (she
seems to have taken some of her images from Wordsworth; cf. her
habit of referring to infancy as a "glory," a "lost vision," a "light,"
etc.). Cathy dies, as she hopes, into a wonderful world of light; she
dies "like a child reviving." The poem beginning "The soft unclouded
blue of air" unites the theme of childhood with the theme of the Hero.
The poem concerns the thoughts of an unnamed "I" on a day "as
bright as Eden's used to be":

> Laid on the grass I lapsed away,
> Sank back again to childhood's day;
> All harsh thoughts perished, memory mild
> Subdued both grief and passion wild.

But, she asks, does the sunshine that bathes the "stern and swarthy brow" of "that iron man" elicit in his memory a sweet dream of childhood, or is

> Remembrance of his early home
> So lost that not a gleam may come?

He sits in silence.

> That stormy breast
> At length, I said, has deigned to rest;
> At length above that spirit flows
> The waveless ocean of repose . . .
> Perhaps this is the destined hour
> When hell shall lose its fatal power
> And heaven itself shall bend above
> To hail the soul redeemed by love.

But all in vain. One glance at the "iron man" reveals

> how little care
> He felt for all the beauty there

and how soon her own breast can grow as cold

> As winter wind or polar snow.

Her futile desire has been to drag the hero back into infancy—perhaps into that "Unique Society" of childish heroes and heroines who perform romantic deeds among the islands of the Pacific in Emily Brontë's juvenile writings. She has wanted to transform the universal energy embodied by the "iron man" into the mild light of the Other World, or "home." She has thought that by detachment from this world she could deprive hell of "its fatal power" and make heaven "hail the soul." But detachment cannot resolve the conflict between the Devil and God; that is work which must be done in This World. Cathy, too, tried to take Heathcliff into "that glorious world" which she sees "dimly through tears" and yearns for "through the walls of an aching heart." But this is only an imaginary Heathcliff, "*my* Heathcliff," she says, not the relentless inquisitor who stands before her. "*My* Heathcliff" is a child returning to what Wordsworth called the "imperial palace" and what Emily Brontë described thus:

> I saw her stand in the gallery long,
> Watching the little children there,
> As they were playing the pillars among
> And bounding down the marble stair.

Virginia Woolf writes that Emily Brontë "looked out upon a world cleft into gigantic disorder and felt within her the power to unite it in a book." *Wuthering Heights* displays the schisms between the forces of the universe; we have a sense of great motions taking place without immediately recognizable relation. Things do not fit together and we are left to contemplate the estrangement of parts. The book is meaningful because it portrays human beings caught in the schisms—caught between the Other World and This World, between Childhood and Adulthood, between Savagery and Civilization, between the Devil and God, between Matter and Spirit, between Stasis and Motion.

## IV

We are asked to consider three pairs of lovers in *Wuthering Heights*: Heathcliff and the elder Cathy, Linton Heathcliff and the younger Cathy, Hareton Earnshaw and the younger Cathy. Nothing could be more Victorian than the marriage of the child lovers, Linton and the younger Cathy, both aged 17, under the baleful influence of Heathcliff. They are sweet, innocent children; they are persecuted and forced into a morbid sex relationship. They are both spoiled—Linton is an invalid who sucks sugar candy and asks Cathy not to kiss him, because it takes his breath away; he is pettish, willful, and mortally afraid of his father. Cathy has some of the vivacity of her mother; she is pretty; but she too is pettish and spoiled. "I should never love anybody better than papa," she says.

In my family there is an illustrated Victorian autograph album, inherited from elder generations. It contains—along with many elaborately scrolled signatures, pictures of doves, and a recipe for smelling salts—an engraving of a smiling and cherubic girl sucking a stick of candy. At first glance she seems perfectly innocent; yet there is an almost wicked knowingness in her expression. Behind her is a dark, bestial face carved heavily in wood; the leg of the table on which she leans is carved in the shape of a menacing griffon or gargoyle. It is exactly the relationship of Linton and Cathy to Heathcliff in those appalling love scenes on the moors. The theme of childhood, voiced by the elder Cathy on her deathbed, is thus continued in the main action of the second half of the book. We begin to see that, in one way or another, childhood is in fact the central theme of Emily Brontë's writing.

There is a childishness too about the love relationship of Hareton and the younger Cathy. They marry when Hareton is twenty-five and Cathy nineteen, but Hareton is still a primitive waif, having been deliberately kept untaught by Heathcliff. Cathy is still a spoiled child.

Their marriage promises to be a happy one, however. Hareton, though in many ways the image of Heathcliff, has little of Heathcliff's force. He can be domesticated. Cathy promises to mature into a responsible woman. As in the marriage of Jane and Rochester, the woman has a strong advantage over her lover; for Cathy is educated and intelligent and she will teach Hareton, who desperately desires to be educated. In *Jane Eyre* the principal lovers finally come together, though in a compromised relationship. *Wuthering Heights* is a more uncompromising book. Heathcliff and the elder Cathy come together only at several removes: Hareton and the younger Cathy are but pale replicas of their elders.

## V

I have said that the Brontës were essentially Victorian. The happy marriages at the end of *Jane Eyre* and *Wuthering Heights* represent the triumph of the moderate, secular, naturalistic, liberal, sentimental point of view over the mythical, religious, tragic point of view. The moral texture of these novels is woven whole cloth out of the social customs of the day. To the heroic marriage of free and God-like souls, to the futurist utopias of sexual society, the Brontës plainly preferred domesticity—and this despite the fact that no one knew better the readiness with which the Victorian family reverted to the primitive horde. They "rebelled" only in the sense that they transmuted the Victorian social situation into mythical and symbolic forms. And this reminds us that the fault of much of our criticism of nineteenth-century literature is to mistake art for rebellion.

# The Image of the Book in
## *Wuthering Heights*

### *by Robert C. McKibben*

Recent critics, reacting against earlier evaluations, have tended to treat *Wuthering Heights* as an art product of a very high order, a work of genius in execution as well as in vision. These commentators have attempted to resolve technical and thematic questions and to clarify the rapport between the two.[1] One of the most successful of them, Dorothy Van Ghent, has effectively demonstrated the relationship between two "figures" in the novel and her conception of its central problem. To cite the opening sentences of her article:

> *Wuthering Heights* exists for the mind as a tension between two kinds of reality, a restrictive reality of civilized manners and codes, and the anonymous unregenerate reality of natural energies. The poetic structure which, in Emily Brontë's novel, associates these two kinds of reality is a structure of variations on the possibility of a break-through from one mode of being into the other.[2]

Like the majority of her predecessors, Mrs. Van Ghent has emphasized the most ambiguous dramatization of this tension in the book, the attraction between Catherine and Heathcliff. Yet Emily Brontë did not wish to leave her reader to puzzle an ultimate tension: she consciously strove to assert the triumph of society in the love of the second Catherine and Hareton. A qualitative difference between the two couples must be recognized, although, as Klingopulos has observed,

"The Image of the Book in *Wuthering Heights*," by Robert C. McKibben. From *Nineteenth-Century Fiction*, XV, no. 2 (1960), 159–69. Copyright © 1960 by The Regents of the University of California. Reprinted by permission of The Regents.

[1] Aside from Mrs. Van Ghent see especially Boris Ford, "*Wuthering Heights*," *Scrutiny*, VII (1939), 375–89; G. D. Klingopulos, "The Novel as Dramatic Poem (II): 'Wuthering Heights,' " *Scrutiny*, XIV (1947), 269–86; Mark Schorer, "Fiction and the Matrix of Analogy," *Kenyon Review*, XI (1949), 539–60; and Melvin R. Watson, "Tempest in the Soul: The Theme and Structure of *Wuthering Heights*," *NCF*, IV (1949), 87–100.

[2] Van Ghent, "The Window Figure and the Two-Children Figure in *Wuthering Heights*," *NCF*, VII (1952), 189–90.

this is not necessarily to imply the presence of a moral judgment: Catherine and Heathcliff take their existence outside the framework of manners and codes; but at the same time a parallelism is unmistakable. If the problem of escape or "breaking-through" functions in terms of certain poetic figures, the theme of reconciliation must be operative in other images. In fact, just as the window figure is primarily identified with the more tempestuous lovers, so the image of the book is the reflection of the stabilizing love of Cathy and Hareton.

The world of the novel is divided into the two rival camps of Edgar and Heathcliff, Thrushcross Grange and Wuthering Heights. It is not surprising, then, that books which appear in the narrative are found in either one or the other of these camps and that, consequently, they operate in different ways and call forth attitudes which are fundamentally in opposition. A more detailed examination of the role of the book image in each environment should serve to illustrate the means of this contention.

The atmosphere of the Heights is dominated by suffering, and the nature of this suffering is to propagate itself. One soul in torment can find relief only in the reproduction of its agony in those around it. A forceful will initiates the process, and the tortured victim becomes in his turn the agent of torture. " 'The tyrant grinds down his slaves and they don't turn against him; they crush those beneath them,' " states Heathcliff (chap. xi). It is important to note that the desire for revenge is willed into actuality, for in the pursuit of perverse ends the will itself is perverted. Thus Isabella, caught in the unremitting psychology of the Heights, says of Heathcliff, " 'I'd rather he suffered *less*, if I might cause his sufferings and he might *know* that I was the cause' " (chap. xvii). But there is no peace in eternal vengeance, no solution in obeying the demands of this spontaneous reaction. The self-injury involved in serving its purposes may be more damaging than the original wrongs of others. As Isabella again comments, " 'treachery and violence are spears pointed at both ends: they wound those who resort to them worse than their enemies' " (chap. xvii).

Catherine Heathcliff is the first to directly introduce the image of the book into the narrative. Early in the novel (chap. ii) she avails herself of "a long, dark book" in order to exorcise Joseph, the spectre of warped Christianity. In the episode immediately following (chap. iii) Lockwood stumbles upon Catherine Earnshaw's library, which acts as link between reality and his significant nightmare. He remarks that it is " 'select' " and has been " 'thought not altogether for a legitimate purpose,' " for Catherine has filled the blank spaces in her books with her own observations. In her diary the book also plays a meaningful role: in the hands of Joseph it is an instrument of oppression, the symbol of arbitrary constraint; in the hands of the two children it is a means of rebellious protest. Catherine declares that she hates a good book and casts a volume into the dog kennel; Heathcliff follows her lead. His attitude towards the book is confirmed when, later in the same chapter, he orders the reading Catherine Heathcliff to " 'Put your trash away and find something to do.' " Bearing these instances in mind, one may proceed to some generalization concerning the function of the image in the environment of the Heights.

In a domain governed by indomitable will engaged in the task of realizing through action the terms of its reality, all objects are regarded as means to that task. In greater or lesser degree, then, depending upon the scope of individual ambition, the examples cited represent a misuse of the image, a subordination of the book to will. If it cannot be made to be the servant of the will, it is banished, ignored, or even destroyed. In a gesture which at once is an affirmation of the useless-ness of the book and a revolt against ill-treatment, Catherine tosses away *Th' Helmet o' Salvation*. And Catherine Heathcliff tells Lock-wood that " 'Mr. Heathcliff never reads; so he took it into his head to destroy my books' " (chap. xxxi). It is not a coincidence that the image which reflects the widening ground between the divergent paths chosen by Heathcliff and Catherine Earnshaw is again that of the book. As Catherine tends towards the world of the other household, she comes to accept that which is the very foundation of the security of Thrush-cross Grange. Ellen Dean gives this description of Heathcliff in the period after the death of old Mr. Earnshaw:

> In the first place, he had by that time lost the benefit of his early edu-cation: continual hard work, begun soon and concluded late, had ex-tinguished any curiosity he once possessed in pursuit of knowledge, and any love for books or learning. . . . He struggled long to keep up an equality with Catherine in her studies, and yielded with poignant though silent regret . . . (chap. viii).

The atmosphere of Thrushcross Grange is one of normalcy and convention; but since convention is merely an accepted method of simplifying reality, and since this simplification usually involves a modification or avoidance of the more unpleasant aspects of life, the Lintons, as they are portrayed by the outcast Heathcliff, exist in a polite and petty play-world. The vision of Edgar and Isabella battling for possession of a lap dog, "a heap of warm hair" (chap. vi), a prize so little desired that it is eventually refused by both, can only arouse contempt in a proud and unregenerate nature which equates battle with life itself.

The book image, insofar as it represents a civilizing force and a bulwark of that convention which seeks to cover naked experience, is the core of the Grange. When with Heathcliff's return domestic strife becomes the rule in his home, Edgar increases the frequency of his visits to his books: the tranquillity of the Grange is upset by the wild energy of the Heights, and he is personally threatened by those forces which his early education failed to take into account. Ellen tells Catherine that he is continually in the library " 'since he has no other society' " (chap. xii). The book becomes the natural heritage of the second Catherine and is closely identified with her. Her father takes her training upon himself, introduces her to reading, and permits her to share his sanctuary. " 'She learned rapidly and eagerly,' " comments Ellen, " 'and did honour to his teaching' " (chap. xviii). By the time of Edgar's final illness it can be asserted that "the library, where her father stopped a short time daily . . . and his chamber, had become her whole world" (chap. xxvii).

If the domain of Heathcliff illustrates an attempt to create a reality, then Thrushcross Grange under Edgar Linton reflects a shrinking from reality, a denial of aggressive will. There, escape from the conditions of an unpleasant status quo is effected by means of withdrawal, and refuge is found in the book. Heathcliff and Catherine may be said to exist solely in terms of active volition; Edgar derives his requirements for life from passive retreat. The book is used to sustain a shallow view of the world, a view rendered false by its omissions, and in this way the image is again misused. When young Catherine first makes the acquaintance of a seemingly inoffensive Heathcliff, her father undertakes to enlighten her as to his true character:

> She appeared so deeply impressed and shocked at this new view of human nature—excluded from all her studies and all her ideas till now—that Mr. Edgar deemed it unnecessary to pursue the subject. He merely added—
> "You will know hereafter, darling, why I wish you to avoid his house and family; now return to your old employments and amusements, and think no more about them" (chap. xxi).

Isabella too indulges in this characteristic misuse of the image (chap. xvii). It is apparent that such a limitation of awareness through the medium of the book may involve dangers greater than those to be feared from the aspects of life which are denied. The book becomes an excuse for weakness; its misuse is confirmed when Ellen states that Edgar " 'shut himself up among books that he never opened' " (chap. xii). In his flight from that experience not admitted by convention, he ends by ignoring the civilizing factor; his "philosophical resignation" is a false peace.

Another approach to the analysis of the role of the image is afforded by the situations of the two Catherines. These heroines are raised in opposite environments but find that each must face her destiny in the

domain of the other. When Heathcliff returns, Mrs. Catherine Linton
reacts violently to her position. In the throes of her self-induced illness
she is told that her husband is " 'among his books,' " and she cries,
" 'What in the name of all that feels has he to do with *books,* when
I am dying' " (chap. xii). This is the appeal of the totally involved,
those who live in the realm of passionate consciousness and willful
action, to the reclusive; and the mind of Catherine for a time strays
back to her childhood when she realizes that the Lintons are alien to
her and exemplify a completely foreign mode of perception. As his wife
slowly regains her health, Edgar uses the logical instrument to bring
her into his household again, the book. But the gulf between their
sensibilities cannot now be bridged, and his gesture is futile:

> A book lay spread on the sill before her, and the scarcely perceptible
> wind fluttered its leaves at intervals. I believe Linton had laid it there:
> for she never endeavoured to divert herself with reading, or occupation
> of any kind, and he would spend many an hour in trying to entice her
> attention to some subject which had formerly been her amusement
> (chap. xv).

As Edgar tries unsuccessfully to reconcile the spirit of the Heights
to that of his own sphere, so his daughter, using the same means, essays
the same feat. For her Wuthering Heights exercises an unavoidable
attraction, and the presence there of young Linton is only another in-
ducement to the creation of a new harmony between the houses. Her
first efforts to send Linton some books are thwarted by Ellen, but
difficulties are overcome, and she is soon able to visit the Heights
regularly. Her marriage to Heathcliff's son is, however, destined to end
unhappily, for in order to assimilate past into present and create a
confident future, she must descend into and emerge from the reality
of Wuthering Heights. Edgar failed to win Cathy's mother to the cause
of an image of withdrawal; now Cathy will have her books, those same
images of an unreal security, confiscated. After she enters the camp of
Heathcliff, the image predominates, a climax is attained, and the book
reappears as reconciliation.

From her lifelong haven Catherine Heathcliff is thrust into a vortex
of abnormal emotion. Her faith in herself has never been forged, and
Zillah asks, " 'what will all her learning and her daintiness do for her
now?' " (chap. xxx). The death of her pitiful husband breaks her only
link to her former home: it is the death of all sense of purpose in her
life. She suddenly awakes, as did her mother before her, to find herself
in an adverse world which threatens the very basis of her identity.
" 'I feel like death!' " she cries (chap. xxx). Shaken by her experience,
she (in unconscious imitation of her father) withdraws. In her heart
she erects a shrine to the illusion of her girlhood, the illusion repre-

sented by the book. When Hareton appropriates some volumes that
she has found, she complains to Lockwood: " 'Those books, both prose
and verse, were consecrated to me by other associations; and I hate to
see them debased and profaned in his mouth!' " (chap. xxxi). The cold
drives her into the midst of the society of the Heights, but she adopts
the rude manners of the household only insofar as they serve her to
keep the present from desecrating her spiritual retreat into the past:
not being able to enforce self-exile, she wishes to exile the world.
" 'Mr. Hareton,' " she informs the company, " 'and the whole set of
you, will be good enough to understand that I reject any pretence at
kindness you have the hypocrisy to offer! I despise you, and will have
nothing to say to any of you!' " (chap. xxx). It is the ultimate sterility
of this attitude which she recognizes when she tells Hareton she is
" 'stalled.' "

It is significant that she addresses this confession to Hareton, as
if she were already aware that he is to be her salvation just as she is
to be his. Heathcliff has formed Hindley's son into a replica of his own
youthful degradation and humiliation, which Ellen pictures in the
following terms:

> Then personal appearance sympathised with mental deterioration:
> he acquired a slouching gait and ignoble look; his naturally reserved
> disposition was exaggerated into an almost idiotic excess of unsociable
> moroseness; and he took a grim pleasure, apparently, in exciting the
> aversion rather than the esteem of his few acquaintance (chap. viii).

It has already been noted that Heathcliff's rejection of the book was
a cause of his gradual estrangement from Catherine Earnshaw, and
it is here seen as the reason for his physical deterioration as well. He
has carefully inculcated this hatred in Hareton (chap. xxxi). Nevertheless, there is a strain of quality in the boy which even the machinations
of Heathcliff cannot alter. Ellen's description of Hareton can be compared to the one of his evil mentor just cited:

> "I could scarcely refrain from smiling at this antipathy to the poor
> fellow; who was a well-made, athletic youth, good-looking in features,
> and stout and healthy, but attired in garments befitting his daily oc-
> cupations of working on the farm. . . . Still, I thought I could detect in
> his physiognomy a mind owning better qualities than his father ever pos-
> sessed. Good things lost amid a wilderness of weeds, to be sure . . . yet,
> notwithstanding, evidence of a wealthy soil, that might yield luxuriant
> crops under other and favourable circumstances" (chap. xviii).

Heathcliff acknowledges the superiority of Hareton only to credit
himself with its eternal subjugation. But this is not to be the case,
for Hareton has within him the seeds of transformation.

Mrs. Van Ghent, as has been seen, refers to the novel as "a tension

40 Robert C. McKibben

between two kinds of reality." It is obvious that both Cathy and Hareton are victims of that tension, each representing a kind of reality. Each is the incarnate ideal of the heroes in opposition, Edgar and Heathcliff; each is a product of a certain misuse of the book. But unlike those who molded them, they conceive of the limitations of their positions and move to counteract absolute stagnation. Only together, mutually aiding one another, can they struggle free of influences which have made them prey to conscious or unconscious misunderstanding. The value of Catherine's inheritance, striving to disassociate itself from false purposes, discovers its proper subject in Hareton; and he, recognizing his own potentialities and needs in it, takes it for his proper object. This value, which resolves an apparently inevitable and insurmountable tension, is, quite logically, expressed by the image of the book.

Hareton is stimulated by his contact with Catherine to desire education, and he tries to make himself agreeable when she begins to frequent the kitchen. There she discovers some volumes which Hareton helps her to reach: "That was a great advance for the lad. She didn't thank him; still, he felt gratified that she had accepted his assistance . . ." (chap. xxx). This is the initial hint of cooperation between the two, and although the event does not conclude happily, it is a portent of times to come. The characteristic misuse of the book at Thrushcross Grange stands between Catherine and her surroundings; but a second and decisive encounter of the two young people and the book is to dissolve the final barrier. Hareton steals Catherine's small library, and she views this as a threat to the truest level of her identity: " 'And he wants me to sink into a dunce, meantime' " (chap. xxxi). She and he argue; the resources of suffering and pride are marshalled and sent into action. In a climactic gesture Hareton, the slave of the psychology of the Heights repeating its distinctive misuse of the image, throws the books into the fire. The conflagration would appear to depict the victory of the ungoverned will over moderation and forgiveness: the image of a possible reconciliation is consumed; discord and brutality triumph.

In 1842, while a student of M. Heger in Brussels, Emily Brontë wrote, as an exercise, a number of short essays in French. One of these curious productions is a philosophical piece on the nature of creation entitled "The Butterfly." [3] In it the first-person protagonist wanders on a summer day through a peaceful wood, but in the processes of nature she can see only an insane mutual destruction. Within a flower she finds "an ugly caterpillar," a symbol of human activity upon the earth, which can only derive its sustenance from annihilation; and she

[3] Emily Brontë, *Five Essays Written in French* (El Paso, 1948), pp. 17–19.

arrives at an unavoidable question: "why was man created? He torments, he kills, he devours; he suffers, dies, is devoured—that's his whole story" (p. 18). From this cycle there is seemingly no escape. She throws flower and insect to the ground and tramples them. But just as she does so, a butterfly, "a symbol of the world to come," flutters before her eyes; and the truth is revealed: "this globe is the embryo of a new heaven and of a new earth whose meagerest beauty infinitely surpasses mortal imagination"; and the greater conclusion is inferred:

> God is the God of justice and mercy; then, assuredly each pain that he inflicts on his creatures, be they human or animal, rational or irrational, each suffering of our unhappy nature is only a seed for that divine harvest which will be gathered when sin having spent its last drop of poison, death having thrown its last dart, both will expire on the funeral pyre of a universe in flame, and will leave their former victims to an eternal realm of happiness and glory (pp. 18–19).

It is through suffering that evil is eventually purged and happiness made possible. A general conflagration separates the two worlds of pain and bliss, a conflagration in which sin and death are forever consumed. So in *Wuthering Heights,* when the prime mover of evil is exhausted, when Heathcliff suffers his *crise de volonté,* the image of the book, abused by two extremes of reality, is fed to the flames; and out of the microcosmic conflagration arises an existence of stability and peace, the ideal of the novel realized in the unheroic terms of Cathy and Hareton, who find in their natures and experience the possibility of reconciliation within the framework of society and who accept the conditions of man's limitations.

It has already been noted that *Wuthering Heights* does not invoke an omnipotent point of view representing some absolute concept of morality; however, a mode of justice does function in the novel, and it is the same justice which is at work in "The Butterfly"; but here the apocalyptic character of the destructive fire is set within one world, only types of reality being differentiated. The collapse of the reality of the Heights takes place immediately after Hareton has consigned the volumes to the blaze. Heathcliff appears and for the first time his resolution falters: " 'It will be odd if I thwart myself' " (chap. xxxi). The fire has returned things to themselves, to the paradise of normalcy: Cathy and Hareton are ready to resume their rightful places, evil is spent. In this new life founded upon acceptance, operating as reconciliation, the book fulfills its proper duty.

When Lockwood returns to the Heights after an absence of nearly a year, he is greeted by its summer aspect, by the sight of the lovers united by the book. Catherine Earnshaw strove in her way to provide an environment for Heathcliff and herself; indeed, this was a principal reason for her marriage to Edgar; but she overestimated the power of her will, the efficacy of her love, and by so doing misjudged the nature of life itself. " 'I thought,' " she exclaims during her spiritual breakdown, " 'though everybody hated and despised each other, they could not avoid loving me' " (chap. xii). Her crisis results in self-discovery, for she perceives that she has attempted what cannot be realized in this world, but only in some world beyond. In order to meet her challenge Heathcliff must disassociate his love from the desire for revenge, and in order to do this he must undermine the very basis of his identity, itself the creation of a thwarted will. No bond in this life can join such lovers. But Cathy Heathcliff is able to accomplish what the first Catherine could not; she places her love not within a self-created environment, the glorification of the will, but within human society, the modification of the will; and Hareton in his turn endows her existence with purpose. The bond which joins them is imaged by the book. " 'The intimacy thus commenced, grew rapidly.' " Ellen reports,

> "though it encountered temporary interruptions. Earnshaw was not to be civilized with a wish, and my young lady was no philosopher, and no paragon of patience; but both their minds tending to the same point— one loving and desiring to esteem, and the other loving and desiring to be esteemed—they contrived in the end to reach it" (chap. xxxii).

Throughout the novel Ellen Dean has remained the calm in the eye of the hurricane. Secure and unassailable in her limited universe, she demonstrates the strengths and weaknesses of convention. She does not hesitate to credit the cause of her stability: " 'I have undergone sharp discipline, which has taught me wisdom; and then, I have read more than you would fancy, Mr. Lockwood. You could not open a book in this library that I have not looked into, and got something out of also . . .' " (chap. vii). She refers to the library at Thrushcross Grange, the same library from which new books arrive after Hareton's destructive act. And from these books comes a world of eternal summer where the individual is reconciled to himself and to reality. Catherine and Hareton both attain their true natures and resolve their animosities to others. This was Emily Brontë's conception of the effectiveness of the book and its rightful use. In another of her French essays, "Lettre d'un frère à un frère," the library is the scene of renunciation and forgiveness, and in one of the Gondal poems, which has been related to the theme of the Palace of Instruction in that imaginary country, she writes:

> All day I've toiled, but not with pain
> In learning's golden mine;

And now at eventide again
The moonbeams softly shine. . . .

True to myself, and true to all,
May I be healthful still,
And turn away from passion's call
And curb my own wild will.[4]

[4] C. W. Hatfield, ed., *The Complete Poems of Emily Jane Brontë* (New York, 1941), p. 35.

# Charlotte Brontë
# as a Critic of
# *Wuthering Heights*

## by Philip Drew

> The faults of *Wuthering Heights* proceed, not from defective knowledge of human nature, but from inferior technique, from an insufficient acquaintance with the craft of fiction. The story is in general ill constructed, and in its detail often complicated and obscure. In parts it is uncertainly conceived, the pattern of it haunted by bad example—the "novel of edification" and the "Tale of Terror" both lend to it vicious elements.
>
> —H. W. Garrod, Introduction to
> World's Classics edition.

Emily Brontë's technique has not lacked defenders in recent years;[1] one may feel that Garrod's objections have been answered in full and that in addition there is now general recognition of the positive virtues of Emily Brontë's style and of the powerful effects of her complex system of narration and of her peculiarly tightly-woven plot, economizing in characters, dispensing with them ruthlessly as soon as they have served their purpose by bearing a child, and generally concentrating the story to a few personages in a single place. The most obvious example of the care with which Emily Brontë works is the ironic correspondence between the two halves of the novel. The younger Catherine, Hareton, and Linton re-enact the parts of Cathy, Heath-

"Charlotte Brontë as a Critic of *Wuthering Heights*," by Philip Drew. From *Nineteenth-Century Fiction*, XVIII, no. 4 (1964), 365–81. Copyright © 1964 by The Regents of the University of California. Reprinted by permission of The Regents and the author.

[1] For example, *The Structure of Wuthering Heights,* by C. P. Sanger [reprinted in this edition, pp. 7–18], (*Hogarth Essays*, XIX); David Cecil in *Early Victorian Novelists* (1934); D. Traversi (*Dublin Review*, CCXXII); J. K. Mathison (*NCF*, XI); Carl Woodring (*NCF*, XI); Miriam Allott (*Essays in Criticism*, VIII).

cliff, and Edgar at Heathcliff's bidding. Catherine's marriage to the sickly and malicious Linton is Heathcliff's bitter caricature of Cathy's marriage to Edgar. This is why the idea of Cathy's ghost is so plausible: in a sense her life is being lived over again.

The effect of this critical preoccupation with Miss Brontë's technique has been to withdraw attention from a direct consideration of the moral implications of the book, although clearly such a consideration is necessary for a judgment of its success or failure, especially of Heathcliff's fitness to stand as the central figure.[2]

Of the critics who comment explicitly on the book's subject and its moral import one of the earliest is Charlotte Brontë. Although her critical powers are disabled by Garrod, the points she makes in her preface to the edition of 1850 are so different from those which trouble modern critics that they are worth careful attention on their own account, to say nothing of their unique value as the comments of an intelligent and informed contemporary, who was peculiarly well placed to understand the nature of the authoress's achievement.

At the beginning of her preface, Charlotte Brontë apologizes ironically to those too delicately brought up to enjoy the story of unpolished moorland people and to those who are offended by seeing words (presumably "damn," "devil," and "hell") written out in full. She continues by apologizing in the same vein for the rusticity of *Wuthering Heights,* although she is in fact defending it as authentic and inevitable.

> With regard to the rusticity of *Wuthering Heights,* I admit the charge, for I feel the quality. It is rustic all through. It is moorish, and wild, and knotty as the root of heath. Nor was it natural that it should be otherwise; the author being herself a native and nursling of the moors. . . . Had Ellis Bell been a lady or a gentleman accustomed to what is called "the world," her view of a remote and unreclaimed region, as well as of the dwellers therein, would have differed greatly from that actually taken by the homebred country girl. Doubtless it would have been wider —more comprehensive: whether it would have been more original or more truthful is not so certain.

This point established, she explains how Emily became obsessed with the more "tragic and terrible traits" of Yorkshire life, and how her character was such that she could not understand why anyone should object to the depiction of scenes so vivid and so fearful. Charlotte's next step is to discuss the characters of the book in the light of her knowledge of her sister's imagination and of the atmosphere of the Yorkshire moors: it is here that she is most at variance with modern criticism.

[2] Mrs. Allott's article is a notable exception.

She begins, "For a specimen of true benevolence and homely fidelity, look at the character of Nelly Dean." A feature of recent criticism of the book has been the suggestion that Nelly is far from an adequate character—that Emily Brontë wishes us to set her uncultivated, unde-manding, homespun, conventional morality in unfavourable contrast to the passion of Heathcliff and the elder Catherine.[3] In support of this, one may observe that she plays a crucial part in the action and that this part is often weak and temporizing. So that Nelly-as-actor often annoys us and disposes us to distrust and even to resist the explicit judgments of Mrs. Dean-as-narrator. There are three reasons for supposing that this is not a deliberate effect contrived by Emily Brontë to cast doubt on Mrs. Dean's value as a source of moral standards. First, she is honest about her own failures, admitting her errors of judgment and her complacency; in fact she so often reflects ironically on her own inadequacies that James Hafley is able to sug-gest, in a most entertaining article,[4] that she is the villain of the book. Second, many of the foolish things she does are required by the neces-sities of the plot, and are more accurately seen as clumsiness or obvious-ness of contrivance than as deliberate devices to discredit her. Third, Lockwood is already set up as the source of conventional urban judg-ments and Joseph as the source of narrow moral judgments. If we must choose either Mrs. Dean's morality or Heathcliff's, there is no doubt which we are to prefer. Nelly Dean is *of* the moors; Heathcliff is an incomer. She is shown to be fairly perceptive, kindly, loyal, and, in particular, tolerant. Thus she finds many good things to say about Heathcliff, but on balance she feels bound to condemn him. Since we see the story through her eyes and she is not presented ironically, her verdict carries great weight with the reader. But for her the book would hardly have any point of normal reference. Isabella uses a significant phrase in her letter to Nelly in Chapter XIII, "How did you contrive to preserve the common sympathies of human nature when you resided here?"

Charlotte's preface continues, "For an example of constancy and tenderness, remark [the character] of Edgar Linton." This view of Edgar is more favourable than that of most modern critics, who generally regard him as "a poor creature," [5] but there is good warrant for it in the novel. For example, in Chapter XVIII Nelly describes Linton's demeanour after Catherine's death: ". . . he was too good to be thoroughly unhappy long. *He* didn't pray for Catherine's soul to haunt him. Time brought resignation and a melancholy sweeter than com-

[3] For example, by Garrod (Introduction to World's Classics edition, p. x), and by J. K. Mathison (op. cit.).
[4] *NCF*, XIII (Dec., 1958).
[5] Cecil.

mon joy. He recalled her memory with ardent, tender love, and hopeful aspiring to the better world, where he doubted not she was gone." A little later she contrasts him favourably with Hindley: "Linton . . . displayed the true courage of a loyal and faithful soul. He trusted God, and God comforted him. One hoped, and the other despaired. They chose their own lots, and were righteously doomed to endure them." I find it impossible to believe that Emily Brontë intended either of those passages to be read as ironical.

Charlotte Brontë's comments on Joseph and young Catherine are unremarkable, but of the older Catherine she has this to say: "Nor is even the first heroine of the name destitute of a certain strange beauty in her fierceness, or of honesty in the midst of perverted passion and passionate perversity." This surprising judgment must be considered in conjunction with Charlotte Brontë's verdict on Heathcliff, which may be summed up by the beginning of its first sentence: "Heathcliff, indeed, stands unredeemed; never once swerving in his arrow-straight course to perdition."

This is the crucial point in her criticism of the novel. Her assessment of Heathcliff depends on a recognition of his superhuman villainy, whereas modern critics, if they move away from a consideration of the book's mechanism to a consideration of the moral relations of the characters, usually choose to minimize or justify Heathcliff's consistent delight in malice in order to elevate him to the status of hero. An article by E. F. Shannon (*NCF*, Sept., 1959) represents this kind of criticism at its strongest. In the course of his article, Shannon says, "Within the ethical context of the novel, he [Heathcliff] is paradoxically accurate when, near death, he replies to Nelly's exhortation to penitence 'As to repenting of my injustices, I've done no injustice, and I repent of nothing.' " To decide between these conflicting views, the first step is to see whether or not Charlotte bases her judgment on an accurate description of Heathcliff's conduct in the course of the novel.

In the early part of the book, we are led to suspect him of nothing worse than a hot temper, a proud nature, and a capacity for implacable hatred. Indeed until he is sixteen the balance of sympathy is with him, since he has been treated so ill. The worst that Nelly says of him is, ". . . without having bad features, or being deficient in intellect, he contrived to convey an impression of inward and outward repulsiveness that his present aspect retains no traces of" (Chapter VIII). But all this (except perhaps the word "inward") could be laid at the door of Hindley's cruel treatment of him.

However, when he returns after three years' absence to find Catherine married to Edgar, it is clear that his character has changed. Catherine herself says (Chapter X) "He's a fierce, pitiless, woolfish man," and

Nelly confirms that he is leading Hindley to perdition. The remarkable thing about this is that Heathcliff has been back at Wuthering Heights for at most four months (September, 1783–January, 1784) and has not yet quarrelled with Catherine: yet she describes his nature so.

He courts Isabella not so much for her property as for revenge on Edgar. That he does not love her he makes plain in Chapter X, when he says of her, "You'd hear of odd things if I lived alone with that mawkish waxen face. The most ordinary would be painting on its white the colours of the rainbow, and turning the blue eyes black, every day or two." Later Catherine says to him, "I won't repeat my offer of a wife. It is as bad as offering Satan a lost soul. Your bliss lies, like his, in inflicting misery" (Chapter XI). She goes on to say that Heathcliff is destroying her happiness with Edgar: his conduct in the succeeding chapters bears this out. He runs off with Isabella through malice, despising her as he does so, and before he leaves, hangs her pet spaniel. He says himself, "The first thing she saw me do on coming out of the Grange was to hang up her little dog, and when she pleaded for it, the first words I uttered were a wish that I had the hanging of every being belonging to her, except one." Isabella writes of him, "He is ingenious and unresting in seeking to gain my abhorrence. I some-times wonder at him with an intensity that deadens my fear; yet I assure you a tiger or a venomous serpent could not rouse terror in me equal to that which he wakens" (Chapter XIII). It may be held that Isabella is not an impartial witness: the point is that her letter, written a bare two months after marriage, expresses nothing but bitter hatred of her husband, and is itself testimony to his treatment of her. Of this treatment Heathcliff says, "I've sometimes relented, from pure lack of invention, in my experiments on what she could endure and still creep shamefully cringing back" (Chapter XIV). Later in the same chapter he says, "I have no pity! I have no pity! The more the worms writhe, the more I yearn to crush out their entrails! It is a moral teething; and I grind with greater energy in proportion to the increase of pain."

Even in his grief for Cathy's death he still behaves cruelly to Isabella; when she had fled from Wuthering Heights after Heathcliff has thrown a dinner-knife at her, she remarks temperately, "Catherine had awfully perverted taste to esteem him so dearly, knowing him so well." Heath-cliff must also fall under strong suspicion of murdering Hindley Earnshaw, whom he has already ruined and driven to the brink of madness. He has also knocked him down and kicked him in the course of a quarrel. Nelly asks herself, "Had he [Hindley] fair play?" and Joseph implies that when he set off for the doctor Hindley was far from dead. Heathcliff says that Hindley was "both dead and cold and stark" before the doctor came, but this must be wrong, since Kenneth reached Thrushcross with the news while it was still early morning (Chapter

XVII). Nelly comments on Heathcliff's bearing after Hindley's death, "He maintained a hard, careless deportment, indicative of neither joy nor sorrow; if anything, it expressed a flinty gratification at a piece of difficult work successfully executed." Thus, having ruined Hindley and made himself master of Wuthering Heights and of young Hareton, and having driven away Isabella and his own child, Heathcliff has completed the first stage of his revenge, much of it during the lifetime of the elder Catherine.

There is then a gap of twelve years while the younger generation grows up. During this time, Heathcliff carries out his plan to degrade and pervert Hareton. Later he insists on possession of his son, Linton, and treats him with notable callousness. Finally he lays his plans to trap the younger Catherine into marriage with his son, first prompting Linton into a correspondence with her, and then telling her that Linton is dying for love of her. He uses his son, who is close to death, simply as a bait for Catherine, not because she will have money (all she will bring Linton is what Edgar has set aside for her, although this is referred to as a "fortune"), but to make her wretched. When Linton is very ill, Heathcliff compels him by terror to lure Catherine into Wuthering Heights. "What was filling him with dread we had no means of discerning; but there he was, powerless under its gripe, and any addition seemed capable of shocking him into idiocy." When they are in the house and the door is locked. Heathcliff says of Linton and Catherine, "It's odd what a savage feeling I have to anything that seems afraid of me. Had I been born where laws are less strict and tastes less dainty, I should treat myself to a slow vivisection of these two as an evening's amusement" (Chapter XXVII). He seizes Catherine and administers "a shower of terrific slaps on both sides of the head"; he then imprisons her for four or five days, although her father is on his deathbed. "Miss Linton, I shall enjoy myself remarkably in thinking your father will be miserable; I shall not sleep for satisfaction." He thus forces her to marry his son (exactly how this was done is not made clear) and then sets him against her: he knocks Catherine down and takes her locket. After Catherine's escape he punishes Linton.

> "I brought him down one evening, the day before yesterday, and just set him in a chair, and never touched him afterwards. I sent Hareton out, and we had the room to ourselves. In two hours I called Joseph to carry him up again; and, since then, my presence is as potent on his nerves as a ghost; and I fancy he sees me often, though I am not near. Hareton says he wakes and shrieks in the night by the hour together . . ." (Chapter XXIX).

When Linton is dying, Heathcliff refuses to send for the doctor ("His life is not worth a farthing, and I won't spend a farthing on him"), and his son dies. When Heathcliff is himself on the point of death, he says, "As to repenting of my injustices, I've done no injustice, and I repent of nothing" (Chapter XXXIV).

His whole career from the time of his return (September, 1783) to his death (May, 1802) is one of calculated malice: during this time he does not perform one single good or kindly action,[6] and continually expresses his hatred of all the other characters. So extreme is his malevolence indeed that one might expect him to impress critics as a grotesque villain, like Quilp in *The Old Curiosity Shop*. But this is far from the case. Melvin R. Watson's article on "*Wuthering Heights* and the Critics" (*NCF*, March, 1949) provides a convenient conspectus. He speaks approvingly of the opinion of Mrs. Robinson: "She insists rightly that Heathcliff is the central figure and that he harms no one seriously who had not either harmed him or asked for trouble." One can see that this is simply an inaccurate account of the novel, but as Watson's article shows, it may fairly be taken as representative of much recent criticism of *Wuthering Heights*. How are we to account for the fact that, although Charlotte Brontë describes Heathcliff's conduct accurately, her judgment of his character has commanded virtually no support from later writers, and the very transactions on which this judgment is based are ignored? Why, in short, have critics responded so readily to Heathcliff as the hero of the novel and paid so little attention to his more conspicuous qualifications to be considered the villain?

Most obviously, the characters set in opposition to him are gentle to the point of weakness. Isabella, the younger Catherine and his own son are powerless to resist him, Hindley seems a frail old man, Edgar is not a man of action, and Nelly herself, who is Heathcliff's most persistent opponent, often behaves foolishly at vital points in the action. The reader is thus tempted to admire Heathcliff, as the Romantic critics admire Satan, for his energy and decisiveness, even his ruthlessness. A closer parallel to this attitude to Heathcliff may be found in *Sanditon,* where Sir Edward Denham speaks approvingly of "the high-toned machinations of the prime character, the potent pervading Hero of the Story," and contrasts them with "the tranquil and morbid virtues of any opposing characters." Of course Jane Austen is here satirizing Sir Edward's modish taste for the extravagances of the Gothic novel. If we discount such highly-charged romantic views of the Hero, what is to be found in *Wuthering Heights* itself which may be supposed to influence the reader in Heathcliff's favour?

---

[6] But notice that E. F. Shannon (op. cit.) makes the following point in Heathcliff's favour: "Although a reluctant host, he provides Lockwood with a glass of wine, tea and dinner on separate occasions; and during the narrator's illness he sends him a brace of grouse and chats amiably at his 'bedside a good hour.'"

It is frequently argued that Heathcliff is redeemed by his passionate love for Catherine Earnshaw. This is Charlotte Brontë's comment:

> . . . his love for Catherine . . . is a sentiment fierce and inhuman: a passion such as might boil and glow in the bad essence of some evil genius; a fire that might form the tormented centre—the ever-suffering soul of a magnate of the infernal world: and by its quenchless and ceaseless ravage effect the execution of the decree which dooms him to carry Hell with him wherever he wanders.

In the rest of this article, I shall hope to show that this is a literally accurate description of Heathcliff's passion for Catherine.

The facts as given by Mrs. Dean are these. When Catherine is fifteen and Heathcliff sixteen, he hears her say that it would degrade her to marry him. She has in fact already accepted Edgar Linton. Heathcliff leaves Wuthering Heights then for over three years: the implication is that he is in love with Catherine. Before she knows that he has left, Catherine makes an impassioned declaration of her feelings for him.

> "If all else perished and *he* remained *I* should still continue to be. And if all else remained, and he were annihilated, the universe would turn to a mighty stranger—I should not seem a part of it. My love for Linton is like the foliage in the woods; time will change it, I'm well aware, as winter changes the trees. My love for Heathcliff resembles the eternal rocks beneath—a source of little visible delight, but necessary. Nelly, I *am* Heathcliff."

This speech is a fine one; it is quoted *ad nauseum,* and part of its power is transferred to Heathcliff. He is supposed to reciprocate Catherine's selfless love for him and to be redeemed by it. In fact, he reveals to Nelly and Isabella the selfishness of his love for Catherine and of the means he uses to convince himself that he is actually behaving more nobly than Edgar. This is especially plain in Chapter XIV, and culminates in Heathcliff's derisive comment on Edgar, "It is not in him to be loved like me." Yet Catherine declares her love for Edgar: "I love the ground under his feet, and the air over his head, and everything he touches, and every word he says. I love all his looks, and all his actions, and him entirely and altogether." When Heathcliff leaves and stays away for three years, Catherine gives no sign that the universe seems empty to her. On the contrary, she marries Edgar Linton, and Nelly comments, "I believe I may assert that they were really in possession of deep and growing happiness." Or as Catherine puts it herself, "I begin to be secure and tranquil." Catherine dies when she is eighteen and Heathcliff nineteen. As adults they are together for barely a sixth of the novel: they meet seldom and when they do they usually quarrel, until finally Heathcliff is goaded into marrying Isabella.

There is no doubt that this bond between Catherine and Heathcliff is extraordinarily powerful, but it is not a *justifying* bond. To describe it as "a love that springs from an elemental and natural affinity between them" and to imply that they act as they do merely through a pardonable excess of love, which is the prime virtue, is to fail to recognize its nature. On Heathcliff's side at least, it is selfish, which should warn us not to confuse it with love; it expresses itself only through violence—notice, for example, the extraordinary series of descriptions of violent physical contact during and immediately after Heathcliff's last meeting with Catherine; their passion for each other is so compounded with jealousy, anger, and hatred that it brings them only unhappiness, anguish, and eventually death; it is described as the instrument of Catherine's damnation by Mrs. Dean when she says, "Well might Catherine deem that heaven would be a land of exile to her, unless with her mortal body she cast away her mortal character also." In short, while we must recognize that the forging and breaking of the bond between Catherine and Heathcliff provides the novel with all its motive energy, it is fallacious to argue that this proves that Emily Brontë condones Heathcliff's behaviour and does not expect the reader to condemn it. Charlotte's phrase "perverted passion and passionate perversity" is exact.

We must consider next the argument, as advanced by Cecil, for example, that it was not Emily Brontë's intention that the reader should condemn Heathcliff, since he dictates the whole course of the novel, brings his schemes to a successful conclusion, and dies happily. A bitter remark of the younger Catherine's is relevant here. In Chapter XXIX she says:

> "Mr. Heathcliff, *you* have *nobody* to love you; and however miserable you make us, we shall still have the revenge of thinking that your cruelty arises from your greater misery! You *are* miserable, are you not? Lonely, like the devil, and envious like him? *Nobody* loves you— *nobody* will cry for you when you die! I wouldn't be you!"

Later in the same chapter, Heathcliff himself admits, talking of the older Catherine,

> "She showed herself, as she often was in life, a devil to me! And, since then, sometimes more and sometimes less, I've been the sport of that intolerable torture—infernal—keeping my nerves at such a stretch that, if they had not resembled catgut, they would long ago have relaxed to the feebleness of Linton's. . . . It racked me. I've often groaned aloud, till that old rascal Joseph no doubt believed that my conscience was playing the fiend inside of me. . . . It was a strange way of killing— not by inches, but by fractions of hairbreadths—to beguile me with the spectre of a hope through eighteen years!"

"Strange happiness," as Nelly says. At the end of the book, Heathcliff's domination over the other characters fails, and he finds himself unable to plan further degradation for Catherine and Hareton.

"It is a poor conclusion, is it not?" he observed . . . "an absurd termination to my violent exertions? I get levers and mattocks to demolish the two houses, and train myself to be capable of working like Hercules, and when everything is ready and in my power I find the will to lift a slate of either roof has vanished! My old enemies have not beaten me. Now would be the precise time to revenge myself on their representatives. I could do it, and none could hinder me. But where is the use? I don't care for striking; I can't take the trouble to raise my hand. That sounds as if I had been labouring the whole time only to exhibit a fine trait of magnanimity. It is far from being the case. I have lost the faculty of enjoying their destruction, and I am too idle to destroy for nothing" (Chapter XXXIII).

This passage leads on at once to Heathcliff's death. It is clear that his thwarted love of and vain grief for Catherine became perverted into the sadistic desire for revenge which sustained him for so many years. As soon as cruelty lost its savour, he lost all that was keeping him alive. At the end of his life, Nelly reproaches him for his wickedness (Chapter XXXIV), and her remarks are clearly just. They accord precisely with the spirit of Charlotte Brontë's preface.

The only point which Charlotte urges in Heathcliff's favour is what she calls "his rudely confessed regard for Hareton Earnshaw— the young man whom he has ruined." There is a strong resemblance between Hareton and Heathcliff, for both were poor dependents— half servant, half adopted son. Heathcliff perceived the likeness at the time of Hindley's death. "Now, my bonny lad, you are *mine!* And we'll see if one tree won't grow as crooked as another with the same wind to twist it" (Chapter XVII). He takes full advantage of the position.

"I've a pleasure in him," he continued, reflecting aloud. "He has satisfied my expectations. If he were a born fool I should not enjoy it half so much. But he's no fool; and I can sympathize with all his feelings, having felt them myself. I know what he suffers now, for instance, exactly. It is merely a beginning of what he shall suffer though. And he'll never be able to emerge from his bathos of coarseness and ignorance. I've got him faster than his scoundrel of a father secured me, and lower, for he takes a pride in his brutishness. I've taught him to scorn everything extra-animal as silly and weak" (Chapter XXI).

The crucial difference is that Hareton does not allow his ill-treatment to make him bitter; he even acquires a kind of fondness for Heathcliff. But this tells in his favour, not Heathcliff's, for it shows that Heathcliff was not *necessarily* brutalized by his environment, but rather that Hindley's ill-treatment of him encouraged a vindictiveness which he later deliberately fostered.

These are the strongest arguments I have found in justification of Heathcliff's conduct, and, as I have shown, none of them is of sufficient force to avert the reader's natural censure of his consistent malice and cruelty. The problem therefore is to reconcile our condemnation of his behaviour with his dominant place in the novel and in the reader's sympathies. Clearly, our attitude to the main character of a work of fiction need not be one of moral approval (e.g., Macbeth, Giles Overreach, Tamburlaine, Giovanni, Beatrice-Joanna, Becky Sharp, Pincher Martin), but he must in some way act with the reader's understanding and sympathy. In the remainder of this article, I should like to suggest one way in which Emily Brontë powerfully develops the reader's feelings in Heathcliff's favour.

In the earlier chapters our sympathies go naturally to Heathcliff (i.e., Lockwood's narrative and the first part of Nelly Dean's story— up to Chapter IX) since he is seen only as the victim of ill-treatment. As Charlotte wrote to W. S. Williams,[7]

> [Heathcliff] exemplified the effects which a life of continued injustice and hard usage may produce on a naturally perverse, vindictive, and inexorable disposition. Carefully trained and kindly treated, the black gipsy-cub might possibly have been reared into a human being, but tyranny and ignorance made of him a mere demon.

Heathcliff vanishes for three years, and these years are wrapped in mystery. Lockwood makes some historically plausible conjectures about them. "Did he finish his education on the Continent, and come back a gentleman? Or did he get a sizar's place at college, or escape to America, and earn honours by drawing blood from his foster-country, or make a fortune more promptly on the English highways?" (Chapter X). Mrs. Dean has to admit that she does not know: all she can say is that between the ages of sixteen and nineteen Heathcliff converted himself from an ignorant penniless servant to a man with money and black whiskers, a man of whom Catherine says, "It would honour the first gentleman in the country to be his friend." The mystery remains throughout the book.

After Heathcliff's return, he dominates the other characters, but, although he is now strong and his enemies weak, his life is one of continual torment. His sufferings engage the reader's natural sympathies, the more so as he suffers in a particular way, and one that accounts for, even if it cannot excuse, his wickedness. For Emily

[7] Letter to W. S. Williams, August 14, 1848, quoted by L. and E. M. Hanson, *The Four Brontës* (p. 260).

Brontë implies very strongly that if Heathcliff during his absence has not in fact sold his soul to the devil, he has effectively done so. Every description of him reinforces this implication, starting from Nelly's first meeting with him on his return. He appears suddenly in a patch of shadow, startling her.

"I have waited here an hour," he resumed, while I continued staring; "and the whole of that time all round has been as still as death. I dared not enter. You do not know? Look, I'm not a stranger!"
A ray fell on his features; the cheeks were sallow and half covered with black whiskers, the brows lowering, the eyes deep-set and singular. I remembered the eyes.
"What!" I cried, uncertain whether to regard him as a worldly visitor, and I raised my hands in amazement. "What! you come back? Is it really you? Is it?"
"Yes, Heathcliff," he replied. . . . "I want to have one word with her—your mistress. Go, and say some person from Gimmerton desires to see her."
"How will she take it?" I exclaimed. "What will she do? The surprise bewilders me. It will put her out of her head. And you *are* Heathcliff, but altered! Nay, there's no comprehending it. Have you been for a soldier?"
"Go and carry my message," he interrupted impatiently. "I'm in hell till you do" (Chapter X).

Thereafter, hardly a chapter passes without some indication that Heathcliff is suffering the torments of a lost soul; from the moment of his return he is referred to as "ghoulish," "a devil," "a goblin," "Judas," and "Satan." Edgar says that his presence is "a moral poison that would contaminate the most virtuous." After his marriage Isabella writes to Nelly, "The second question I have great interest in; it is this—Is Mr. Heathcliff a man? If so, is he mad? And if not, is he a devil?" Hindley calls Heathcliff "hellish" and "a fiend." "Fiend" or "fiendish" is applied to him some seven times thereafter. Hindley is a powerful instrument for stressing the damnation of Heathcliff. He says,

"Am I to lose *all* without chance of retrieval? Is Hareton to be a beggar? Oh, damnation! I *will* have it back, and I'll have his gold too, and then his blood, and hell shall have his soul! It will be ten times blacker with that guest than ever it was before!"

Heathcliff himself makes a revealing comment when he learns of Catherine's illness. He says that if he were ever to lose her, if, for example, she forgot him completely, "Two words would comprehend my future—*death* and *hell*; existence after losing her would be hell." Shortly afterwards Isabella introduces the other word commonly used to refer to Heathcliff—"diabolical." Heathcliff is described as "diabolical" or "devilish" no fewer than six times: some comment on his infernal powers is thus made virtually every time he appears. Heathcliff's own outburts to Catherine have a similar effect.

> "Are you possessed with a devil," he pursued savagely, "to talk in that manner to me when you are dying? Do you reflect that all those words will be branded in my memory and eating deeper eternally after you have left me? You know you lie to say I have killed you; and, Catherine, you know that I could as soon forget you as my existence! Is it not sufficient for your infernal selfishness that, while you are at peace, I shall writhe in the torment of hell?"

Similarly, shortly afterwards:

> "Yes, you may kiss me, and cry, and wring out my kisses and tears; they'll blight you—they'll damn you. . . . So much the worse for me that I am strong. Do I want to live? What kind of living will it be, when you—O God! would *you* like to live with your soul in the grave?" (Chapter XV).

This idea of souls being separated from bodies and its extension into the idea of ghosts walking the earth because there is no peace for them in the grave are pervasive in the book, and do much to reinforce the suggestion that evil powers are abroad. Heathcliff is particularly given to a belief in ghosts (Chapter XXIX).

For the rest of the book, Heathcliff is referred to variously as "an incarnate goblin," "a monster," "not a human being," and "a hellish villain"; Isabella refers to his "kin beneath," and talks of Hell as "his right abode." She says to Hindley, "His mouth watered to tear you with his teeth, because he's only half man—not so much—and the rest fiend!" (Chapter XVII).

Other characters refer to him as a "devil" (twice) and "a goblin." Nelly wonders whether he is wholly human. " 'Is he a ghoul or a vampire?' I mused. I had read of such hideous incarnate demons." He says of himself to Catherine, "To you I've made myself worse than the devil." And through his adult life he undergoes what he describes as "that intolerable torture—infernal!" He says to Nelly when he is near death, "Last night I was on the threshhold of hell," and when he dies Joseph exclaims, "Th' divil's harried off his soul."

This network of references and comment serves to mark out Heathcliff as a possessed soul. If the story were expressly narrated on a supernatural level, his career could be described by saying simply that he sells his soul to the devil in exchange for power, power over others, and specifically power to make himself fit to marry Catherine. When however he attempts to claim his share of the bargain he finds that the devil is, as always, a cheat. He has the power he asked for but loses Catherine herself. He is left simply with power, the exercise of which he finds necessary but intolerably painful. Thereafter, he is consumed inwardly by hell-fire and the knowledge of his own damnation.

This would be a metaphorical way of describing what in fact happens. Heathcliff's personality begins to disintegrate when he allows himself to become obsessed by a physical passion for Catherine and deliberately fosters this passion to the point of mania. He sacrifices every other part of his personality to the satisfaction of his passion, until by its very violence it destroys its own object. Once Catherine has gone, Heathcliff is left with no possible emotions except those into which he can pervert his previous obsession with Catherine. He finds that he can demonstrate that he has feelings only by expressing them as cruelty. This brings him no happiness: on the contrary his power for wickedness *is* his punishment, rather than his prize, just as his passion for Catherine was not a blessing but a curse. In short, he is destroying himself throughout the book: each act of wanton brutality is a further maiming of himself. "Treachery and violence are spears pointed at both ends. They wound those who resort to them worse than their enemies" (Chapter XVII). Time moves swiftly on the moors, and senility sets in very early (Hindley is only twenty-seven at his death), but nobody else ages as fast as Heathcliff. Towards his death, he seems to be consuming his life ever more rapidly, as if the processes of nature had been accelerated by the fires within. He acts like a fiend incarnate, but his actions torture him as much as they torture his victims: they are a part, and the worst part, of the torments of the damned which Heathcliff suffers during his life. When he finds himself capable of a good act, even one so neutral as not persecuting Hareton and Catherine, it is as though his sentence had been at last worked out, and he dies almost joyfully.

The sympathy that we give to him is thus not the sort that we give to the noble tragic hero, nor is it the same as our reluctant admiration of a powerfully defiant villain like Vittoria. It is more nearly akin to the compassion we feel for those who are fated to work out their doom in torment and despair, characters such as Satan himself, Marlowe's Faustus and Mephistopheles, the Wandering Jew, Vanderdecken, or even Captain Ahab.[8] It does not lead us to approve of Heathcliff's actions or even to condone them. Emily Brontë's achievement is to arouse our sympathy for a lost soul while making it quite clear that his actions are damnable.

All this is comprehended in Charlotte's preface. She sees that Heathcliff is embarked on an "arrow-straight course to perdition," and that

[8] Mrs. Allott (op. cit.) suggests that Heathcliff sometimes reminds us of Byron's Manfred or Cain. Muriel Spark and Derek Stanford (*Emily Brontë*, London, 1953) note this also, but as a major weakness in the drawing of Heathcliff who, they say, "is Byron in prose dress."

his love for Catherine is a fire "that might form the tormented centre
—the ever-suffering soul of a magnate of the infernal world" doomed
"to carry Hell with him wherever he wanders." She concludes her
remarks on his character by saying that but for one or two slight re-
deeming features "we should say he was child neither of Lascar nor
gipsy, but a man's shape animated by demon life—a Ghoul—an
Afreet." She thus identifies the novel's main source of evil energy and
its central metaphor, which is the parallel between diabolical possession and embittered passion. Her concluding paragraph expresses
with some subtlety the extent of Emily Brontë's achievement in liber-
ating this terrifying energy and yet controlling it.

> *Wuthering Heights* was hewn in a wild workshop, with simple tools,
> out of homely materials. The statuary found a granite block on a solitary
> moor: gazing thereon, he saw how from the crag might be elicited a
> head, savage, swart, sinister; a form moulded with at least one element of
> grandeur—power. . . . With time and labour, the crag took human
> shape; and there it stands colossal, dark, and frowning, half statue, half
> rock: in the former sense, terrible and goblin-like; in the latter, almost
> beautiful, for its colouring is of mellow grey, and moorland moss clothes
> it; and heath, with its blooming bells and balmy fragrance, grows faith-
> fully close to the giant's foot.

# Control of

# Sympathy in

# *Wuthering Heights*

## *by John Hagan*

One of Emily Brontë's major achievements in *Wuthering Heights* is to keep alive the reader's sympathy for both Catherine and Heathcliff, even though their behavior after the former's marriage to Edgar Linton becomes increasingly bizarre and frightening akin to the demonic. From the time in Chapter X of Heathcliff's return to Thrushcross Grange after his three-year absence to the end of the novel, we are sustained in a double view: far from condoning the hideous spiritual transformation which Catherine and Heathcliff undergo, Emily Brontë evokes our moral revulsion by employing all the resources of her art to bring its viciousness into the sharpest relief; at the same time, however, she never allows her hero and heroine to forfeit our compassion. This double view is essential if the final effect of the novel is to be tragic and not merely distasteful. We must condemn the sin, but pity the sinner. The view that Emily Brontë is an amoral writer results in large part from a confusion between ethical neutrality and this pity she enlists on behalf of a hero and heroine whose behavior is allowed at the same time to shock us profoundly. (It is also a consequence of attributing to Catherine and Heathcliff a factitious metaphysical status, as I shall try to show later.) The confusion can be removed if we come to understand the precise means by which Emily Brontë accomplishes the delicate task of making us respond in this complex way.

The only critic to have specifically addressed himself to this problem in any detail is Arnold Kettle, who justly observes that "despite everything he does and is, we continue to sympathize with Heathcliff —not, obviously, to admire him or defend him, but to give him our

"Control of Sympathy in *Wuthering Heights*," by John Hagan. From *Nineteenth-Century Fiction*, XXI, no. 4 (1967), 305–323. Copyright © 1967 by The Regents of the University of California. Reprinted by permission of The Regents and the author.

inmost sympathy. . . ."[1] But valuable as Kettle's discussion is for
focusing attention on the issue, it is unsatisfactory both because he
neglects to apply the question to Catherine as fully as her part in the
novel requires and, more important, because his explanation of how
this effect is achieved rests on a curious, Marxist-oriented interpretation of Heathcliff as an "outcast slummy" and a "conscious rebel"
(144, 145). On this reading Heathcliff wins our sympathies because
"he is on the side of humanity and we are with him just as we are
with Oliver Twist, and for much the same reasons"; ". . . what
Heathcliff stands for is morally superior to what the Lintons stand
for . . . and [the] Earnshaws"; we "continue in an obscure way to
identify ourselves with him *against* the other characters"; "instinctively we recognize a rough moral justice in what he has done to
his oppressors . . ." (145–146, 149–150). Not only is this thesis quite
inconsistent with the assertion that we neither "admire" nor "defend"
Heathcliff (for if he is "on the side of humanity" like Oliver Twist
and "morally superior" to the Lintons and Earnshaws, why shouldn't
we admire and defend him?), but it is wholly unacceptable on the
grounds of ordinary morality and the evidence of the text alike because it implies that Heathcliff is the moral superior of *all* his enemies.
How, for instance, can it be made to apply to the second Catherine
and Hareton Earnshaw? They have not been Heathcliff's "oppressors";
he has been theirs. To argue that Heathcliff's subjugation of Catherine and Hareton is only a by-product of his laudable attempt to
beat Hindley and Edgar "at their own game . . . to turn on them
. . . their own standards . . . their own weapons of money and ar-
ranged marriages"—in short, to get "power over them by the classic
methods of the ruling class, expropriation and property deals" (150)
—still does not demonstrate these youngsters' moral inferiority. Indeed, only on the assumption of a primitive eye-for-eye morality are
these tactics defensible for Heathcliff to use even against those who
have really injured him. If they are proof of the corruption of who-
ever uses them, then Heathcliff must stand condemned as much as the
"ruling class" itself. Kettle himself is uneasily aware of this, for no
sooner has he spoken of Heathcliff's revenge as having "moral force"
(149) than he contradictorily concedes that it is the result of his enemies having "entrapped him in their own values" (150).

But all of this only raises the larger question of the fairness of
lumping together Isabella and Edgar Linton as mere specimens of
a corrupt "ruling class" in the first place. Isabella's only "crime"
against Heathcliff is her youthful and foolish infatuation. How this
can cause us to feel any sympathy for Heathcliff's barbaric treatment

---

[1] *An Introduction to the English Novel*, 2 vols. (London, 1951), I, 149. Hereafter,
page references to this work will be given parenthetically in the text.

of her after their marriage is a problem which Kettle refuses squarely to face. One would suppose that, if the moral edge had to be given to one or the other, Isabella's trust, however naive, would surely stand up as well as Heathcliff's cynical calculation. As for Kettle's excessively disparaging view of Edgar, this appears to rest not on all the evidence offered by the text, but on no better authority than the bitter, highly biased denunciations uttered by Catherine and Heathcliff in Chapters x–xii, when they are in the throes of the frustration which has followed their impassioned reunion. A far juster view of his character may be found in Mary Visick's *Genesis of Wuthering Heights* (Hong Kong, 1958). Kettle's error in handling the Lintons is to ignore almost completely the particularities of Emily Brontë's characterization and to make them mere papier-mâché representatives of a class to which he believes moral inferiority can be attributed a priori.

The critical problem which confronted us at the outset, therefore, still challenges us for a solution.


## II


The central fact about Catherine after Heathcliff's return is that she becomes actively malignant and perverse. Her behavior between now and her death resolves itself into a succession of harrowing mad-scenes. A lesser novelist of Emily Brontë's day would have allowed the heroine gently and beautifully to pine away in unfulfilled longing. But Emily Brontë softens nothing. She carries our aversion to Catherine so far as to bring our sympathies near the breaking-point. This is the artistic risk she must run if her story is to transcend sentimental melodrama.

The first sign of Catherine's moral and psychological deterioration is her wholly unreasonable expectation in Chapter x that Edgar should welcome Heathcliff back to the Grange with open arms. When the former naturally resists this demand, she shows herself wholly unable to grasp his point of view and accuses him of being "sulky," of uttering nothing but "pettish, silly speeches," of always contriving "to be sick at the least cross," of "whining for trifles," of displaying "idle petulance," and the like.[2] To accept these charges as a valid criticism of Edgar's character would, of course, be very wide of the mark. What Emily Brontë is rendering here, with no attempt to minimize the moral ugliness, is Catherine's blind self-pity, self-right-

---

[2] *Wuthering Heights*, ed. William M. Sale, Jr. (Norton Critical Editions; New York, 1963), p. 86. Henceforth, page references to the novel will be to this virtually definitive edition and will be given parenthetically in the text.

eousness, and injustice. This state of mind becomes even more intense later in the same chapter when she discovers Isabella's infatuation with Heathcliff. Her first response, prompted by her fierce jealousy, is to slander the latter unconscionably. " 'Tell her what Heathcliff is' " she orders Nelly; " 'an unreclaimed creature, without refinement, without cultivation; an arid wilderness of furze and whinstone. . . . He's a fierce, pitiless, wolfish man. . . . I know he couldn't love a Linton; and yet he'd be quite capable of marrying your fortune and expectations. Avarice is growing with him a besetting sin . . .' " (89–90). Again, though it is easy to read this passage as if it were an interpretation of Heathcliff endorsed by Emily Brontë, the context and language alike make it clear that it is both a calculated effort to discourage Isabella by painting her idol in the most lurid colors and a kind of manic hallucination in which Catherine herself has come to half-believe. Heathcliff's roughness (for which, significantly, Catherine has never shown anything but short-lived distaste before now) is grossly overstated; his cruelty is only a presumption; and the contention that avarice is becoming his "besetting sin" is a misinterpretation of his motives for gambling with the truly avaricious Hindley. Catherine's jealous response to her discovery of Isabella's infatuation does not stop here, however. On the following day, she loses no time in brutally humiliating the girl by forcibly detaining her and exposing her passion in the presence of Heathcliff himself (91–92).

The breaking-point finally comes in Chapters XI and XII as a result of Catherine's second discovery—that Isabella's infatuation is apparently being reciprocated. In the angry confrontation with Heathcliff which follows, Catherine tries to make light of her jealousy and implies that if Heathcliff now went away she would return to a happiness with Edgar which she enjoyed before his return (98), but the reader sees that these are mere rationalizations. This becomes even clearer when Edgar intervenes and threatens to have Heathcliff put out of the house: instead of supporting her husband, as her remarks have led us to suppose she would, she turns on him, and, when he shows his weakness, joins Heathcliff in showering him with contempt (99–100). So confused are her emotions, however, that, immediately after Heathcliff has left, she addresses to Nelly an extraordinary speech, which concludes with her threatening to revenge herself on both men by committing suicide:

> "Well, if I cannot keep Heathcliff for my friend, if Edgar will be mean and jealous, I'll try to break their hearts by breaking my own. That will be a prompt way of finishing all, when I am pushed to extremity! But it's a deed to be reserved for a forlorn hope; I'd not take Linton by surprise with it. To this point he has been discreet in dreading to provoke me; you must represent the peril of quitting that policy, and re-

mind him of my passionate temper, verging, when kindled, on frenzy. I wish you could dismiss that apathy out of your countenance, and look rather more anxious about me!" (101).

In its shockingly blind and unscrupulous self-righteousness and self-pity this speech brings Catherine to a moral nadir. Almost at once she grows hysterical, locks herself in her room, falls into a fit, and, upon recovering, subjects herself to the three-day fast that fatally undermines her health. She ceases to starve herself only when she becomes maniacally suspicious that her death is precisely what Edgar desires (103–4) and that everyone else in the household has become her enemy too (104). Thus, the vital and vivacious Catherine of childhood is transformed into a histrionic, vindictive harridan—an egomaniac and a paranoiac on the verge of insanity, reduced at last by "feverish bewilderment" to tearing the pillow "with her teeth" (104). Emily Brontë is ruthless in systematically stripping her heroine of almost every shred of attractiveness and dignity.

She cannot, however, allow this impression to last for long. If she does, Catherine will no longer seem pitiful and tragic to us, but merely repulsive. Accordingly, from the beginning she has subtly qualified our response by leading us to see that Catherine's sense of having been betrayed by everyone, Heathcliff included, is not without a grain of truth. In Chapter xv, when she and Heathcliff are reunited for the last time and he upbraids her for having abandoned him at the prompting of her " 'poor fancy' " for Edgar (135), she retaliates by charging him with having abandoned *her* (135). Though this feeling is expressed later than the scenes I have just considered, we can hardly suppose that Catherine has hitherto been a stranger to it: the assumption that it has been rankling in her consciousness over a long period helps to account for the fierce intensity of her jealousy. Nor can we regard this feeling as wholly irrational. If we examine the account in Chapter ix of how her marriage to Edgar actually came about and correlate with it an important passage in Chapter x, we cannot avoid noticing that on the assumption of Catherine's sole responsibility for her separation from Heathcliff the plot is unnecessarily complicated. On the night she accepts Edgar's proposal and confesses her feelings to Nelly, Heathcliff is invisibly and silently present "on the other side of the settle . . . on a bench by the wall" (69), where he can hear whatever she has to say. Since he gets up and leaves as soon as she declares that to marry him in his present state would "degrade" her (72), he fails to hear her confess her impassioned sense of their affinity. But he *has* heard her say that " 'I've no more business to marry Edgar Linton than I have to be in heaven' " (72), and this is enough to assure him that her choice of Edgar is causing her deep misgivings. He runs away from Wuthering Heights, then, not in anger, but, as we learn later, to seek his fortune and thereby make himself worthy of Catherine's preference. Like Pip in Dickens's *Great Expectations,* he has been made ashamed of his low condition by the girl he loves, and he seeks to transform himself into a gentleman (85). Obviously, his hope was that she would not marry Edgar before he returned. But he was gone for three years, and Catherine, apparently having given up all expectation of seeing him again, went through with the marriage after all. There is a presumption, then, that if Heathcliff had come back earlier it might never have taken place. It remains true, of course, that Catherine's acceptance of Edgar's proposal is the necessary condition for all that happens subsequently, but we cannot ignore the part in her fate played, however unwittingly, by Heathcliff's wounded pride and ambition. It is her awareness that he "abandoned" her once before at a critical juncture in her life that lends plausibility as well as intensity to her fears that he may be reciprocating Isabella's love and imparts to her manic rages a measure of justification which enlists our sympathy.

An analogous method is used by Emily Brontë to modify our outraged response to Heathcliff's atrocious career of revenge. Whatever romantic glamour may have been attached to him earlier, it is dispelled by his outright savagery. No casuistry can in the least win our moral approval of his brutality, especially toward Isabella and the three members of the second generation, including his own son Linton. Nothing shows more clearly the level to which he descends than his perverse description of his pitiless behavior as " 'a moral teething' " (128). Nevertheless, there is something in the situation which, though it does not cause us to renounce our moral judgment, does induce us to apply it with compassion. This is the way in which Heathcliff's plan of revenge actually originates. It develops only gradually—in three stages—taking shape in his mind not when he runs away from Wuthering Heights in Chapter ix, but only three years later after his reunion with the married Catherine in Chapter x. As I have just noted, he runs away only in the hope of transforming himself into a gentleman. This transformation is eventually effected, but then he discovers to his dismay that Catherine has discarded him for Edgar. His struggles now seem wholly vain, and his first plan, therefore, is simply to avenge himself in some unspecified way on Hindley (the man who caused the degradation which has cost him his happiness) and then commit suicide (85; cf. his speech to Nelly on 125–26). The moment Catherine's ardent welcome proves she still loves him, however, he abandons this plan and adopts another—that of taking up residence again at Wuthering Heights in order to be once more in her vicinity (87). His third and final plan is, of course, his dual revenge against all the Earnshaws and Lintons by which he hopes to become master of the Heights and the Grange alike. Precisely when this plan occurs to him is not specified, but its evolution can easily be inferred. The crucial point is that the suggestion for it actually comes unwittingly from his victims themselves. His originally vague idea of "settling his score" with Hindley is given definite content only when the latter, out of greed for Heathcliff's newly acquired money, encourages him in that gambling at the Heights which eventually leaves Hindley stripped of his property (87). Similarly, Heathcliff conceives the idea and method of revenging himself upon the Linton family only after he has been made aware by Catherine that the naive Isabella has fallen in love with him (93).

The importance of these details cannot be ignored. They make clear that Heathcliff develops his plan of revenge against the houses of his two enemies only after they first put themselves in his power by their own volition. Though he takes the fullest advantage of the position in which they place themselves, he does not force them into this position originally. As his increasingly frequent meetings with Catherine after his return convince him that she loves him more than her husband, the need for revenge naturally grows more intense, until it reaches a climax in Chapter xi when Edgar threatens to have him thrown out of the house and strikes him in the throat. From this moment on nothing can deflect Heathcliff from his destructive course. But the essential point is that his violence has been building up only gradually and only under the stress of provocation. For this reason, though we may deplore his subsequent actions, he never entirely forfeits our sympathy.

## III

Important though these plot manipulations are for determining our double view of Catherine and Heathcliff with its blend of moral disapproval and compassion, they are not fundamental. The decisive factor is Emily Brontë's ability to convince us that cruelty is not innate in the characters of her hero and heroine, but is the consequence of their extreme suffering. In this respect there is a very close similarity between *Wuthering Heights* and Euripides' *Medea*: in both the novel and the play the force that drives the protagonists to their outrageous behavior is their personal misery. In the case of *Wuthering Heights* this causal nexus is often obscured, as in the following interpretation by Dorothy Van Ghent:

> What ever could happen to these two [Catherine and Heathcliff], if they could be happily together, would be something altogether asocial,

amoral, savagely irresponsible, wildly impulsive: it would be the en-
thusiastic, experimental, quite random activity of childhood, occult to
the socialized adult. But since no conceivable *human* male and female,
not brutish, not anthropologically rudimentary, could be together in
this way as adults, all that we can really imagine for the grown-up
Catherine and Heathcliff, as "characters" on the human plane, is what
the book gives of them—their mutual destruction by tooth and nail
in an effort, through death, to get back to the lost state of gypsy freedom
in childhood.[3]

The fallacy here is to confuse what Catherine and Heathcliff are
*before* Catherine's marriage with what they are *after* it. It is implied
that they are "altogether asocial, amoral, savagely irresponsible, wildly
impulsive" *by nature*—nothing less, as it were, than a case of retarded
development—and that this must have inevitably led to "their mutual
destruction by tooth and nail" *even if a marriage between Catherine
and Edgar had never taken place.* This mistake is easy to make because so much more space in the novel is given to representing Catherine and Heathcliff after the marriage than before it; but, by the
same token, it is impossible to support such a reading with adequate
evidence. (Indeed, Mrs. Van Ghent contradicts her thesis later when
she declares that though "some alluring and astonishing destiny seems
possible" for Catherine and Heathcliff, *"what that phenomenon might
be or mean, we cannot know, for it is frustrated by Catherine's marriage to Edgar"* [168; my italics].) That Catherine and Heathcliff are
wild and rebellious as children goes without saying. But Emily Brontë
takes great pains to show us that the tyranny of Hindley under which
they are forced to live has given them good reason to be. At this stage,
there is nothing sinister in their behavior at all. On the contrary, it
is their only source of consolation. Nor is it ever implied that, had
circumstances been different, they would never have matured beyond the "quite random activity of childhood." Such an assumption
is wholly gratuitous and runs squarely in the face of the fact that
everything is done by Emily Brontë early in the novel to set forth
these characters in the most sympathetic light. Indeed, it is only because she does this so well that we can accept their separation by
Catherine's marriage as a calamity. The pride, hardness, and sullen-
ness which Heathcliff displays as a child is significant only because
these traits make his later violence *possible;* there is never any suggestion that they would *necessitate* it without provocation. His nature
is a soil capable of nourishing violence (if this were not demonstrated
early in the story the plot would be wholly implausible), but the seed
of frustration has to be planted first.

[3] *The English Novel: Form and Function* (New York, 1953), pp. 157–58. Hereafter, page references to this work will be given parenthetically in the text.

What stands in the way of a clear recognition of these facts for some readers is the time-honored tradition of attributing to Catherine and Heathcliff a unique metaphysical status. They are said to be not merely human beings, with recognizably human needs, capabilities, and failings, but the embodiment of special cosmic "forces," "energies," or "principles." These views betray their weaknesses because their proponents are unable to give any consistent account of precisely what these forces or principles are supposed to be. In Lord David Cecil's famous interpretation, for instance, Catherine and Heathcliff are said at one moment to incarnate a "spiritual principle" which lives on after their deaths in the form of an "immortal soul," and at another to be "a manifestation of natural forces" like a "mountain torrent," which, when it is "frustrated of its natural outlet . . . inevitably becomes destructive." [4] What identity there is between a "natural force" and a "spiritual principle" is not explained. Similarly, Mrs. Van Ghent seems undecided whether the strange "otherness" which Catherine and Heathcliff manifest is "the raw, inhuman reality of anonymous natural energies" (157; cf. 154, 163, and 164), the unconscious mind (163), or some literal demonism (168; cf. 154 and 163). The clue to the critical confusion here is the way in which each critic seems wholly unaware, as he moves from one to another, that all these different forces and principles cannot be regarded as identical, if terms are being used with any precision at all. These are not statements to the effect that Emily Brontë herself is confused; they are the inevitably confused results of trying to discover in the novel more metaphysical concreteness than it can yield.

Ultimately, the evidence on which such readings appear to rest consists of Catherine's famous utterances to Nelly Dean in Chapter IX where, in lyrical prose, she contrasts her feelings for Edgar with those for Heathcliff; the lovers' expectation of prolonging their passion for each other after death; Heathcliff's sense, near the end of the novel, of Catherine's ghostly presence; and the local legend that, after his death, the ghosts of both may be seen walking together on the moors. None of this leads to anything nearly as definite as the critics would make out. If we look closely at Catherine's speeches, for instance, and refrain from importing into them our own metaphysical preferences or those given cachet by fashionable criticism, we can hardly avoid seeing how little they lend themselves to precise formulation. They tell us simply that Catherine's feeling for Heathcliff is one of the closest, apparently most instinctive affinity—even identity; that this feeling is extraordinarily intense; that it is, indeed, the deepest kind of passion she knows; and that she experiences it as

---

[4] *Early Victorian Novelists* (Indianapolis, 1935), pp. 168, 175. Hereafter, page references to this work will be given parenthetically in the text.

an absolute necessity of her being. All of this is perfectly intelligible
and probable as an expression both of her character and of her desper-
ate situation at the time. But, if we try to deduce from it an elaborate
metaphysical doctrine, or attribute such to the author herself, we
become only subjective and arbitrary.

It can be reasoned, of course, that many of Catherine's sentiments
must be more than merely dramatically appropriate—that they must
be endorsed to some extent by the author herself—because they are
echoed in a number of Emily Brontë's lyrics. But one of the difficulties here is that since most of these lyrics themselves appear to be
the dramatically appropriate utterances of characters in the Gondal
saga and since the nature of this saga can only be conjectured, the
lyrics offer us no more certain a guide to Emily Brontë's own metaphysical persuasions than Catherine's speeches themselves. Moreover,
even allowing—what is surely likely—that the lyrics often do express
ideas and attitudes endorsed by the author, they would still be largely
irrelevant to the issue because they have nothing to say about that
crucial conception of immortality on the basis of which the claims
for Catherine and Heathcliff's unique metaphysical status seem frequently to rest. Death, revolt, moorland nature, moorland ecstasy,
the grief of separated lovers, yearnings for childhood freedom and
joy—these certainly are the preoccupations of Catherine and the
poems alike; but on the subject of that unorthodox conception of an
immortality of fierce passion which Catherine and Heathcliff anticipate for themselves the poems are quite silent. In verses like "The
Philosopher's Conclusion," indeed, death is conceived by the speaker
simply as oblivion. And when immortality *is* envisaged, as in the
famous "No coward soul is mine," it is something much closer to the
orthodox immortality of peace in God conceived at various times by
Edgar, Nelly Dean, and Lockwood.

This raises the question of the status of the apparently supernatural
elements in the novel itself. David Cecil states unequivocally that
when Catherine dies "her spirit does take up its abode at Wuthering
Heights. And not just as an ineffective ghost: as much as in life she
exerts an active influence over Heathcliff, besieges him with her passion" (168). But the text gives no warranty to this kind of certainty
in the least. What defines Emily Brontë's method in this matter is
precisely its circumspection. Catherine begins to reveal her longing
for what she later calls " 'that glorious world' " beyond the grave and
the " 'shattered prison' " of her body (134) only in Chapter xii—at
a time, that is, when, her mind and body alike having been wrecked
by the ordeal of her hysteria and her fast, she is on the threshold of
"brain fever" and already "doomed to decay" (131). It is her remarks
to the same effect in Chapter xv that also implant the idea of a tran-

scendental reunion in the mind of Heathcliff, who heretofore has given no sign of entertaining any such notion whatsoever. After she dies he takes up the idea in earnest and feverishly prays to her that she will haunt him for the rest of his life (139). At first his prayer appears to be answered: no sooner is she buried than he "sees" her ghostly presence with him at the graveside (229–30). Whether he is suffering from a delusion at this time we are not, of course, explicitly told, but the point is that, in the light of his extreme grief and longing, this is left open as a distinct possibility. Indeed, in the eighteen years which follow, though he yearns continually for a repetition of his experience, none is forthcoming (230). Furthermore, his expectations suddenly abate at the end of this period when, upon the death of Edgar, he opens Catherine's coffin and looks upon her " 'passionless features' " (229), for this sight persuades him that his hopes have been in vain—that, as Lockwood affirms at the end of the novel, Catherine has been for all these years only a quiet sleeper in the quiet earth. Convinced now that the only kind of reunion with her which he can expect is the purely material one of mutual dissolution (228–29), he loosens a side of her coffin and bribes the sexton " 'to pull it away, when I'm laid there, and slide mine out too' " (228). But two months later, when Lockwood arrives at Wuthering Heights and dreams of Catherine's ghost at the window, all of Heathcliff's anguished yearning is revived (33). The reader knows that Lockwood has had only a nightmare, but Heathcliff is convinced that his visitor has really seen the spectre he himself had hoped to see for all those eighteen years. Most significantly, it is on precisely this delusion that Emily Brontë arranges for the dénouement of the novel to hinge, for from this point onward Heathcliff can think of nothing but joining Catherine in death (xxxiii). He now begins to see her presence again just as he did when he stood at her grave after her burial. But by this time, in order to achieve his desire, he has also begun to starve himself, and thus the possibility that he is suffering only from a hallucination is distinctly left open once more. Why, we must ask, if Emily Brontë wanted us to accept the "supernatural" in the novel as a certainty, has she so systematically hedged it round with these ironic ambiguities? There remains, of course, the local legend that Heathcliff and Catherine may still be seen walking the moors. But a less conclusive way of persuading us of their immortality than by the testimony of superstitious rustics could hardly be imagined. These tales, at any rate, are given no more authority than Lockwood's contrary conviction that Heathcliff has joined Catherine and Edgar in an eternally quiet sleep.

Finally, we cannot overlook still another objection to the metaphysical-supernaturalist reading. This is simply that it is inconsistent with the novel's total emotional effect. If Catherine and Heathcliff are merely the channels through which pour immense "spiritual" or "natural" or "demonic" energies over which they have no control, our reaction to them may be one of awe, but hardly of pity: we do not pity blind natural or supernatural forces, but only their victims. I submit, however, that this is not our principal reaction to the novel at all. On the contrary, *Wuthering Heights* is such a remarkable work partly because it persuades us so forcibly to pity victims and victimizers alike. The revealing fact about readings like those of David Cecil and Dorothy Van Ghent is that though they lay great emphasis upon Catherine and Heathcliff's power for destruction, they say next to nothing about their equally great capacity for suffering. The ultimate effect of such readings on these characters is to dehumanize them.

On our awareness of their suffering, however, and especially of this suffering as the cause of their destructive power, our entire emotional reaction to Emily Brontë's hero and heroine depends. *Wuthering Heights* is an extravagant novel, but its extravagance is not in its metaphysics. Catherine and Heathcliff are destructive not because they are blind natural forces obeying the same impersonal cosmic economy as a mountain torrent or a storm, or because they are mysterious "spiritual principles" which are not of this world, or because Heathcliff is really a demon, but because of their eminently human frustration. As we watch the step-by-step descent of these characters into their inferno and contemplate the whole ruinous process in retrospect, our dominant impression is one of tragic waste: we feel that we have witnessed the destruction of two human lives which might have been both happier and better in *this* world. The central fact of the novel is that when Catherine betrays her own and Heathcliff's deepest self by marrying Edgar Linton she creates a disorder in their souls which spreads to the entire society around them. Tragically, by her misguided choice of Edgar as her husband, she places herself and Heathcliff in a situation which exacts from each the most atrocious frustration and suffering and, in consequence, brings out the worst in both of them. Whenever Catherine and Heathcliff's cruelty threatens to drown all our sympathy in moral revulsion, this is the vital conception to which Emily Brontë returns.

A crucial matter is her timing. With great deliberation she builds up our moral aversion, carrying it (as we have already seen) to the point where it is about to stifle every other response. At this moment, however, she effects a sudden reversal: a new element is thrust into our awareness, and our horror is transformed into compassion.

Let us go back to the sequence of Catherine's mad-scenes in Chapters x–xii and take up where our earlier analysis left off. No sooner has Catherine reached the moment of "feverish bewilderment" when she is tearing the pillow "with her teeth" than there is a startling transition; the storm suddenly gives way to an almost unearthly calm (105). There follows for almost four pages an extremely poignant section in which, in her half-delirium, she lives again through some of the ecstasies and miseries of her childhood. The climax of this is a terrible confession of despair. Catherine tells Nelly that when she recovered from the fit into which she had fallen upon fleeing to her room at the end of the preceding chapter, the last seven years of her life became a blank. Shutting out of her mind everything connected with the Lintons and her marriage, she was, as it were, transported back over this period to the time of her father's death, when she and Heathcliff were forced by Hindley to sleep separately for the first time. The agony of being "enclosed in the oak-panelled bed" as in a coffin came back to her with all the Proustian vividness of a present reality. This sensation did not last long; her memory of the intervening years was soon restored. But then she was overwhelmed by an anguish even greater, analogous to what she would have felt seven years earlier if, instead of having merely been separated from Heathcliff in bed, she " 'had been wrenched from the Heights, and every early association, and my all in all, as Heathcliff was at that time, and been converted at a stroke into Mrs. Linton, the lady of Thrushcross Grange, and the wife of a stranger; an exile, and outcast, thenceforth, from what had been my world' " (107). It is to this world, the world she shared with Heathcliff before her father's death, that she now longs to return. Thus, at the end of her confession, when she commands Nelly to open the window again and is refused, she leaps out of bed and, throwing it open herself, imagines that she can see in the distance the glow of lights from her old home, and that she and Heathcliff are children wandering at night on the moor. It is now that the whole section reaches its remarkable conclusion. Addressing the boy Heathcliff as if he were actually present, she challenges him to invoke the ghosts in Gimmerton churchyard and promises that if he does so she will never desert him even in death: " 'I'll not lie there by myself; they may bury me twelve feet deep, and throw the church down over me, but I won't rest till you are with me. I never will' " (108).

Probably no words in *Wuthering Heights* are more familiar than these. But what needs to be stressed is their decisive structural significance. The essential point is their *placement:* they are the climax of a whole section which occurs at precisely that moment in the novel when Catherine's frenzied, self-righteous cruelty has threatened to cost her all our sympathy and respect. The effect of this section is to right the reader's emotional balance, both by poignantly imaging what Catherine was like before her hideous transformation and by persuading us that the cause of this transformation has been her terrible frustration. Immediately afterwards Edgar enters the room, and all her cruelty and maniacal fury revive (109–10), but now our reaction to her behavior is quite different from what it was earlier, for we cannot forget what we have just seen. This structuring of Catherine's poignant memories and yearnings between the two scenes of her greatest moral deterioration is one of the triumphs of Emily Brontë's bold fictional rhetoric.

The technique of emotional reversal is used again in Chapter xv at the critical moment of Catherine and Heathcliff's last reunion. Catherine's initial display of petulance, selfishness, and vindictiveness is only a prelude to the lovers' passionate reconciliation, which reaches its climax when Edgar's impending arrival threatens once more to separate them. In dread of this prospect Catherine falls again into delirium and dies shortly after while giving premature birth to her child. Her sufferings have literally destroyed her.

At the same time Emily Brontë is similarly controlling our response to Heathcliff. A few pages before this culminating scene a very black picture of his behavior had been painted by Isabella in her long letter to Nelly (xiii). And almost immediately after this (xiv) he was shown in Nelly's presence mercilessly reviling Edgar's "duty and humanity" and contrasting it with his own passion (125–26). Arnold Kettle takes this passage as a serious judgment on Edgar endorsed by Emily Brontë herself and finds in it a "moral passion" which "has the quality of great poetry" (146). But this is quite unfair. If Edgar is not Heathcliff's equal for passion, neither is he so merely contemptible. Heathcliff's speech is a piece of special pleading and deplorable vainglory, particularly outrageous in the light of the fact that he has just become guilty of what Kettle himself calls "the first of his callous and ghastly acts of revenge, his marriage to Isabella" (146). Kettle's error comes from recognizing that Emily Brontë wants to keep alive our sympathy for Heathcliff, but failing to perceive just how she succeeds in doing so; he has, therefore, to explain away passages which morally revolt us. The real corrective to our moral aversion comes not from any justice in Heathcliff's words, but from what we are shown in the two chapters which follow of his passionate reunion with Catherine and his frustration and despair in the face of her mortal illness and death. Our sympathies are enlisted by his anguished prayer that her ghost return to haunt him, his self-inflicted injuries at the tree, his cries of pain like those of "a savage beast getting goaded to death with knives and spears" (139), his surreptitious visit to Catherine's corpse, when he substitutes his hair for Edgar's in her locket, and the testimony to his overwhelming suffering offered even by his enemy-wife (148).

Heathcliff performs, of course, still another action which reveals his great grief and frustration at this time: Catherine is no sooner buried than, driven to madness by the thought that only " 'two yards of loose earth . . . [are] the sole barrier between us' " (229), he tears open her grave in the hope of holding her once more in his arms. But this episode is not described until twelve chapters later. Why? Just as our hostile response to his cruel treatment of Isabella and his unjust scorn of Edgar must be modified by the description of his anguish at the time of Catherine's illness and death and just as our response to Catherine herself was similarly modified, so too must Emily Brontë modify our hostile response to Heathcliff's fanatically brutal career of revenge—the counterpart in the second half of the novel of Catherine's infernal rages in the first. The beginning of this revenge coincides in time with the various events just mentioned, but Emily Brontë can hardly hope, as she subsequently focuses more and more exclusively on Heathcliff's cruelty to the second generation, that our memory of these events will weigh sufficiently heavy. Indeed, if Heathcliff's story is going to be truly tragic, she must render the barbarous extent of that cruelty as fully and sharply as possible. Thus, she resorts still once more to the method of sudden reversal. For almost a quarter of the novel we see and hear of Heathcliff practically nothing but his villainy, the climax of which is the outrageous marriage he forces upon Cathy and the dying Linton. It is then, in Chapter XXIX, without warning, that he discloses to Nelly the story of his violation of Catherine's grave eighteen years before. Now too he recounts how, throughout that period, he longed in vain for proof of her ghostly presence and how he has allayed this longing only by opening her grave again and gazing upon her " 'passionless features.' " But these were the eighteen years, we realize with something of a shock, during which he was also pursuing his revenge. Thus, Emily Brontë suddenly makes us see this revenge retrospectively in a wholly new light: his cruelty, in large measure, was tragically inseparable from his futile yearning.

But the technique of reversal is not Emily Brontë's only resource for making us aware of the suffering at the root of the cruelty. Its effectiveness at this point depends, in fact, on a quite different strategy. Heathcliff's vengeful actions are so protracted that if he fails to enlist our sympathy until the end and only in retrospect, he runs the risk of forfeiting it entirely. Something must be done to modify our aversion to his revenge while he is pursuing it. Emily Brontë's solution to this problem is to set before us throughout the novel a number of other characters who, when faced with circumstances analogous to his own, behave in a similar way. Because we are likely to attend only to the main functions of these characters in the plot, she can manipulate our judgment of Heathcliff very unobtrusively.

The most obvious parallel to him is, of course, Hareton Earnshaw, who is gradually transformed by his subjugation to Heathcliff into a replica of the latter as he was under the domination of Hindley. But other parallels are equally important. The chief function of Hindley himself, for instance, is to serve as Heathcliff's persecutor, and yet for one moment in the action, immediately after the death of his wife, we glimpse him as something more—the bereaved husband:

> . . . he grew desperate; his sorrow was of that kind that will not lament. He neither wept nor prayed—he cursed and defied—execrated God and man, and gave himself up to reckless dissipation.
>
> The servants could not bear his tyrannical and evil conduct long: Joseph and I [Nelly] were the only two that would stay (61).

The crucial point is that, just as in Heathcliff's case, Hindley's "tyrannical and evil conduct" is the direct result of his overwhelming sorrow. Even more sympathetic characters are transformed in this way. The mild and genteel Isabella's response to Heathcliff's cruelty is a savage desire to claim an eye for an eye (148–49). Even more startling, but no less consistent with Emily Brontë's psychological premises, is what happens to the tender and maternal Cathy as she remains Heathcliff's prisoner at the Heights after the death of her father and Linton. According to the housekeeper, Zillah,

> ". . . She has no lover, or liker among us—and she does not deserve one—for, let them say the least word to her, and she'll curl back without respect of any one! She'll snap at the master himself, and as good as dares him to thrash her; *and the more hurt she gets, the more venomous she grows*" (236; my italics).

What could be a more distinct clue than this last sentence for our understanding of Heathcliff himself? Finally, there is the fastidious Lockwood and his surprisingly violent dream of Catherine's ghost at the window in Chapter III. Dorothy Van Ghent holds that Lockwood's action of pulling the ghost's wrist back and forth over the broken glass until it bleeds is "unmotivated" and therefore proof of some demonic element inherent in human nature itself (159–60). But the definitive answer to this fanciful interpretation has been given by Edgar F. Shannon, Jr., who shows, quite to the contrary, that the violence of Lockwood's dream is the logical result of "the physical and emotional outrages he has sustained" at the Heights during his visits of the last two days.[5] None of these characters is evil or vicious by nature. They become so only under extreme provocation. One of their principal functions in the novel is to persuade us that the dynamics of Heathcliff's violence and cruelty is to be understood in the same way.

The dominant image of Heathcliff that emerges, then, is neither

---

[5] "Lockwood's Dreams and the Exegesis of *Wuthering Heights*," *NCF*, XIV (Sept., 1959), 97–99.

that of a "moral force" nor a "demon," but that of a tragic sufferer. And this is finally our image of Catherine too. We do not condone their outrages, but neither do we merely condemn them. We do something larger and more important: we recognize in them the tragedy of passionate natures whom intolerable frustration and loss have stripped of their humanity.

# The Place of Love in
# *Jane Eyre* and *Wuthering Heights*

## by Mark Kinkead-Weekes

New styles of architecture, a change of heart
—W. H. Auden

*Jane Eyre* and *Wuthering Heights* are love stories—so much is commonplace. The love of Catherine and Heathcliff is admittedly very different from the love of Jane and Rochester; but we all point to Charlotte Brontë's criticism of Jane Austen to register how love has become more passionate and more central in the Brontës than in earlier novelists. To the author of *Jane Eyre,* the author of *Emma* seems essentially superficial. "She does her business of delineating the surface of the lives of genteel English people curiously well; there is a Chinese fidelity, a miniature delicacy in the painting. . . . What sees keenly, speaks aptly, moves flexibly, it suits her to study, but what throbs fast and full, though hidden, what the blood rushes through, what is the unseen seat of Life and the sentient target of death—*this* Miss Austen ignores. . . . Jane Austen was a complete and most sensible lady, but a very incomplete, and rather insensible (*not senseless*) woman; if this is heresy—I cannot help it." If the life of the heart is not made central, the novelist deals only with the surface of living.

When we look more closely, however, it seems less important to argue the injustice to Jane Austen than to examine the implications of what Charlotte Brontë actually says. There seems no reason indeed why much of what has been written in praise of Jane Austen should not be comprehended under Charlotte Brontë's allowances, especially when one learns that she had not read *Persuasion.* Jane Austen (we might expand) has all the values of shrewd observation, pointed wit, flexible style, the civilized intelligence and insight of a late Augustan lady, a connoisseur of social behaviour and its implications. To call this "superficial" is only possible in the sense that we would have to call nine-tenths of human life, of our own lives, superficial: the life of behavior and relationship in society, wherever two or three are gathered together. To Charlotte Brontë, however, it is the last tenth that is all-important, and that Jane Austen cannot reach; and the language tells us that this is the life of the heart. What is significant, however, is how much more is implied than the old metaphor of the passions. For the right to claim the life of the heart as the essential one is registered by calling it "the unseen seat of Life and the sentient target of death." It is in the heart that each of us ultimately lives and dies alone. It follows that the all-important dimension of the human being must be individual, personal, private. It not only exists below the surface of social behavior, it must be a life of the self deeper even than intimate relationships, however these may thwart or fulfill the heart.

We begin to see why *Jane Eyre* should be so concerned to break through the public and social, in order to free the personal selfhood of the heroine and probe the hidden forces in the heart itself which make for its life or death. While Emma's progress is through false situations and misreadings of social and moral value to the discovery of a true relationship, Jane's is a pilgrim's progress from depth to depth in her own heart to reveal the nature of her ultimate self, before it can be fulfilled in love. Both novels end in marriage, but love for Emma is an adjustment between "Hartfield" and "Don(e)well," whereas the last house of Jane's heart is a very private place.

Yet what divides Charlotte Brontë from Jane Austen divides her no less from her sister. It is no accident that Charlotte's novels have titles that refer to individual selves, while Emily's novel does not. Even if it were called *Thrushcross Grange* it would be less individualistic, more "Augustan" perhaps, than *Jane Eyre*. For though life in "Thrushcross Grange" is concerned with the power of love to fulfill the self, it is also concerned to bring loving relationship into harmony with a continuing social, moral, and religious order, still to some extent public. (In *Jane Eyre* moral and religious values have to be discovered within the heart itself; society is dismissed as conventional.) In *Wuthering Heights*, however, the life of "the Grange" is placed against quite another way of looking, that of "the Heights." Here the language of love is not only antisocial, it is also impersonal. Now it is individual selfhood that is broken through, in order to liberate a mode of being and loving beyond personality, beyond life, beyond death—something almost as mysterious and horrifying to Charlotte Brontë as it might have been to Jane Austen.

It seems that we need a way of exploring these radical differences in the place of "love" within the "story" of *Jane Eyre* and *Wuthering*

*Heights,* a way of relating the different ways of looking at love to the basic structures of the novels. It may be that the metaphor of the "house" (which can be an expression of self, or an expression of relationship, or something enduring beyond both) will help us to establish the different architectures of the fiction. It may be, as Auden's line implies, that what "new styles of architecture" amount to is "a change of heart."

The emphasis on personal selfhood explains why *Jane Eyre* must be told in the first person, from the awakening of self-assertion as the necessary beginning, to the consummation of self in marriage as the desirable end. The novel's ancestor is *Pamela,* which is mentioned in the opening chapter. We have the same basic situation of a dependent girl determined to win her right to be treated as a self-respecting individual, conveyed with the same direct experience of a developing self from the inside. Moreover, Charlotte Brontë repeats the basic fault of *Pamela,* which springs from over-concentration on the heroine: failure to create the hero convincingly. If Rochester strikes us as "Gothick," if the story of his past is almost continuously embarrassing, and his part in the developing relationship scarcely less so, it is because the remorseless concentration on the first person creation of Jane never permits him to be done as a character from the inside. He is continually used for a projection of her or for a focus on her, rather than as a self in his own right. Her consciousness becomes a prison from which he never escapes and in which, in a sense, he is finally cut down to size.

The differences, however, are as striking as the similarities. The most obvious point, touched on already in her criticism of Jane Austen, is that Charlotte Brontë shows little sense of society as a web of interrelationships, obligations, and shared sustaining values. Pamela has to win her integrity from her world, but her victory reforms it, and she finally takes her place as a social being. In *Jane Eyre* the half-glimpsed society behind the Reeds and the Brocklehursts, the society of the Ingrams and the Eshtons, the European and West Indian societies through which Rochester has moved, the society from which Diana and Mary Rivers have to be rescued, are all seen as essentially corrupt and inferior, and the art which deals with them is an art of stereotype or caricature. On the one hand, we see society as the enemy against which the selfhood of Jane has to be won; on the other hand, the enemy turns out to be a set of straw men and women, seen in a lurid light that only half creates them as bogeys. We are left, then, with mere conventions, sterile habituations that have to be broken through before the buried life of the heart can flower. (It is interesting to notice, however, that Jane continues to extract a piquancy from playing with a master-servant relationship which—unlike Pamela—she essentially denies.) Only in the two schools, at Lowood and Morton, do we see Jane as a member of a community; in both cases what comes across is a sense of ultimately intolerable limitation; nowhere can be found a society bound together by shared values, sustaining the individual in a system of communal relationships. We may contrast with this situation that in Jane Austen's *Mansfield Park*, where likewise a lonely and unloved girl is placed as a dependent in a great house, and is eventually established as a center of value. Mansfield Park and all the other houses in that novel provide a language of adjustment, a series of metaphors in an analysis of the proper relation between private feeling and a public moral order. The heart is educated in public value, the house is educated by the suffering heart. Eventually, because the foundations have been inspected to test their strength against stress from within and without, the Great House can be renovated, and offered as an image of both the heart civilized and society made sensitive. In Charlotte Brontë, by contrast, houses are metaphors of the private heart, stages in its pilgrim's progress towards the revelation of its ultimate nature.

This brings up another essential difference of the world of *Jane Eyre* from the world of *Pamela* or *Mansfield Park*. For Charlotte Brontë the life of the heart is not only private, but "hidden," "unseen." It is necessarily mysterious. The relationships it can create even after it has broken through society's convictions will remain the tip of an iceberg. Hence the only kind of art that can momentarily bring up what lies so far below the surface is an art of poetic revelation, of symbol, vision, and dream. The real register of Jane Eyre's selfhood is not the Quakerish little figure before Rochester; it lies in the paintings that reveal the dimensions of her heart's secret life. On the level of character (outside Jane herself), of dramatic scene and dialogue, the book often fails lamentably, and some of the language is absurdly pedantic. There is a persistent tendency to lapse into the realm of the woman's magazine. Yet we are also aware of a totally different kind of power, a poetic power, which stills one's witticisms as they rise and finally compels respect. It begins to seem less important to point to the faults than to try to tap the poem within the novel, the glimpses we get of the hidden life of the heart and of the nature of its progress.

I am not sure that I understand the pictures, but that they should continue to be mysteriously powerful is, I think, part of their meaning. Out of a swollen sea a foam-flecked cormorant plucks from a drowned body a brilliant jewelled bracelet. The sea of mutability (may we say?) wrecks and drowns the body; the cormorant—devouring time—perches on the wreckage; yet something indestructible and

precious remains silhouetted against the dark beak, the swollen
flood. In the third picture an iceberg shows its tip, a frozen shape,
against which leans the ghastly apparition of Death in *Paradise Lost,*
but both are defined against the Aurora Borealis. In the center picture of the tryptych there is land, windswept, but recognizable as
the hill of the poet of Revelation, and from it rises in woman's shape
a vision of the Evening Star. The pictures show us that Jane's inner
landscape is bleak and much concerned with death, the heart frozen
or submerged—but the points of light, precious, definitive, spiritu-
alized, make it plain that a life of the heart is asserted against its
winter. The pictures refer back to the icy winter at Gateshead and
the little girl in the window-seat looking at *Bewick's Birds.* They
also refer forward to the terrible inner flood that will sweep through
her after the travesty of her wedding-day; to the icy death of hope
but also the unearthly light of her dream and to the barren life in
the wilderness from which she will eventually be recalled by the
revelation of her woman's shape, and by that miraculous voice calling
her name and manifesting her true identity. It is in these pictures,
and in her nightmare wanderings with the dream-child of her love of
Rochester, and in the final mysterious telepathy that takes her from
the inadequate St. John to the green place where the true life of the
heart can be revealed and renewed, that we get the hidden dimension
of selfhood from which Charlotte Brontë accuses Jane Austen of
superficiality.

This poem within the novel has a structure that allows us to explore the inner landscape in terms of five places of the heart: Gateshead, Lowood, Thornfield, Moor End, and Ferndean. Each of the
houses is a metaphor, not of social order or disorder, but of a condition of the private heart, and a stage in its progress towards the liberation of its buried life. I propose to beg the question of how successfully these metaphors are translated into novelistic presentation, in
terms of character, action, and dialogue. Instead, I shall devote what
space I have to the question of what kind of stage each represents—
for only in this way, I believe, can we perceive what Charlotte Brontë
is attempting, and find an adequate basis for a comparison with
*Wuthering Heights.*

In Gateshead, hidden behind the scarlet draperies of the window-
seat, the heart contemplates a wintry world. It is summoned from that,
and from the wintry imagination of scenes from Bewick—ice-white,
death-cold, with intimations of horror and evil—to face the cruelty
and frozen-heartedness of the Reeds: the blows, the cut welling blood,
the confinement in the Red Room. There, red carpet, red curtains,
red tablecloth, red hangings are set against the snowy white bed and
chair, the bewildered face reflected in the mirror like a pale phantom.

As the last daylight ebbs, so do the sustaining embers of Jane's rage. The life of the heart in this prison seems to present only a choice between frozen wintriness and red passion. And then there falls across the wall what the little girl takes to be an unearthly light from the ghost world of death where Mr. Reed has gone, and for her this is unendurable terror, the extinguishing of self. When she is thrust back into the room by Mrs. Reed, she has a fit which rends her heart-strings and is something like a death of the old submissive Jane. From this experience she gathers the anger to rise in passionate rebellion against her persecutors, bloodying John Reed's nose, denouncing Mrs. Reed with a force that seems to come from beyond her own volition and control, and winning her freedom from this first prison. Yet the price of that kind of "life" of the heart is underlined. "A ridge of lighted heath, alive, glancing, devouring, would have been a good emblem of my mind when I accused and menaced Mrs. Reed; the same ridge, black and blasted after the flames are dead, would have represented as meetly my subsequent condition. . . . Something of vengeance I had tasted . . . warm and racy; its afterflavour . . . gave me a sensation as if I had been poisoned."

In Lowood, the winter of cold and physical deprivation that had been outside the window becomes the whole medium of life under the Brocklehurst regime, and the injustice of Gateshead is repeated and even intensified by her public exposure as a liar. Yet the red passion and the flaming heath do not re-materialize, because the unearthly light to which she had reacted with such horror in the Red Room is given a spiritual embodiment in the smile of Helen Burns. The Jane who had told Helen, "If others don't love me, I would rather die than live—I cannot bear to be solitary and hated," is given two new perspectives. The first arises from discovery of an inner conscience, a self-respect: "If all the world hated you and believed you wicked, while your own conscience approved you and absolved you from guilt, you would not be without friends"; the second from a faith that the inner conscience is connected to a world of spirit, a God, a Heaven. Helen's own brief life is an enactment of the endurance and control which come from the strength these two convictions give the heart. The frozen life leaned on by death is seen against the miraculous light at the pole; and since "God waits only a separation of spirit from flesh to crown us . . . why then should we sink overwhelmed with distress?" the cormorant and bracelet also get a gloss. Helen Burns is the first revelation of the evening star. When Jane tells her story to Miss Temple, she controls the "gall and wormwood" that gave her vindictiveness such a bitter aftertaste, and is believed in consequence. And though Helen dies in the spring that changes Lowood into a place where Jane begins to find herself in new life,

she dies in peace and hope, with the first words of love that Jane has
ever heard. Lowood, though stern still, becomes a greener place, and
"Better is a dinner of herbs where love is, than a stalled ox and hatred
therewith." Nevertheless, if Lowood becomes a liberation from Gateshead in the growing life of the heart, it remains restrictive, offering
insufficient scope. Jane does not hope for true liberty yet, but she
longs for a wider servitude.

So she reaches Thornfield, and Rochester. This is the long central
phase of the novel, and in my attempt to register merely the inner
"poetic" dimension I can only outline the ways in which the house
is used as a metaphor for the heart, and touch on the nature of the
choice which is now offered in the name of love.

The house itself is a metaphor of Rochester's heart, a physical embodiment of the tropical hell he has tried to escape, enclosed within
the half-life which is all he has found. The hell of mindless and uncontrolled passion is barred into the attic, hidden away in the form
of his lunatic wife. The floor below is an empty and deserted mau-
soleum of antiques, for the family life of the Fairfaxes and the society
to which they belonged are gone for ever, meaningless, a departed
world. A floor below again is the modern world of the rich land-
owner, the social life that Rochester could have if it were not for the
attic and what is has done to him—a glamorous, richly beautiful set
of rooms which strike Jane as a kind of heaven, but which remain
empty until Rochester fills them with the country families, but which
even then are shown to be only a setting for charades of one kind or
another. Finally, there is the ground floor, where Mrs. Fairfax and
Adele represent the last residue of the life of the heart, but the advent
of Jane here will cause floor after floor above to be thrown open,
all the doors unlocked from top to bottom, for good or ill. Most of
the "Thornfield" section is a development in Rochester of the deliberate will to throw open all but the attic to Jane, to defy what he sees
as the meaningless sanctions of society, and marry her despite what
is in the final chamber. We can put this exactly in terms of the
metaphor of the house. "Lifting his eyes to the battlements, he cast
over them a glare such as I never saw before or since. Pain, shame,
ire—impatience, disgust, detestation—seemed momentarily to hold
a quivering conflict . . . but another feeling rose and triumphed:
something hard and cynical, self-willed and resolute." He defies the
hag of his destiny whom he imagines writing "lurid hieroglyphics
all along the house front, between the upper and the lower windows,
"Like it if you can! Like it if you dare!" He will dare; "to break
obstacles to happiness, to goodness—yes, goodness." This can be
put in terms of social morality: he believes that all he will be
doing is overleaping "an obstacle of custom, a mere conventional

impediment which neither your conscience sanctifies nor your judgement approves." Yet the wedding will turn out to be the final charade, not because of any exterior sanction, but because to Charlotte Brontë, and her heroine, the only true life the heart can have must come from the opening of every chamber, the plumbing of full depth and height. In fact the locked room can never remain locked: from it the inner fiend issues forth to set the bed on fire, to plunge knife and teeth into Mason, sucking his blood, to tear the wedding-veil in two. Moreover, it is essential to realise what the "story" level of the book does not clarify until later: that the mad woman does not simply represent an external impediment, but also something within Rochester himself which he tries to deny, to escape, to imprison. When Jane finally enters that attic she is penetrating the most secret chamber of Rochester's own heart—an inner dimension in which the chained bestiality growls like a yahoo, held in check by the sardonically named "Grace," while the candlelight plays across the antique carvings of Christ's apostles, and the face of the betrayer, the Judas.

For Jane, Thornfield becomes an image of passage from winter to an apparent "Italian" summer and harvest of the heart. We see the antisocial drive of the novel again in the fact that, from the beginning, it is the rudeness of Rochester, his rupture of social convention, that sets Jane's selfhood free. He is capable of recognizing the inner life that is so much more important than her appearance or her position; he allows her to be a person. So, at the novel's first climax, she speaks of being freed from a kind of burial. "I love Thornfield: I love it because I have lived in it a full and delightful life—momentarily at least. I have not been trampled on. I have not been petrified. I have not been buried with inferior minds, and excluded from every glimpse of communion with what is bright and energetic and high." To be torn from Thornfield-Rochester "is like looking on the necessity of death." When she misunderstands him about Blanche Ingram, she speaks from the heart and spirit, breaking through custom and convention, and even through the flesh, to claim an essential inner equality. "I have as much soul as you—and full as much heart!" And when he offers her what seems the full life of the heart, Thornfield becomes a heaven, and Rochester an idol.

The heaven is false, the idol betrays. The relationship imaged by the great chestnut tree is split apart, as the wedding veil is torn from top to bottom, because of that secret chamber. Once again, though this is partly a matter of the sanctions of the church and the law, it is ultimately not an outer but an inner crisis. Jane is asked to give herself, to the man whose heart is now revealed to its innermost, as though sexual passion and mutual possession were foundation enough for the full life of the heart. It is her own self-respect that forbids her to do so, though separation is, as she had said it would be, a kind of death. The beautiful harvest world of her love is inundated by a terrible Flood: "the waters came into my soul; I sank in deep mire; I felt no standing; I came into deep waters; the floods overflowed me." There is no help from outside, and she does not pray. It is from within herself that she hears an implacable voice telling her what she must do—pluck out her own eye, cut off her own hand, sacrifice her own heart rather than found its life on sexual relationship. It is from within herself in dream that she draws the vision that reorchestrates her pictures and her past once more. She dreams of the red room, but the unearthly light which now turns into the radiance from the cloud, the voice of revelation, resolves itself into the shape of Woman. The God-in-Womanhood mothers the heart, and directs its flight into the wilderness. The false heaven of Thornfield becomes purgatory, "full of blackness, burning," from which she must voyage as a pilgrim, without the consolation of moral applause. Whitcross is the beginning of self-crucifixion, the moors are the desert of the heart.

The world Jane now enters at Moor End is dominated by St. John, but he cannot be the Revelation of her true selfhood either, for his is simply the opposite extreme from the Rochester she has renounced. The kind of Christianity he lives by is built in heroic self-denial and self-control; but sex itself is a shame to him, as we see in his attitude to Rosamund. Because he has no conception of the relation of self to self in the life of the heart, the "marriage" he offers Jane would be the death of frost instead of the death of fire. He is an ice-man. She scorns his idea of love as, in its way, as deeply destructive of her inner self as the relationship with Rochester would have been. It would kill her, her own inner being—and it is in passionate rejection of this that she hears, from a mysterious source at her heart's core, the final voice of her nature, which she believes is God too, the God within the self. "My heart beat fast and thick: I heard its throb. Suddenly it stood still to an inexpressible feeling that thrilled it through, and passed at once to my head and extremities. The feeling was not like an electric shock, but it was quite as sharp, as strange, as startling . . . eye and ear waited while the flesh quivered on my bones." The cry she hears is her own name, the annunciation of full identity in the call to fuse sex, spirit, and mind in the heart, and complete full womanhood in love.

When she returns to Thornfield, the false heaven has burnt itself out in flaming hell, leaving only charred remains like the heath after her own first blaze of uncontrolled passion. Rochester could not pluck out his own offending eye, cut off his own offending hand, but it has been done to him and for him—the unregenerate chamber has been purged, at mutilating cost. The last place of the heart, Ferndean, images a constriction and decay in one sense, if we compare it with Thornfield. Yet it also images a greenness, a new growth still possible for the shattered tree of their relationship; the life of the heart can finally be consummated in marriage because it is founded, through deprivation and suffering, in a fuller and regenerate selfhood. On this basis, love can be a completion of the self in relationship with another. "I know what it is to live entirely for and with what I love best on earth . . . I am my husband's life as fully as he is mine . . . ever more absolutely bone of his bone and flesh of his flesh. . . . I know no weariness of my Edward's society: he knows none of mine, any more than we do of the pulsation of the heart that beats in our separate bosoms. . . . to talk to each other is but a more animated and an audible thinking. . . . we are precisely suited in character—perfect concord is the result." Love fulfils all the modes of being one's self; the "concord" is within as well as between the lovers, and between them and God.

Charlotte Brontë, then, insists that the full life of the heart (so defined) is the only true selfhood—but she fears the extremes of fire and ice, the heart's power to burn up the self or freeze into rigidity. The life of the heart can only be consummated in relationship, but it must be a relationship of individual persons, each respecting his own integrity and the selfhood of the other, accepting also an inner control. Public society and value are stripped away to release the personal self, and that self finds the only real society in love; but love must purge the offending eye and hand lest the self be consumed, and must resist the overbearing spirit lest the self be denied. The language of Christianity is still deeply meaningful, but not in terms of commandments or sanctions—it is a language for the inner evolution of the true self, and the full nature of the free individual in relationship. For all its faults, *Jane Eyre* is a cry from the heart and of the heart, a passionate book that works by involving us with the inner development of its heroine, and is at its strongest (I believe), not in the world of character and dialogue, but in the submerged poem that is the architecture of the fiction.

What strikes one most powerfully in turning to *Wuthering Heights* is the length that Emily Brontë goes to in order to prevent the immersion within a single developing focus that is basic to *Jane Eyre*. It is absolutely of the essence of Emily's novel that we should be given, in the narratives of Lockwood, Nellie Dean, and Isabella, three points of view which not only differ in some respects from one another, but are also united in opposition to the nature and implications of the world of Catherine and Heathcliff that they record. This is more than a technique of authorial self-control. It is more even than a way of making what we shall eventually see more acceptable by revealing its implications only gradually and through eyes so near our own normative vision that they enable us to believe what we see and keep our balance while we watch. Both explanations seem true, but less than the whole truth; for what they do not sufficiently emphasize is that Emily Brontë *has* no single vision of the world. Her way of telling the novel is inseparable from what is told, in that what is told amounts to a dualistic vision, one way of seeing opposed to another. Indeed the great strength of *Wuthering Heights* is that the opposition is balanced with the most delicate and scrupulous fairness. Any choice between "the Heights" and "the Grange," any writing up and writing down, will be the manufacture of the critic, not the novelist. Emily Brontë's places of the heart are not stages in the development of the highest self, but different worlds, totally different ideas of the self, totally different ideas of love, speaking totally different languages. What we have to do in reading the book is learn to understand the two architectures, and begin to measure the full and complex implications of their opposition, revealed to us with scrupulous objectivity.[1]

We might start with the language of Love, looking at that crucial passage in which Catherine tries to explain to Nellie the difference between her "love" for Edgar and her "love" for Heathcliff. Loving Edgar is love in the world of the Grange. It is love for a personality, pleasant, young, handsome, cheerful. It is love in a relationship where contact with that personality creates a pleasant and happy ambiance, and behavior is loving and lovable. "I love the ground under his feet and the air over his head, and everything he touches, and every word he says. I love all his looks and all his actions, and him entirely and altogether." It is love in a society too, where income and status also have a place in the quality of life. Now it is true that Cathy is very superficial if we compare her with Jane Eyre. She is spoilt and immature, her love has neither the responsibility nor the depth of Jane's. It is true also that the young Edgar we have seen up till now has been a fairly shallow and unsympathetic character, equally pampered, and less decisive. It is true most of all, as we are about to confirm, that

---

[1] Mrs. Leavis' essay (*Lectures in America*, 1969, pp. 85–152) seems to me to be likely to become the classic statement of the view from Thrushcross Grange. It establishes the central features of "Grange Criticism" as: a lack of interest in the formal structure, the total endorsement of Nellie's vision, dismissive criticism of Cathy and Heathcliff, impatience with "metaphysics," and the love of Catherine and Hareton as a final positive. I question, not the validity of this view, for on its own terms it is valid enough, but its exclusiveness, its denial that there are other terms deserving attention. The only oddness in Mrs. Leavis' account is her feeling for Joseph, who seems to me demonstrably a "Heights" figure.

Cathy is the kind of self that belongs to the Heights and not the Grange; so that she is not really fitted to know, or share, or do justice to the kind of love that the Grange can offer. The point I wish to make, however, is that if we respond to the Edgar we learn to know in the book as a whole, we find not only that he might have been the hero of another kind of novel, but that he points towards a kind of heroism in this one. We grow to understand what Nellie means by thinking of him as a rich and fertile valley, like the one in which the Grange stands in relation to the community; or what Catherine means when she associates him with a kind of heaven, to which however she does not belong. As Edgar matures, his "heroism" turns out to be a matter of character, which we could gesture towards in the language of moral value: justice, compassion, sympathy, loving-kindness, responsibility, courage, and so on. It is a strength of the novel that we should eventually see very clearly that the kind of love that Edgar offers, that the Grange offers, is a fine thing in human terms: the happiness and fertile growth of personalities fitted to each other in a relationship of loving behavior, founded on mutually supplying traits of character, and capable of taking its place in society. It is this kind of loving relationship that begins to bring the stunted hearts of Hareton and the younger Catherine to flower even in the unpropitious soil at the Heights; but, being a "Grange" relationship, it is there that we are to imagine them after the novel ends, building a fertile life of the heart in terms not dissimilar to those of *Jane Eyre*. ("We are precisely suited in character—perfect concord is the result." The "concord" is less "romantic" in that it is not the outcome of so radical an enquiry into the depths of the individual self, and more "Augustan" in that it is more sociable, but the affinity is recognizable enough.) This is also the world of Nellie, who voices a traditional and communal wisdom while being a highly sympathetic character in her own right; it is the world of Lockwood too, once he has shaken off his sham pose of "Gothick" and Byronic misanthropy through contact with the real thing. And Edgar and Nellie between them allow us to assimilate the happiness of earth to the humanized Christian promise of happiness in heaven, after the death of the loving heart in the body.

Cathy's "love" for Heathcliff, however, has nothing to do with any of the terms one uses to describe her "love" for Edgar Linton. It has nothing to do with happiness, or fertile growth. "My love for Linton is like the foliage in the woods. . . . My love for Heathcliff resembles the eternal rocks beneath, a source of little visible delight . . . not as a pleasure, any more than I am always a pleasure to myself." It is impersonal—indeed has nothing to do with personality, or character. Catherine will tell Isabella that Heathcliff is "a fierce, pitiless,

wolfish man," avaricious, "an arid wilderness of furze and whinstone"
—and he is just as clear and just as careless about her defects of personality and character. Such things seem curiously irrelevant to the
meaning of Love in the world of the Heights. Nor can we discuss
their love in terms of loving behavior; it is unaffected by violence,
cruelty, vindictiveness. Their behavior looks as much like hate as
love—that lock of hair in Cathy's fingers, torn from Heathcliff's scalp,
those fierce caresses that hasten her death and make them look to
Nellie like creatures of another species, which is exactly what, in a
serious sense, they are. I don't think this is a matter of sexuality.
Though Emily Brontë is reticent, I should be inclined to say that
all the love relationships in the novel are sexual. Only, the nature of
sexuality differs as radically between the Grange and the Heights as
everything else does. With Catherine and Heathcliff it seems to have
nothing to do with sexual attraction and physical desire as such.
Like all other aspects of their love, it seems to be concerned with a
breaking through beyond the self, metaphysical and impersonal as
(in Lawrence whom this side of the novel often anticipates.)

The terms one uses in the language of the Grange, then, simply
do not seem relevant to love at the Heights. Or perhaps one does:
the term "relationship"—but it is when we begin to think about this
that a whole opposed range of meanings comes into focus. The language we are now forced to use seems curiously modern. "He's more
myself than I am. . . . I cannot express it; but surely you and everybody have a notion that there is or should be an existence of yours
beyond you. What were the use of my creation if I were entirely contained here? . . . If all else perished and *he* remained, *I* should still
continue to be; and if all else remained, and he were annihilated, the
universe would turn to a mighty stranger." Heathcliff is, like "the
eternal rocks beneath," *necessary:* "Nellie, I *am* Heathcliff! He's always, always in my mind: not as a pleasure, any more than I am
always a pleasure to myself, but as my own being." The self is not
contained in an "I"; has no sustaining "existence" or "being" in itself.
She can only fully exist, be herself, in existing and being beyond herself in Heathcliff; as he can only fully exist, be, live in her. They
are to each other, as the language makes clear, what Heidegger means
by the necessary "ground" of being, that without which there is
nothing, meaninglessness. It does not suffice to think of a self fulfilling
its being by complementing itself with another, for the point is that
the self only exists meaningfully *in* the other; without whom it becomes "L'etranger" in an alienated universe. But the other side of the
relationship is that, not being confinable to the individual self within
its body and personality, it is impervious to time, to flux and change,
to death itself. "My love for Linton is like the foliage in the woods:

time will change it, I'm well aware, as winter changes the trees. My love for Heathcliff resembles the eternal rocks beneath. . . . So don't talk of our separation again: it's impracticable." We shall indeed confirm that it is.

Because there are these two languages, there are two consistent and opposite readings of the book, each with its objective truth, each inevitably less than the whole truth. I begin, as the narrative structure is designed to make us do, by looking through the eyes of the Grange.

We are plunged by Lockwood into the Wuthering Heights of 1801, peopled by unintelligible "Gothick" figures; but then the long backward sweep of Nellie's narrative allows us to build up a credible and intelligible understanding of what we have seen, according to the perspective of Thrushcross Grange. The people we have met are slowly developed into what they have become, in terms of social environment, personality, character, behavior, relationship. We begin to understand how Catherine grows from the pampered child into the fascinating, but solipsistic, irresponsible and hysterical woman, who brings destruction on the inhabitants of both houses. Heathcliff too becomes credible, unlike Rochester, who remains "Gothick" as a character precisely because he is not given this gradual process of becoming, this placing within a dense and convincing environment. We begin to understand (or think we understand) why Heathcliff has become the monster we see; why he should have become the boy that he was, because of the way that both Mr. Earnshaw and Hindley treated him; why he should have conceived his revenge; and in what terms he has carried it out. To see through Nellie's eyes is to judge firmly (in social, moral and Christian terms); but it is also to judge with humane understanding because we share her insight into the whole process of becoming. If Cathy remains adolescent, destructively self-enclosed, and Heathcliff a monster, because he distorts his humanity into sadism, we never lose sympathy with them entirely, because Nellie enables us to see them whole, connected indissolubly with the childhood she shared with them.

Nevertheless, in the eyes of the Grange their story can never be fully de-Gothicised. The melodrama is found in intelligible process, but it remains melodramatic. Heathcliff and Cathy do behave like creatures of another species, hysterical, savage, or demonic. And the end of the story cannot be made intelligible or acceptable in terms of the Grange—it is, and must be, monstrous. Charlotte Brontë had to confess that she found it so. She can say something for Catherine, who is not "destitute of a certain strange beauty in her fierceness, or of honesty in the midst of perverted passion and passionate perversity." But "Heathcliff, indeed, stands unredeemed; never once swerv-

ing in his arrow-straight course to perdition. . . . His love for Catherine . . . is a sentiment fierce and inhuman; a passion such as might
boil and glow in the bad bosom of some evil genius . . . a man's
shape animated by demon life—a Ghoul—an Afreet. Whether it is
right or advisable to create beings like Heathcliff, I do not know:
I scarcely think it is."

Yet we might reflect that the most terrible and inhuman moment
in the novel is not Heathcliff's, but Lockwood's—that nightmare
moment no reader ever forgets, when the civilized city man rubs the
ghost-child's arm against the broken glass of the window, until blood
soaks the bed. One's next choice of the most brutal experience might
be the episode in which, with blood again pouring from a severed
artery, in Hindley's arm, Heathcliff holds Isabella off while he kicks
the prostrate man almost to death, deliberately stopping (it seems)
just short of murder. Significantly, this scene is also concerned with
a window, between two worlds, and it is the one scene where the world
outside the window is given its say, the only scene in the entire book
that we are given from Heathcliff's point of view, long after Isabella's
narrative has given us the Grange's. We are obviously required to
juxtapose the two accounts, but when we do, what is most remarkable
is how they scarcely touch. Not only can neither supplant the other—
the whole crux of the scene, to Isabella, is no more than a momentary,
if disastrous, parenthesis to Heathcliff. In Isabella's story, we learn dramatically how she and Hindley bar him out of the Heights, how he
appears at the window like a demon, with sharp cannibal teeth,
how he bursts through and executes his murderous violence with deliberation. The next morning she vengefully taunts him with Catherine until he hurls the knife at her, and she escapes past Hareton
hanging a whole litter of puppies, escaping from a Hell and a Fiend.
The reaction is Charlotte Brontë's. What we learn from Heathcliff,
however, puts the whole affair in an entirely different light. He has
been trying to open Cathy's coffin when, for the first time since her
death, he becomes sure that she is beside him, substantially, though
he cannot see her. Totally absorbed in the intensity of being with
her and his growing certainty that when they reach the Heights he
will actually see her, he finds himself locked out. "I remember stopping to kick the breath out of him, and then hurrying upstairs—but
when he gets there, she is gone, and he is condemned to his hell of
separation and torture, beguiled "with the spectre of a hope" always
disappointed, for the next twenty years (until the night in April 1802,
four nights before his death, when she appears to him again). To
re-read Isabella's tauntings the next morning is to be surprised that
she gets away as lightly as she does. Yet Isabella's horror at the violence

and the brutality remains valid, even when we can "explain" what happens in very different, and undemonic, terms.

What seems really significant about the episode however, when we juxtapose it with the Lockwood nightmare, is the way that the *window* seems the crux of both, and prevents us from using a purely moral language about either. We understand, I think, how Lockwood's frantic brutality is caused by his terror of the clutch which seeks to pull him into a world that is not his world. Yet if that is so, then Heathcliff's frantic brutality can equally be seen as caused by his fury at the attempt to keep him from the world that *is* his world, and hold him in one that is antipathetic and unreal. It is a maddening interruption in the overwhelming intensity of reunion with Cathy, but when he pauses to kick the prostrate figure before hurrying upstairs, the parenthesis proves disastrous, for it commits him to twenty years of unreality. It is no accident that it is only when he loses all interest in completing his revenge that Cathy manifests herself to him again.

We begin to glimpse a radical reinterpretation of the whole story, which fully allows for the irresponsibility and destructiveness of Cathy's behavior and the brutal cruelty of Heathcliff's revenge, but judges them in terms as different from those of Thrushcross Grange as the language of love at the Heights had been, and for the same reasons. The judgement of Cathy is indeed fully voiced by Heathcliff before she dies, and its language is not that of social ethics, or Christianity, though it uses words drawn from these. "You teach me now how cruel you have been—cruel and false. *Why* did you despise me? *Why* did you betray your own heart, Cathy? I have not one word of comfort. You deserve this. You have killed yourself. . . . You loved me—then what *right* had you to leave me? What right—answer me—for the poor fancy you felt for Linton? Because misery and degradation and death, and nothing that God or Satan could inflict would have parted us, *you*, of your own will, did it. I have not broken your heart— *you* have broken it; and in breaking it, you have broken mine. So much the worse for me that I am strong. Do I want to live? What kind of living will it be when you— Oh God! would *you* like to live with your soul in the grave?" The charge is that Cathy has betrayed the whole ground of being that sustains them both and gives them their only true life, their only standard of "right." In betraying herself she must betray him and "kill" or "damn" them both, since they can only really exist in each other. Her "cruelty" and "irresponsibility" are not conceived in moral terms, but rather in terms we do not greatly distort by calling "existential." She has tried to live in two worlds, but they are separated by an impassable divide. As was the case with the Lockwood nightmare, and the near-murder of Hindley, nothing but violence and destruction results when a being from one world is drawn into the other.

This forces us to reconsider Heathcliff's revenge in a new light too, for it is surely the same kind of betrayal—what Sartre would call *mauvais fois*. In seeking to revenge himself on the world of the Grange, because that was what Cathy betrayed him for, he makes his existence over into the terms of the world he hates—which is death for him, and hell. On this view he is not a demon, but becomes melodramatic precisely because he commits himself to a world that is not real for him. He bars himself inevitably from his true being in and with Catherine, losing faith that death cannot separate them, because he repeats her betrayal. He is melodramatic not only in Grange terms (as seen through the uncomprehending eyes of Nellie), but also in Wuthering Heights terms, because he increasingly registers the unreality of a world false to his real existence. "I have no pity! I have no pity! The more the worms writhe, the more I yearn to crush out their entrails! It is a moral teething; and I grind with greater energy, in proportion to the increase of pain."

We are now in a position to see the marvelously tactful irony of the final days of his life. He gives up his revenge, not through any form of moral change, nor through a new feeling for Hareton and the younger Catherine (though we do detect the first signs of this), but because the very success of his plans reveals to him their meaninglessness. "I don't care for striking; I can't take the trouble to raise my hand! That sounds as if I had been labouring the whole time only to exhibit a fine trait of magnanimity. It is far from being the case. I have lost the faculty of enjoying their destruction, and I am too idle to destroy for nothing." The last word is the crucial one. It is where a "life" of increasing unreality has led. Now the "strange change" he feels approaching makes him register the unreality of everything but his increasing obsession with the one reality of Catherine. If Hareton and her daughter are "the only objects which retain a distinct material appearance," it is because they remind him of himself and Cathy as they were. If he has "to remind myself to breathe—almost to remind my heart to beat," it is because he is utterly taken up again with "one universal idea," reunion with Catherine: 'it has devoured my existence: I am swallowed up in the anticipation of its fulfilment." The true language of the Heights, its kind of love, its kind of fulfilment, has reappeared. *Mauvais fois* is renounced; and with this final turning aside from unreality, reality manifests itself again at last in Catherine's presence. The irony is that the melodrama of the final chapter is no longer Heathcliff's—it is Nellie's. As Heathcliff turns from his falsity to his reality, he becomes totally matter-of-fact, normal and sensible; while her voice becomes more and more nervous and high-pitched. "He didn't notice me, and yet he smiled. I'd rather have seen him gnash his teeth than smile so. 'Mr. Heathcliff! master!' I cried, 'don't, for God's sake, stare as if you saw an unearthly vision.' 'Don't, for God's sake, shout so loud,' he replied. 'Turn round and tell me, are we by ourselves?' " She wonders whether he is a ghoul or a vampire, is shocked at his "godless indifference"; but the truth is simply that she cannot grasp the growing intensity of his happiness. So sane and wise in her judgement of all that falls within the scope of the Grange, she has never been capable of understanding Wuthering Heights, and now her incomprehension is revealed in its full extent. What she sees in her terms as soul committing suicide and marching to hell, is a soul moving in its own terms from a false hell to a real heaven. When Heathcliff dies it is into full life, completing the process of becoming real in union with Cathy. The window is open, there is no blood on the hand, the wind and rain have swept elementally across the still face, the eyes are startlingly alive, the face is *smiling*, life-like, exultant. Nellie cannot bear what she cannot understand: she tries to make the face look as death should look at the Grange, asleep and peaceful, but it will not. So she interprets its expression as a frightful Gothic sneer, and Charlotte Brontë follows suit, as all Grange readers will do if they are not careful.

Yet we are surely not to take the vision of the Heights as supplanting or disqualifying the vision of the Grange. The novel is one of those that immediately expose the reader's most personal preconceptions, but its strength is its imaginative challenge to transcend them. To Grange readers, the critic must insist on the vitality and intensity of the "life" in which Cathy and Heathcliff have their being, and the power of their presentation. To Heights readers he must no less insistently point to Nellie, to Edgar, and to the vivid and "life"-enhancing relationship of Hareton and the younger Catherine, as an image of Heathcliff and Cathy in Grange terms. One kind of life must not blind us to the claims of the other, in either direction. One kind of reader has to be warned against taking Nellie as a reliable witness in all respects, not in moral terms, but because there are dimensions she is incapable of understanding and can only distort. Another kind of reader has to be reminded of the genuine warmth, human wisdom, and moral value of her insight. Looking from one angle, Hareton and his Catherine are maturing adults, while Cathy and Heathcliff are fixed in a mode of being forged in childhood, where intensity is all. (Emily Brontë's sense of this is shown by the fact that the ghost outside Lockwood's window is a child, though she calls herself Catherine Linton.) If we do compare them with Lawrence, there is neither the rich reverence for life through the body, enhancing the whole relationship of man to the physical universe; nor the concern for independent selfhood enriching relationship; which together make his kind of "impersonality" so unsolipsistic. Heathcliff and Catherine are not only enclosed in themselves; their full "being" requires a rejection of society, of any kind of public morality, of all human relationship save one, of individual selfhood and personality, of the body, and hence finally of life itself as we know it. We need to measure the cost of saying "I am Heathcliff" as well as the cost of betraying it. Yet from another angle, Hareton and Catherine are no kind of "might-have-been," for they are a different kind of being, and in some respects at least, a smaller kind. They have incorporated as much of the intensity of the Heights as the Grange will hold, but they remain blind to anything beyond. Heathcliff and Cathy are not finally adolescent, they meet as man and woman under the 'nab,' they become adults who have retained and still further intensified the child's knowledge of the numinous. If we wish to talk of the child's intensities, we confront the Romantic certainty that these allow a deeper and truer insight in some respects than the normal socialized man's—one that vitalizes the universe, retains a sense of mystery, taps powers and dimensions that can raise human life to "heights" that dwarf the civilized landscape. Through the foliage of Thrushcross Grange, the bells that even in Gimmerton announce the existence of a numinous world beyond cannot be heard except in winter, but they can always be heard at the Heights. In the fertile valley the humanized and civilized Church of England falls into decay, the Methodist chapel is going too, but the last inhabitant of Wuthering Heights retains, in gnarled and twisted form, the certainty that the final judgement and election will not be in human, social, or ethical terms. Joseph's Calvinism sees Heathcliff as damned, but shares with him the renunciation of the world for a higher truth, and the certainty of eternal heaven for the special souls who remain true to their mysterious election.

We have to hold the comparison true, finely balanced. We must not attempt to "unify" the conflicting visions by trying to make one prevail; but try instead to encompass the whole landscape, the two houses, the different ways of looking, in their opposition. The last paragraphs of the novel do this with scrupulous delicacy. Each of them not only can but must be read from two points of view. Emily Brontë secures our eyes in line with the windowpane that separates the worlds, so that one eye sees the one, and the other the other.

As we move from *Mansfield Park* to *Wuthering Heights*, the changing styles of architecture of the fictions do seem to reflect changing conceptions of the place of the heart in human life; the houses are metaphors for widely differing ideas of love. *Mansfield Park* and *Emma* are the last Augustan novels, adjusting private feeling to public order; but the increasing interiorization, the exploration of the individual, point forward to a new mode. In *Persuasion* we are in a world of flux, Jane Austen's Mutability Canto. The public order represented by the Great House has atrophied, and the question of who is to inherit, and on the basis of what Constancy, is the central question of the novel. The answer is found in the enduring heart, which can incorporate conscience in feeling, and sense in sensibility. If Charlotte Brontë had read *Persuasion,* she might well have judged Jane Austen differently. In *Jane Eyre,* however, all sense of shared public value has gone, society is merely conventional where it is not corrupt. The house becomes a metaphor of the private heart; a stage in the liberation of its buried life, and the revelation of the ultimate nature of the self before it can be fulfilled in love. Value can only be discovered within the self, but marriage can consummate the full life of the heart in a relationship of spiritual, moral, and sexual concord. In *Wuthering Heights,* two visions are set in irreconcilable conflict. The world of Thrushcross Grange is less Romantic and more Augustan than *Jane Eyre,* because it is less concerned to probe the depths of the individual self, and because it retains a sense of community and shared traditions of value, but its portrait of love and marriage has strong affinities with Charlotte Brontë's. But there is opposed to Thrushcross Grange another architecture, where it is not only public value, but also the language of character, personality, and individual selfhood that is broken through, to release a concept of being and loving that is antisocial, impersonal, impervious to time, to flux, to death. In Emily Brontë we might even say that the early nineteenth-century and the twentieth-century novel seem to challenge each other within the same covers; but she does not resolve, she encompasses, ensuring vision through both eyes.

# Charlotte Brontë's "New" Gothic

## by Robert B. Heilman

In that characteristic flight from cliché that may plunge him into the recherché the critic might well start from *The Professor* and discover in it much more than is implied by the usual dismissal of it as Charlotte Brontë's poorest work. He might speculate about Charlotte's singular choice of a male narrator—the value of it, or even the need of it, for her. For through William Crimsworth she lives in Héger, making love to herself as Frances Henri: in this there is a kind of ravenousness, inturning, splitting, and doubling back of feeling. Through Crimsworth she experiences a sudden, vivid, often graceless mastery. But these notes on the possible psychology of the author are critically useful only as a way into the strange tremors of feeling that are present in a formally defective story. Pelet identifies "a fathomless spring of sensibility in thy breast, Crimsworth." If Crimsworth is not a successful character, he is the channel of emotional surges that splash over a conventional tale of love: the author's disquieting presence in the character lends a nervous, off-center vitality. The pathos of liberty is all but excessive (as it is later in Shirley Keeldar and Lucy Snowe): Crimsworth sneers, ". . . I sprang from my bed with other slaves," and rejoices, "Liberty I clasped in my arms . . . her smile and embrace revived my life." The Puritan sentiment (to be exploited partially in Jane Eyre and heavily in Lucy Snowe) becomes tense, rhetorical, fiercely censorious; the self-righteousness punitive and even faintly paranoid. Through the frenetically Protestant Crimsworth and his flair for rebuke Charlotte notes the little sensualities of girl students ("parting her lips, as full as those of a hot-blooded Maroon") and the coquettish yet ugent sexuality of Zoraide Reuter perversely responding to Crimsworth's ostensible yet not total unresponsiveness to her: "When she stole about me with the soft step of a slave, I felt at once barbarous and sensual as a pasha."

"Charlotte Brontë's 'New' Gothic," by Robert B. Heilman. From *From Austen to Conrad*, ed. R. C. Rathburn and M. Steinmann (Minneapolis, Minn.: The University of Minnesota Press, 1958), pp. 118–32. Reprinted by permission of the author.

Charlotte looks beyond familiar surfaces. In Yorke Hunsden she notes the "incompatibilities of the 'physique' with the 'morale.' " The explosive Byronic castigator has lineaments "small, and even feminine" and "now the mien of a morose bull, and anon that of an arch and mischevous girl." In this version of the popular archetype, "rough exterior but heart of gold," Charlotte brilliantly finds a paradoxical union of love and hate; she sees generosity of spirit sometimes appearing directly but most often translated into antithetical terms that also accommodate opposite motives—into god-like self-indulgence in truth-telling; almost Mephistophelian cynicism; sadism and even murderousness in words.

Charlotte's story is conventional; formally she is for "reason" and "real life"; but her characters keep escaping to glorify "feeling" and "Imagination." Feeling is there in the story—evading repression, in author or in character; ranging from nervous excitement to emotional absorption; often tense and peremptory; sexuality, hate, irrational impulse, grasped, given life, not merely named and pigeonholed. This is Charlotte's version of Gothic: in her later novels an extraordinary thing. In that incredibly eccentric history, *The Gothic Quest,* Montague Summers asserts that the "Gothic novel of sensibility . . . draws its emotionalism and psychology . . . from the work of Samuel Richardson." When this line of descent continues in the Brontës, the vital feeling moves toward an intensity, a freedom, and even an abandon virtually nonexistent in historical Gothic and rarely approached in Richardson. From Angria on, Charlotte's women vibrate with passions that the fictional conventions only partly constrict or gloss over—in the center an almost violent devotedness that has in it at once a fire of independence, a spiritual energy, a vivid sexual responsiveness, and, along with this, self-righteousness, a sense of power, sometimes self-pity and envious competitiveness. To an extent the heroines are "un-heroined," unsweetened. Into them there has come a new sense of the dark side of feeling and personality.

*The Professor* ventures a little into the psychic darkness on which *Villette* draws heavily. One night Crimsworth, a victim of hypochondria, hears a voice saying, "In the midst of life we are in death," and he feels "a horror of great darkness." In his boyhood this same "sorceress" drew him "to the very brink of a black, sullen river" and managed to "lure me to her vaulted home of horrors." Charlotte draws on sex images that recall the note of sexuality subtly present in other episodes: ". . . I had entertained her at bed and board . . . she lay with me, . . . taking me entirely to her death-cold bosom, and holding me with arms of bone." The climax is: "I repulsed her as one would a dreaded and ghastly concubine coming to embitter a husband's heart

toward his young bride . . . ," This is Gothic, yet there is an integrity
of feeling that greatly deepens the convention.

From childhood terrors to all those mysteriously threatening sights,
sounds, and injurious acts that reveal the presence of some malevolent
force and that anticipate the holocaust at Thornfield, the traditional
Gothic in *Jane Eyre* has often been noted, and as often disparaged. It
need not be argued that Charlotte Brontë did not reach the heights
while using hand-me-down devices, though a tendency to work through
the conventions of fictional art was a strong element in her make-up.
This is true of all her novels, but it is no more true than her counter-
tendency to modify, most interestingly, these conventions. In both
*Villette* and *Jane Eyre* Gothic is used but characteristically is undercut.
Jane Eyre hears a "tragic . . . preternatural . . . laugh," but this
is at "high noon" and there is "no circumstance of ghostliness"; Grace
Poole, the supposed laugher, is a plain person, than whom no "apparition less romantic or less ghostly could . . . be conceived"; Charlotte apologizes ironically to the "romantic reader" for telling "the
plain truth" that Grace generally bears a "pot of porter." Charlotte
almost habitually revises "old Gothic," the relatively crude mechanisms
of fear, with an infusion of the anti-Gothic. When Mrs. Rochester
first tried to destroy Rochester by fire, Jane "baptized" Rochester's
bed and heard Rochester "fulminating strange anathemas at finding
himself lying in a pool of water." The introduction of comedy as a
palliative of straight Gothic occurs on a large scale when almost
seventy-five pages are given to the visit of the Ingram-Eshton party to
mysterious Thornfield; here Charlotte, as often in her novels, falls
into the manner of the Jane Austen whom she despised. When Mrs.
Rochester breaks loose again and attacks Mason, the presence of guests
lets Charlotte play the nocturnal alarum for at least a touch of comedy:
Rochester orders the frantic women not to "pull me down or strangle
me"; and "the two dowagers, in vast white wrappers, were bearing down
on him like ships in full sail."

The symbolic also modifies the Gothic, for it demands of the reader
a more mature and complicated response than the relatively simple
thrill or momentary intensity of feeling sought by primitive Gothic.
When mad Mrs. Rochester, seen only as "the foul German spectre—
the Vampyre," spreads terror at night, that is one thing; when, with
the malicious insight that is the paradox of her madness, she tears the
wedding veil in two and thus symbolically destroys the planned marriage, that is another thing, far less elementary as art. The midnight
blaze that ruins Thornfield becomes more than a shock when it is
seen also as the fire of purgation; the grim, almost roadless forest sur-

rounding Ferndean is more than a harrowing stage-set when it is also felt as a symbol of Rochester's closed-in life.

The point is that in various ways Charlotte manages to make the patently Gothic more than a stereotype. But more important is that she instinctively finds new ways to achieve the ends served by old Gothic—the discovery and release of new patterns of feeling, the intensification of feeling. Though only partly unconventional, Jane is nevertheless so portrayed as to evoke new feelings rather than merely exercise old ones. As a girl she is lonely, "passionate," "strange," "like nobody there"; she feels superior, rejects poverty, talks back precociously, tells truths bluntly, enjoys "the strangest sense of freedom," tastes "vengeance"; she experiences a nervous shock which is said to have a lifelong effect, and the doctor says "nerves not in a good state"; she can be "reckless and feverish," "bitter and truculent"; at Thornfield she is restless, given to "bright visions," letting "imagination" picture an existence full of "life, fire, feeling." Thus Charlotte leads away from standardized characterization toward new levels of human reality, and hence from stock responses toward a new kind of passionate engagement.

Charlotte moves toward depth in various ways that have an immediate impact like that of Gothic. Jane's strange, fearful symbolic dreams are not mere thrillers but reflect the tensions of the engagement period, the stress of the wedding-day debate with Rochester, and the longing for Rochester after she has left him. The final Thornfield dream, with its vivid image of a hand coming through a cloud in place of the expected moon, is in the surrealistic vein that appears most sharply in the extraordinary pictures that Jane draws at Thornfield: here Charlotte is plumbing the psyche, not inventing a weird *décor*. Likewise in the telepathy scene, which Charlotte, unlike Defoe in dealing with a similar episode, does her utmost to actualize: "The feeling was not like an electric shock; but it was quite as sharp, as strange, as startling: . . . that inward sensation . . . with all its unspeakable strangeness . . . like an inspiration . . . wondrous shock of feeling. . . ." In her flair for the surreal, in her plunging into feeling that is without status in the ordinary world of the novel, Charlotte discovers a new dimension of Gothic.

She does this most thoroughly in her portrayal of characters and of the relations between them. If in Rochester we see only an Angrian-Byronic hero and a Charlotte wish-fulfillment figure (the two identifications which to some readers seem entirely to place him), we miss what is more significant, the exploration of personality that opens up new areas of feeling in intersexual relationships. Beyond the "grim," the "harsh," the eccentric, the almost histrionically cynical that super-

ficially distinguish Rochester from conventional heroes, there is something almost Lawrentian: Rochester is "neither tall nor graceful"; his
eyes can be "dark, irate, and piercing"; his strong features "took my
feelings from my own power and fettered them in his." Without using
the vocabulary common to us, Charlotte is presenting maleness and
physicality, to which Jane responds directly. She is "assimilated" to
him by "something in my brain and heart, in my blood and nerves";
she "must love" and "could not unlove" him; the thought of parting
from him is "agony." Rochester's oblique amatory maneuvers become
almost punitive in the Walter-to-Griselda style and once reduce her
to sobbing "convulsively"; at times the love-game borders on a power-
game. Jane, who prefers "rudeness" to "flattery," is an instinctive
evoker of passion: she learns "the pleasure of vexing and soothing him
by turns" and pursues a "system" of working him up "to considerable
irritation" and coolly leaving him; when, as a result, his caresses become grimaces, pinches, and tweaks, she records that, sometimes at
least, she "decidedly preferred these fierce favors." She reports, "I
crushed his hand . . . red with the passionate pressure"; she "could
not . . . see God for his creature," and in her devotion Rochester
senses "an earnest, religious energy."

Charlotte's remolding of stock feeling reaches a height when she
sympathetically portrays Rochester's efforts to make Jane his mistress;
here the stereotyped seducer becomes a kind of lost nobleman of
passion, and of specifically physical passion: "Every atom of your flesh
is as dear to me as my own. . . ." The intensity of the pressure which
he puts upon her is matched, not by the fear and revulsion of the
popular heroine, but by a responsiveness which she barely masters:
"The crisis was perilous; but not without its charm. . . ." She is
"tortured by a sense of remorse at thus hurting his feelings"; at the
moment of decision "a hand of fiery iron grasped my vitals . . .
blackness, burning! . . . my intolerable duty"; she leaves in "despair";
and after she has left, "I longed to be his; I panted to return . . ."—
and for the victory of principle "I abhorred myself . . . I was hateful
in my own eyes." This extraordinary openness to feeling, this escape
from the bondage of the trite, continues in the Rivers relationship,
which is a structural parallel to the Rochester affair: as in Rochester
the old sex villain is seen in a new perspective, so in Rivers the clerical
hero is radically refashioned; and Jane's almost accepting a would-be
husband is given the aesthetic status of a regrettable yielding to a
seducer. Without a remarkable liberation from conventional feeling
Charlotte could not fathom the complexity of Rivers—the earnest
and dutiful clergyman distraught by a profound inner turmoil of conflicting "drives": sexuality, restlessness, hardness, pride, ambition
("fever in his vitals," "inexorable as death"); the hypnotic, almost in-

human potency of his influence on Jane, who feels "a freezing spell," "an awful charm," an "iron shroud"; the relentlessness, almost the un- scrupulousness, of his wooing, the resultant fierce struggle (like that with Rochester), Jane's brilliantly perceptive accusation, ". . . you almost hate me . . . you would kill me. You are killing me now"; and yet her mysterious near-surrender: "I was tempted to cease struggling with him—to rush down the torrent of his will into the gulf of his existence, and there lose my own."

Aside from partial sterilization of banal Gothic by dry factuality and humor, Charlotte goes on to make a much more important—indeed, a radical—revision of the mode: in *Jane Eyre* and in the other novels, as we shall see, that discovery of passion, that rehabilitation of the extra-rational, which is the historical office of Gothic, is no longer oriented in marvelous circumstance but moves deeply into the lesser known realities of human life. This change I describe as the change from "old Gothic" to "new Gothic." The kind of appeal is the same; the fictional method is utterly different.

When Charlotte went on from *Jane Eyre* to *Shirley*, she produced a book that for the student of the Gothic theme is interesting precisely because on the face of things it would be expected to be a barren field. It is the result of Charlotte's one deliberate venture from private in- tensities into public extensities: Orders in Council, the Luddites, tech- nological unemployment in 1811 and 1812, a social portraiture which develops Charlotte's largest cast of characters. Yet Charlotte cannot keep it a social novel. Unlike Warren, who in the somewhat similar *Night Rider* chose to reflect the historical economic crisis in the private crisis of the hero, Miss Brontë loses interest in the public and slides over into the private.

The formal irregularities of *Shirley*—the stop-and-start, zig-zag move- ment, plunging periodically into different perspectives—light up the divergent impulses in Charlotte herself: the desire to make a story from observed outer life, and the inability to escape from inner urgencies that with centrifugal force unwind outward into story almost autonomously. Passion alters plan: the story of industrial crisis is re- peatedly swarmed over by the love stories. But the ultimate complica- tion is that Charlotte's duality of impulse is reflected not only in the narrative material but in two different ways of telling each part of the story. On the one hand she tells a rather conventional, open, pre- dictable tale; on the other she lets go with a highly charged private sentiency that may subvert the former or at least surround it with an atmosphere of unfamiliarity or positive strangeness: the Gothic impulse.

For Charlotte it is typically the "pattern" versus the "strange." She describes "two pattern young ladies, in pattern attire, with pattern deportment"—a "respectable society" in which "Shirley had the air of a black swan, or a white crow. . . ." When, in singing, Shirley "poured round the passion, force," the young ladies thought this "strange" and concluded: "What was *strange* must be *wrong* . . . ." True, Charlotte's characters live within the established "patterns" of life; but their impulse is to vitalize forms with unpatterned feeling, and Charlotte's to give play to unpatterned feeling in all its forms. She detects the warrior in the Reverend Matthew Helstone; reports that Malone the curate "had energy enough in hate"; describes Shirley weeping without apparent reason; recounts Mrs. Yorke's paranoid "brooding, eternal, immitigable suspicion of all men, things, creeds, and parties"; portrays Hiram Yorke as scornful, stubborn, intolerant of superiors, independent, truculent, benevolent toward inferiors, his virtues surrounding an aggressive *amour propre*.

Shirley is given a vehement, sweeping, uninhibited criticalness of mind; in her highly articulate formulations of incisive thought is released a furious rush of emotional energy. Within the framework of moral principles her ideas and feelings are untrammeled. She vigorously debunks clichés against charity, but against the mob she will defend her property "like a tigress"; to Yorke's face she does a corrosive analysis of his personality; she attacks Milton in a fiery sweeping paean to Eve, the "mother" of "Titans"; in an almost explosive defense of love she attacks ignorant, chilly, refined, embarrassed people who "blaspheme living fire, seraph-brought from a divine altar"; when she insists that she must *"love"* before she marries, her "worldly" Uncle Sympson retorts, "Preposterous stuff!—indecorous—unwomanly!"

Beside the adults who in ways are precocious are the precocious children—the Yorkes who have their parents' free-swinging, uninhibited style of talk; Henry Sympson, having for his older cousin Shirley an attachment that borders on sexual feeling; and most of all Martin Yorke, aged fifteen, to whose excited pursuit of Caroline, almost irrelevant to plot or theme, Charlotte devotes two and a half zestful chapters. Martin is willing to help Caroline see Robert Moore, "her confounded sweetheart," to be near her himself, and he plans to claim a reward "displeasing to Moore"; he thinks of her physical beauties. Once he gets between Robert and Caroline at goodbye time; "he half carried Caroline down the stairs," "wrapped her shawl round her," and wanted to claim a kiss. At the same time he feels "power over her," he wants her to coax him, and he would like "to put her in a passion—to make her cry." Charlotte subtly conveys the sexuality of his quest—a rare feat in the nineteenth-century novel.

In Robert Moore, the unpopular mill-owner, Charlotte finds less social rightness or wrongness than his strength, his masculine appeal;

her sympathy, so to speak, is for the underside of his personality. It "agreed with Moore's temperament . . . to be generally hated"; "he liked a silent, sombre, unsafe solitude"; against the vandals his "hate is still running in such a strong current" that he has none left for other objects; he shows "a terrible half" of himself in pursuing rioters with "indefatigable, . . . relentless assiduity"; this "excitement" pleases him; sadistically he likes to "force" magistrates to "betray a certain fear." He is the great lover of the story; he almost breaks Caroline's heart before he marries her, and he even has a subtle impact on Shirley, teasingly communicated, though officially denied, by Charlotte. What Caroline yields to is his "secret power," which affects her "like a spell." Here again Charlotte records, as directly as she can, simple sexual attractiveness. From the problem novel she veers off into "new Gothic"; in old Gothic, her hero would have been a villain.

True to convention, the love stories end happily. But special feelings, a new pathos of love, come through. Louis Moore demands in a woman something "to endure, . . . to reprimand"; love must involve "prickly peril," "a sting now and then"; for him the "young lioness or leopardess" is better than the lamb. There is that peculiarly tense vivacity of talk between lovers (the Jane-Rochester style), who discover a heightened, at times stagey, yet highly communicative rhetoric, drawing now on fantasy, now on moral conviction, verging now on titillating revelation, now on battle; a crafty game of love, flirting with an undefined risk, betraying a withheld avowal, savoring the approach to consummation, as if the erotic energy which in another social order might find a physical outlet were forcing itself into an electric language that is decorous but intimately exploratory. Between Louis Moore, who has "a thirst for freedom," and Shirley, to whom finding love is the Quest for the Bridle (for "a *master* [whom it is] impossible not to love, and very possible to fear"), there is an almost disturbingly taut struggle, a fierce intensification of the duel between Mirabel and Millamant, complex feelings translated into wit, sheer debate, abusiveness of manner, and a variety of skirmishings; Louis, the lover, adopting the stance of power and consciously playing to fright; the pursuit of an elusive prey ending in a virtual parody of "one calling, Child!/ And I replied, My Lord"; over all of this a singular air of strained excitement, of the working of underlying emotional forces that at the climax leads to a new frenetic intensification of style in Louis's notebook:

> "Will you let me breathe, and not bewilder me? You must not smile at present. The world swims and changes round me. The sun is a dizzying scarlet blaze, the sky a violet vortex whirling over me."
> I am a strong man, but I staggered as I spoke. All creation was exag-

gerated: colour grew more vivid: motion more rapid; life itself more
vital. I hardly saw her for a moment; but I heard her voice—pitilessly
sweet. . . . Blent with torment, I experienced rapture.

Nor does Charlotte's flair for "unpatterned feeling" stop here: Shirley,
the forceful leader who has already been called "a gentleman" and
"captain," languishes under the found bridle of the masterful lover,
whom she treats chillily and subjects to "exquisitely provoking" post-
ponements of marriage; he calls her a "pantheress" who "gnaws her
chain"; she tells him, "I don't know myself," as if engagement had
opened to her eyes a previously undetected facet of her nature. Though
"these freaks" continue, she is "fettered" at last; but not before the
reader is radically stirred by the felt mysteries of personality. Before
Charlotte, no love story tapped such strange depths, no consummation
was so like a defeat.

Here Charlotte is probing psychic disturbance and is on the edge of
psychosomatic illness. The theme draws her repeatedly. When Caroline
thinks Robert doesn't love her, she suffers a long physical decline,
described with painful fullness. She "wasted," had a "broken spirit,"
suffered "intolerable despair," felt the "utter sickness of longing and
disappointment," at night found "my mind darker than my hiding-
place," had "melancholy dreams," became "what is called nervous,"
had "fears I never used to have," "an inexpressible weight on my
mind," and "strange sufferings," believed at times "that God had
turned His face from her" and sank "into the gulf of religious despair."
Charlotte divines this: "People never die of love or grief alone; though
some die of inherent maladies which the tortures of those passions
prematurely force into destructive action." Caroline lingers in illness,
has fancies "inscrutable to ordinary attendants," has a hallucination
of talking to Robert in the garden. Shirley, having been bitten by a
dog which she believes to be mad, becomes seriously ill; psychosomatic
illness springs directly from Charlotte's special sensitivity to the neurotic potential in human nature. A complementary awareness, that
of the impact of the physical on the psychic, appears when she observes
the "terrible depression," the "inexpressible—dark, barren, impotent"
state of mind of Robert when he is recovering from a gunshot wound.

To give so much space to a lesser work is justifiable only because
some of its contents are of high historico-critical significance. Though
*Shirley* is not pulled together formally as well as *Jane Eyre* or even
the more sprawling *Villette,* and though the characters are as wholes
less fully realized, still it accommodates the widest ranging of an
extraordinarily free sensibility. Constantly, in many different direc-
tions, it is in flight from the ordinary rational surface of things against
which old Gothic was the first rebel in fiction; it abundantly contains

and evokes, to adapt Charlotte's own metaphor, "unpatterned feeling."
It turns up unexpected elements in personality: resentfulness, malice,
love of power; precocities and perversities of response; the multiple
tensions of love between highly individualized lovers; psychic dis-
turbances. And in accepting a dark magnetic energy as a central virtue
in personality, Charlotte simply reverses the status of men who were
the villains in the sentimental and old Gothic modes.

Of the four novels, *Villette* is most heavily saturated with Gothic—
with certain of its traditional manifestations (old Gothic), with the
undercutting of these that is for Charlotte no less instinctive than the
use of them (anti-Gothic), and with an original, intense exploration of
feeling that increases the range and depth of fiction (new Gothic).
As in *Jane Eyre*, Charlotte can be skillful in anti-Gothic. When
Madame Beck, pussyfooting in espionage, "materializes" in shocking
suddenness, Lucy is made matter-of-fact or indignant rather than
thrilled with fright. "No ghost stood beside me . . ." is her characteristic response to a Beck surprise. Once the spy, having "stolen" upon
her victims, betrays her unseen presence by a sneeze: Gothic yields to
farce. Technically more complex is Charlotte's use of the legend of
the nun supposedly buried alive and of the appearances of a visitant
taken to be the ghost of the nun: Charlotte coolly distances herself
from this by having Lucy dismiss the legend as "romantic rubbish"
and by explaining the apparitions as the playful inventions of a giddy
lover. True, she keeps the secret long enough to get a few old Gothic
thrills from the "ghost," but what she is really up to is using the apparitions in an entirely new way; that is, for responses that lie beyond
the simplicities of terror.

First, the apparitions are explained as a product of Lucy's own
psychic state, the product, Dr. John suggests, of "long-continued
mental conflict." In the history of Gothic this is an important spot,
for here we first see the shift from stock explanations and responses to
the inner human reality: fiction is slowly discovering the psychic
depths known to drama for centuries.

Then, when Lucy next sees the nun, she responds in a way that lies
entirely outside fictional convention: "I neither fled nor shrieked . . .
I spoke . . . I stretched out my hand, for I meant to touch her." Not
that Lucy is not afraid, but that she is testing herself—an immense
change from the expectable elementary response: the *frisson* disappears
before the complexer action that betokens a maturing of personality.

Finally, Paul and Lucy both see the spectre and are thus brought
closer together: they have had what they call "impressions," and
through sharing the ghost they assume a shared sensibility. Paul says,
"I was conscious of rapport between you and myself." The rapport is

real, though the proof of it is false; the irony of this is a subtle sophistication of Gothic.

The responsiveness, the sensitivity, is the thing; many passages place
"feeling" above "seeing" as an avenue of knowledge. Reason must be
respected, for it is "vindictive," but at times imagination must be
yielded to, like a sexual passion at once feared and desired. There is
the summer night when the sedative given by Madame Beck has a
strange effect:

> Imagination was roused from her rest, and she came forth impetuous
> and venturous. With scorn she looked on Matter, her mate—
> "Rise!" she said; "Sluggard! this night I will have *my* will; nor shalt
> thou prevail."
> "Look forth and view the night!" was her cry; and when I lifted the
> heavy blind from the casement close at hand—with her own royal ges-
> ture, she showed me a moon supreme, in an element deep and splendid.
> . . . She lured me to leave this den and follow her forth into dew,
> coolness, and glory.

There follows the most magnificent of all Charlotte's nocturnes: that
vision of the "moonlit, midnight park," the brilliance of the fete, the
strange charm of places and people, recounted in a rhythmical, en-
chanted style (the "Kubla Khan" mode) which at first reading gives the
air of a dream mistaken for reality to what is in fact reality made like
a dream. This is a surrealistic, trance-like episode which makes
available to fiction a vast new territory and idiom. The surrealistic is,
despite Montague Summers, one of the new phases of Gothic, which in
its role of liberator of feeling characteristically explores the non-
naturalistic: to come up, as here, with a profounder nature, or a nature
freshly, even disturbingly, seen.

The surrealism of Lucy's evening is possible only to a special sensitivity, and it is really the creation of this sensitivity, in part patho-
logical, that is at the apex of Charlotte's Gothic. In *The Professor*
the tensions in the author's contemplation of her own experience come
into play; in *Shirley* various undercurrents of personality push up into
the social surfaces of life; in *Jane Eyre* moral feeling is subjected to the
remolding pressures of a newly vivid consciousness of the diverse impulses of sexuality; and in *Villette* the feeling responses to existence
are pursued into sufferings that edge over into disorder. The psychology of rejection and alienation, first applied to Polly, becomes
the key to Lucy, who, finding no catharsis for a sense of desolation,
generates a serious inner turmoil. She suffers from "a terrible oppression" and then from "anxiety lying in wait on enjoyment, like a
tiger crouched in a jungle . . . his fierce heart panted close against
mine; . . . I knew he waited only for sun-down to bound ravenous
from his ambush." Depression is fed by the conflict between a loveless

routine of life and her longings, which she tried to put down like "Jael to Sisera, driving a nail through their temples"; but this only "transiently stunned" them and "at intervals [they] would turn on the nail with a rebellious wrench: then did the temples bleed, and the brain thrill to its core."

These strains prepare us for the high point in Charlotte's new Gothic—the study of Lucy's emotional collapse and near breakdown when vacation comes and she is left alone at the school with "a poor deformed and imbecile pupil." "My heart almost died within me; . . . My spirits had long been gradually sinking; now that the prop of employment was withdrawn, they went down fast." After three weeks, storms bring on "a deadlier paralysis"; and "my nervous system could hardly support" the daily strain. She wanders in the street: "A goad thrust me on, a fever forbade me to rest, . . ." She observes a "growing illusion" and says, ". . . my nerves are getting overstretched, . . ." She feels that "a malady is growing upon" her mind, and she asks herself, "How shall I keep well?" Then come "a peculiarly agonizing depression"; a nine-days storm: "a strange fever of the nerves and blood"; continuing insomnia, broken only by a terrifying nightmare of alienation. She flees the house, and then comes the climactic event of her going to a church and despite the intensity of her Protestant spirit entering the confessional to find relief.

From now on, overtly or implicitly, hypochondria and anxiety keep coming into the story—the enemies from whose grip Lucy must gradually free herself. At a concert she spotted the King as a fellow-victim of "that strangest spectre, Hypochondria," for on his face she saw its marks, whose meaning, "if I did not *know*, at least I *felt* . . . ," When, after her return to Beck's on a rainy night, things are not going well, a letter from Dr. John is "the ransom from my terror," and its loss drives her almost to frenzy. She describes night as "an unkindly time" when she has strange fancies, doubts, the "horror of calamity." She is aware of her "easily-deranged temperament." Beyond this area of her own self-understanding we see conflicts finding dramatic expression in her almost wild acceptance of Rachel's passionate acting of Phèdre ("a spectacle low, horrible, immoral"), which counterbalances her vehement condemnation of a fleshy nude by Rubens (one of the "materialists"). Paul identifies her, in a figure whose innocence for him is betrayed by the deep, if not wholly conscious, understanding that leads Charlotte to write it: "a young she wild creature, new caught, untamed, viewing with a mixture of fire and fear the first entrance of the breaker in."

There is not room to trace Lucy's recovery, especially in the important phase, the love affair with Paul which is related to our theme by compelling, as do the Jane-Rochester and Louis Moore-Shirley relationships in quite different ways, a radical revision of the feelings exacted by stereotyped romance. What is finally noteworthy is that Charlotte, having chosen in Lucy a heroine with the least durable emotional equipment, with the most conspicuous neurotic element in her temperament, goes on through the history of Lucy's emotional maturing to surmount the need for romantic fulfillment and to develop the aesthetic courage for a final disaster—the only one in her four novels.

Some years ago Edmund Wilson complained of writers of Gothic who "fail to lay hold on the terrors that lie deep in the human soul and that cause man to fear himself" and proposed an anthology of horror stories that probe "psychological caverns" and find "disquieting obsessions." This is precisely the direction in which Charlotte Brontë moved, especially in Lucy Snowe and somewhat also in Caroline Helstone and Shirley Keeldar; this was one aspect of her following human emotions where they took her, into many depths and intensities that as yet hardly had a place in the novel. This was the finest achievement of Gothic.

Gothic is variously defined. In a recent book review Leslie Fiedler implies that Gothic is shoddy mystery-mongering, whereas F. Cudworth Flint defines the Gothic tradition, which he considers "nearly central in American literature," as "a literary exploration of the avenues to death." For Montague Summers, on the other hand, Gothic was the essence of romanticism, and romanticism was the literary expression of supernaturalism. Both these latter definitions, though they are impractically inclusive, have suggestive value. For originally Gothic was one of a number of aesthetic developments which served to breach the "classical" and "rational" order of life and to make possible a kind of response, and a response to a kind of thing, that among the knowing had long been taboo. In the novel it was the function of Gothic to open horizons beyond social patterns, rational decisions, and institutionally approved emotions; in a word, to enlarge the sense of reality and its impact on the human being. It became then a great liberator of feeling. It acknowledged the nonrational—in the world of things and events, occasionally in the realm of the transcendental, ultimately and most persistently in the depths of the human being. (Richardson might have started this, but his sense of inner forces was so overlaid by the moralistic that his followers all ran after him only when he ran the wrong way.) The first Gothic writers took the easy way: the excitement of mysterious scene and happening, which I call old Gothic. Of this Charlotte Brontë made some direct use, while at the same time tending toward humorous modifications (anti-Gothic); but what really counts is its indirect usefulness to her: it released her from the patterns of the novel of society and therefore permitted the flowering of her real talent—the talent for finding and giving dramatic form to impulses and feelings which, because of their depth or mysteriousness or intensity or ambiguity, or of their ignoring or transcending everyday norms of propriety or reason, increase wonderfully the sense of reality in the novel. To note the emergence of this "new Gothic" in Charlotte Brontë is not, I think, to pursue an old mode into dusty corners but rather to identify historically the distinguishing, and distinguished, element in her work.

# Fire and Eyre: Charlotte Brontë's
# War of Earthly Elements

## by David Lodge

> 'I have brought you a book for evening solace,' and he laid
> on the table a new publication—a poem: one of those genuine
> productions so often vouchsafed to the fortunate public of
> those days—the golden age of modern literature (XXXII).

The "new publication" which St. John Rivers brings Jane Eyre,
at that stage in her life when she is a village schoolmistress, is *Marmion* (1808), and this is, I believe, the only precise indication in the
book of the date of its action. The allusion to *Marmion* suggests that,
without intending to create any sense of "period" in her novel (in
which case she would have referred much more extensively to dates
and historical events), Charlotte Brontë almost instinctively placed
her heroine in that period whose literature she found most inspiring,
the hey-day of Romanticism, the "golden age of modern literature."
It is inconceivable that *Jane Eyre* could have been written without
the Romantic Movement. The "gothic" elements so often noted by
commentators on the novel—the Byronic hero-with-a-past, the mad
wife locked up in an attic, and so on—constitute only a small part of
Charlotte's debt to Romantic literature. Far more important is the
characteristically Romantic theme of the novel—the struggle of an
individual consciousness towards self-fulfilment—and the romantic
imagery of landscape, seascape, sun, moon and the elements, through
which this theme is expressed.

On the other hand, the particular interest and strength of *Jane
Eyre* is that it is not a pure expression of Romanticism. The instinctive, passionate, nonethical drive of Romanticism towards self-fulfilment at whatever cost, is held in check by an allegiance to the ethical

"Fire and Eyre: Charlotte Brontë's War of Earthly Elements." From *The Language of Fiction*, by David Lodge (London: Routledge & Kegan Paul, Ltd.,
1966), pp. 114–43. Copyright © 1966 by David Lodge. Reprinted by permission
of Routledge & Kegan Paul, Ltd. and John Cushman Associates, Inc.

precepts of the Christian code and an acknowledgement of the necessity of exercising reason in human affairs. Jane's comment after Rochester's first marriage has been revealed and she realizes her duty to leave him, epitomizes the struggle within her between these two systems of value: "conscience, turned tyrant, held passion by the throat" (XXVII).

It is clear that the dominant energies and sympathies of the novel are on the side of passion. "Feeling without judgment is a washy draught indeed; but judgment untempered by feeling is too bitter and husky a draught for human deglutition," Jane opines (XXI). We are frequently reminded that she herself is primarily a creature of passion and feeling. " '[Y]ou are passionate, Jane, that you must allow' " says Mrs. Reed (IV), and she does allow it. "I know no medium: I never in my life have known any medium in my dealings with positive, hard characters, antagonistic to my own, between absolute submission and determined revolt. I have always faithfully observed the one, up to the very moment of bursting, sometimes with volcanic vehemence, into the other" (XXXIV).

On the other hand Rochester, early in his relationship with Jane, perceives resources of reason and moral strength in her which can control the passions. Reading her character in her physiognomy (in the scene where he is disguised as a gypsy) he says her eye is " 'soft and full of feeling' " and her mouth " 'mobile and flexible.' " But, prophesying future events, he reads a different message in the brow:

> "I see no enemy to a fortunate issue but in the brow; and that brow professes to say,—'I can live alone, if self-respect and circumstances require me so to do. I need not sell my soul to buy bliss' . . . the forehead declares, 'Reason sits firm and holds the reins, and she will not let the feelings burst away and hurry her to wild chasms. The passions may rage furiously, like true heathens, as they are; and the desires may imagine all sorts of vain things: but judgment shall still have the last word in every argument, and the casting vote in every decision. Strong wind, earthquake-shock, and fire may pass by: but I shall follow the guiding of that still small voice which interprets the dictates of conscience' " (XIX).

Rochester's association of the passions with elemental disturbance has a significance I shall explore later. I am concerned immediately to draw attention to the dialogue which is sustained throughout the novel between passion and reason, feeling and judgment, impulse and conscience. At the beginning of the story Jane is an underprivileged, oppressed child. She rebels against the tyrannical authority of Mrs. Reed, and experiences the romantic glow of released passion: "My soul began to expand, to exult, with the strangest sense of freedom, of triumph, I ever felt" (IV). She is sent to Lowood School where she is more oppressed than before. But for the first time she encounters an alternative attitude to suffering and injustice, the Christian stoicism of Helen Burns (whose favourite reading is *Rasselas,* antithesis of Romantic literature). Jane says to her, " 'When we are struck at without a reason, we should strike back again very hard; I am sure we should—so hard as to teach the person who struck us never to do it again.' " To which Helen replies, " 'You will change your mind, I hope, when you grow older: as yet you are but a little, untaught girl,' " and quotes the Christian precept about loving one's enemies (VI). Inspired by the sanctity of Helen Burns, and supported by the example and encouragement of the teacher, Miss Temple, Jane patiently endures her life at Lowood. "I' had imbibed from her [Miss Temple] something of her nature and much of her habits: more harmonious thoughts: what seemed better regulated feelings had become the inmates of my mind. I had given in allegiance to duty and order; I was quiet; I believed I was content" (X). But when Miss Temple leaves the school to be married:

> I was left in my natural element, and beginning to feel the stir of old emotions . . . now I remembered that the real world was wide, and that a varied field of hopes and fears, of sensations and excitements, awaited those who had courage to go forth into its expanse, to seek real knowledge of life amidst its perils (X).

This yearning is expressed through a characteristically Romantic gaze at the landscape:

> My eye passed all other objects to rest on those most remote, the blue peaks: it was those I longed to surmount; all within their boundary of rock and heath seemed prison-ground, exile limits. I traced the white road winding round the base of one mountain, and vanishing in a gorge between the two: how I longed to follow it further! (X).

She follows it to Thornfield Hall, as governess to Rochester's ward. Rochester is a kindred spirit: passionate, vital, unconventional. He represents for Jane the possibility of realizing her vague, romantic aspirations in a concrete human relationship. But the life of the passions is hedged about with potential danger and disaster, personified in the haunting presence at Thornfield Hall of Rochester's mad malevolent wife.

The first great crisis of Jane's life is when she has to choose between following the law of passion by living as Rochester's mistress, and following the law of conscience and duty by renouncing him. She takes the second course, but her renunciation is only passive. St. John Rivers, a reincarnation, in a much more extreme and forbidding form, of Helen Burns, and, in a less grotesque form, of Mr. Brocklehurst, calls her to a life of complete renunciation—a loveless marriage to him and work in the mission fields. This is the second great crisis of Jane's life. She refuses; and is finally rewarded by being reunited with Rochester, now free to offer her a lawful love, though tamed and mutilated by the purgatorial fire of Thornfield.

In his highly perceptive and stimulating essay, "The Brontës, or, Myth Domesticated," [1] Richard Chase remarks that *Jane Eyre* and *Wuthering Heights* end similarly: "a relatively mild and ordinary marriage is made after the spirit of the masculine universe is controlled or extinguished." [2] This he considers a weakness, and to some extent a betrayal of the mythical force behind both novels.

> It was the Victorian period which supposed that the primeval social order consisted of a murderous old man and his company of females and weaker males and which bequeathed the idea to Freud. We may almost say that the Brontë household *was* this primeval social order. The purpose of the Brontë culture heroine is to transform primeval society into a humane and noble order of civilization. . . . Our Brontë culture heroine, then, is the human protagonist of the cosmic drama. Rochester and Heathcliff are portrayed as being at once godlike and satanic. In them the universal enemies may be set at war by a culture heroine. Then if the devil is overcome, a higher state of society will have been achieved. The tyrannical Father-God will have been displaced. The stasis will have been smashed by the creative *élan* of sex and intelligence. The Brontë heroines fail in their missions; they refuse to venture so much; they will not accept the challenge of the God-Devil. They will not accept the challenge, for fear the Devil should win. Yet when we understand these heroines in some such terms as the foregoing, they acquire a new significance: it had not occurred to us that the stakes were so great.[3]

The reservations one has about Chase's argument, which is brilliantly conducted, are the reservations one commonly has about "myth-criticism"—that it tends to assume that literary work accumulates more value the more closely it approximates to "pure myth." [4] "The Brontës' tremendous displacement of the domestic values towards the tragic and mythical, though it falls short of ultimate achievement, gives their work a margin of superiority over that of other Victorian novelists," [5] says Chase. This displacement is certainly the source of the enduring interest of the Brontës' work, but it does not follow that a complete displacement would have resulted in complete achievement. To leave *Wuthering Heights* aside, the domestication

---

[1] Richard Chase, "The Brontës, or Myth Domesticated," *Forms of Modern Fiction,* ed. Willian Van O'Connor (Bloomington: Midland Book edition, 1959), pp. 102–19.

[2] Ibid., p. 110.

[3] Ibid., pp. 111–12.

[4] See Walter J. Ong's essay, "The Myth of Myth," *The Barbarian Within* (New York, 1962), pp. 131–45, for some cautionary words on the concept of "myth" in literary criticism.

[5] Chase, op. cit., p. 119.

of the mythical or, as I would term it, the Romantic element in *Jane Eyre,* is the resolution to which the whole novel points. Such a resolution need not be a cowardly compromise. It engages with the great Faustian dilemma bequeathed by Romanticism to modern man: how to reconcile the free development of the individual consciousness with the acceptance of the checks and restraints necessary to social and individual moral health—how to buy bliss without selling one's soul. The really interesting question is how Charlotte Brontë created a literary structure in which the domestic and the mythical, the realistic world of social behaviour and the romantic world of passionate self-consciousness, could coexist with only occasional and local lapses into incongruity.

For if we try to gather together our impressions of *Jane Eyre,* we are likely to recall two very different kinds of scene: on the one hand, the loneliness and misery of the young child in the Reed household, or the humiliations and discomforts of Lowood School, or the description of Jane, destitute and drenched with rain, peering through a window into the snug interior of Moor House; and on the other hand, the descriptions of Jane's paintings, or the scene of Rochester's proposal, when the chestnut tree is struck by lightning, or the extended image of a summer landscape invaded by icy winter through which Jane expresses her feelings when her marriage is prevented; on the one hand, writing which is firmly realistic and literal, keenly sensitive to common emotions and sensations, insisting on the value of animal comfort, domestic happiness, ordinary human affection; and on the other hand, writing which is visionary and poetic, evocative of heightened states of feeling, insisting on the value of individual self-fulfilment won from a conflict between passion and reason conducted at an extraordinary pitch of imaginative perception. I shall not be concerned in this essay, except incidentally, to demonstrate how Charlotte Brontë realizes these two orders of experience independently, but to suggest how she unites them. For she has not only to contain them within a single structure, but to persuade us that they can coexist in a single consciousness, and that they can be reconciled.

This sense of unity pervading a novel which embraces such diverse elements, and which, when analysed in conventional terms of "character" and "plot," seems to reveal only glaring weaknesses and absurdities, has, I think, been acknowledged by most critics of *Jane Eyre.* "Childish naïveté, rigid Puritanism, fiery passion, these would seem incongruous elements indeed; and it is their union which gives Charlotte Brontë's personality its peculiar distinction," says Lord David Cecil.[6] And according to Walter Allen, "If it were not for the unity

---

[6] David Cecil, *Early Victorian Novelists* (Penguin edition, 1948), p. 105.

of tone, *Jane Eyre* would be incoherent, for as a construction it is artless." [7] "Unity of tone" is a useful hint towards an understanding of the artistic coherence of *Jane Eyre*, yet on the surface there is a very striking variation of tone in the novel—between, for instance, this:

> I then sat with my doll on my knee, till the fire got low, glancing round occasionally to make sure that nothing worse than myself haunted the shadowy room; and when the embers sank to a dull red, I undressed hastily, tugging at knots and strings as I best might, and sought shelter from cold and darkness in my crib (IV).

and this:

> "And you will not marry me? You adhere to that resolution?"
> Reader, do you know, as I do, what terror those cold people can put into the ice of their questions? How much of the fall of the avalanche is in their anger? of the breaking up of the frozen sea in their displeasure? (XXXV).

Yet there is some kind of community between these two passages.

*Jane Eyre* is, it will be generally agreed, a novel about the emotional life: manners and morals, the characteristic concerns of the novel-form, are of interest to Charlotte Brontë only in so far as they shape the inner life of her heroine. Adopting T. S. Eliot's well-known term for the means by which emotions are expressed in art,[8] I want to suggest that Charlotte Brontë succeeds in uniting the diverse elements of her novel by employing a system of "objective correlatives" susceptible of equally diverse treatment, ranging from the prosaic and realistic to the poetic and symbolic. At the core of this system are the elements—earth, water, air, and fire; these, by a logical and linguistic association, are manifested in weather; this leads to images of nature as affected by weather, and the extensive use of the pathetic fallacy;[9] finally the system incorporates the sun and moon, which affect the weather, and, traditionally, human destiny.

[7] Walter Allen, *The English Novel* (Penguin edition, 1958), p. 190.

[8] "The only way of expressing emotion in the form of art is by finding an "objective correlative"; in other words, a set of objects, a situation, a chain of events which shall be the formula of that *particular* emotion; such that when the external facts, which must terminate in sensory experience, are given, the emotion is immediately evoked." "Hamlet," *Selected Essays* (3rd edition, 1951), p. 145.

[9] "All violent feelings . . . produce in us a falseness in our impressions of external things, which I would generally characterise as the 'pathetic fallacy.'" Ruskin, *Modern Painters*, IV, xii. Ruskin, though acknowledging the persistence of the pathetic fallacy, particularly in modern literature, and recognizing that as a literary device it must be judged by the use made of it in any particular case, regards it in general as a fault. I use the term, here and elsewhere, in a neutral, descriptive sense.

As E. M. W. Tillyard's summary shows,[10] the Elizabethans placed the four elements in a hierarchical order, beginning at the bottom with earth (cold and dry), followed by water (cold and moist), air (hot and moist), and finally fire (hot and dry), "the noblest element of all . . . which next below the sphere of the moon enclosed the globe of air that girded water and earth."[11] As Shakespeare's Cleopatra says:

> I am fire and air; my other elements
> I give to baser life.                                    (V, ii)

This scheme corresponds roughly with the way the elements are used in *Jane Eyre*. Earth (particularly as rock or stone) and water (particularly as ice, snow and rain) are associated with discomfort, unhappiness, alienation. Air has a punning association with the heroine. Fire is certainly the dominant element in the novel, and the one most commonly associated with happy or ecstatic states of being.

But Charlotte Brontë was not an Elizabethan; nor was she a highly self-conscious and deliberate symbolist novelist like Joyce or Conrad; and we should be mistaken in looking for a rigidly schematic system of elemental imagery and reference in *Jane Eyre*. She seeks in the natural world, not order, but a reflection of the turbulent, fluctuating inner life of her heroine. The elements have a constantly changing, and often ambivalent aspect in the novel, sustained by its basic rhythms, the alternation of night and day, storm and calm. To explore all the ramifications of this complex of elemental imagery and reference in detail would occupy too much space. I shall therefore focus attention on *fire*, which I take to have a central importance in *Jane Eyre*, and show how its meanings are developed out of the interplay of the whole complex.

Fire is a source of heat and light. It is, as the Prometheus myth tells us, necessary to civilized human life. It cheers us in the dark, when evil and unknown things threaten. It is, in the British climate, the focal point of social and domestic life—the most privileged members of the family have the seats nearest to the hearth. Fire is often applied metaphorically to the passions, particularly sexual passion. It burns and destroys as well as giving warmth and comfort. Religious, particularly Christian, concepts of spiritual purgation and eternal punishment are commonly described in terms of fire. All these denotations and connotations can be traced in *Jane Eyre*, which contains about eighty-five references to domestic fires (plus about a dozen separate references to "hearths"), about forty-three figurative allusions

---

[10] E. M. W. Tillyard, *The Elizabethan World Picture* (1943).
[11] Ibid., p. 57.

to fire, about ten literal references to fire as conflagration (in connection with Bertha's incendiarism), and four references to Hell-fire. I intend to show that hearth-fires are important points of reference in the depiction of Jane's struggle towards a life of decent animal comfort, human acceptance, and domestic happiness, while metaphors of fire express the exciting, invigorating, frightening inner life of passionate self-fulfilment, and at the same time the disaster and punishment that wait upon an excessive indulgence in passion.

I am not aware that the imagery of fire and associated elemental imagery has been remarked on by previous critics of *Jane Eyre,* but to point it out is to engage in a fairly familiar kind of criticism. Metaphorical language naturally alerts us to the possibility of larger thematic meanings. It is less usual, perhaps, to attribute a quasi-metaphorical significance to literal descriptions of literal objects, and it may be as well to anticipate some objections to such a procedure in respect of hearth-fires in *Jane Eyre.*

The large number of references to ordinary hearth-fires in the novel is indeed explicable on a very simple environmental level. Charlotte Brontë lived in a generally cold, bleak part of England, where the open hearth-fire was an essential creature comfort, shedding light as well as warmth into the dark rooms. Mrs. Gaskell's account of a visit to Charlotte Brontë at Haworth late in September includes the following appreciative note:

> Then we rested, and talked over the clear bright fire; it is a cold country, and the fires were a pretty warm dancing light all over the house.[12]

Coal was relatively cheap and, as Lowood remarks in *Wuthering Heights,* fires were kept going even in summer. "Both doors and lattices were open; and yet, as is usually the case in a coal district, a fine, red fire illuminated the chimney; the comfort which the eye derives from it renders the extra heat endurable." [13] References to hearth-fires in *Jane Eyre,* then, have an obvious function in contributing to that effect of concrete particularity which is a staple of the novel form. They follow naturally from Charlotte Brontë's undertaking to describe realistically a certain milieu.

However, . . . no item of concrete detail in a fiction can be totally arbitrary, totally neutral in effect; and I think there are clear indications in *Jane Eyre* that hearth-fires attract a very significant cluster of emotions and values. There is, for instance, a lavishness of epithet in descriptions of fires which seems in excess of the demands of func-

[12] Mrs. Gaskell, *Life of Charlotte Brontë* (Everyman edition, 1960), p. 384.
[13] Emily Brontë, *Wuthering Heights* (Penguin edition, 1946), Chapter XXXII.

tional realism. Fires in *Jane Eyre* are "good" (VIII), "cheerful" (ibid.), "brilliant" (ibid.), "excellent" (XI), "genial" (XII), "superb" (ibid.), "large" (XVII), "clear" (ibid.), "reviving (XVII), "glaring" (XXVIII), "generous" (XXIX). There is a vivid appreciation of the effect of fires on interiors, for example:

> The hall was not dark, nor yet was it lit, only by the high-hung bronze lamp: a warm glow suffused both it and the lower steps of the oak staircase. This ruddy shine issued from the great dining room, whose two-leaved door stood open, and showed a genial fire in the grate, glancing on marble hearth and brass fire-irons, and revealing purple draperies and polished furniture in the most pleasant radiance (XII).

(This, incidentally, is Jane's first intimation that the master of Thornfield has returned; the ritual of fire-making accompanies all significant domestic events of homecoming and reunion—cf. Jane's preparations for the return of the Rivers sisters to Moor house: " 'I shall go near to ruin you in coals and peat to keep up good fires in every room' " . . . "They were expected about dark, and ere dust, fires were lit up stairs and below" (XXXIV).

The prevalence of imagery of fire in *Jane Eyre* tends to give a special resonance to literal descriptions of fires. In this respect *Jane Eyre* differs from *Wuthering Heights,* which has proportionately at least as many literal references to fires, but only half-a-dozen figurative references.[14] What is particularly striking in *Jane Eyre* is that the meanings of both literal and figurative references to fire are defined by a context of opposite and conflicting elemental phenomena. As I show below, the passionate relationship existing between Jane and Rochester is characterized by imagery of fire, and disruption of this relationship—whether by the separation of the two lovers or by the rival relationship offered by St. John Rivers—is characterized by imagery of earth and water—stone, ice, rain, snow, etc. Literal references to domestic fires occur in the same kind of context. Let me give three examples.

We first meet Jane as a small child, excluded from the fireside circle of Mrs. Reed and her children, perched on the window seat, alternately looking out at "the drear November day. . . . Afar, it offered a pale blank of mist and cloud; near, a scene of wet lawn and storm-beat shrub, with ceaseless rain sweeping away wildly before a long and lamentable blast," and glancing at her book, Bewick's *History of British Birds,* with a particular attention to the descriptions of arctic

---

[14] This is not to imply that domestic fires in *Wuthering Heights* are unimportant: they have a significant function which overlaps at some points with their function in *Jane Eyre,* but they do not have such an important place in the thematic organization of the novel.

regions, " 'those forlorn regions of dreary space,—that reservoir of frost and snow, where firm fields of ice, the accumulation of centuries of winters, glazed in Alpine heights above heights, surround the pole, and concentre the multiplied rigours of extreme cold' " (I). When Jane is reunited with Rochester at the very end of the novel, it is on a similar day—"an evening marked by the characteristics of sad sky, cold gale, and continued small, penetrating rain" (XXXVII). She finds the blinded Rochester by "a neglected handful of fire" and her first practical gesture is to mend it:

> "Now, let me leave you an instant, to make a better fire, and have the hearth swept up. Can you tell when there is a good fire?"
> "Yes; with the right eye I see a glow—a ruddy haze" (XXXVII).

The latter remark is the first hint of Rochester's recovery of his sight. In the middle of the book there is a description of Mrs. Reed on her deathbed:

> . . . the patient lay still, and seemingly lethargic, her livid face sunk in the pillows: the fire was dying in the grate. I renewed the fuel, rearranged the bed-clothes, gazed awhile on her who could not now gaze on me, and then I moved away to the window.
> The rain beat strongly against the panes, the wind blew tempestuously. "One lies there," I thought, "who will soon be beyond the war of earthly elements" (XXI).

In these passages the domestic fire is plainly associated with human vitality, and cold and damp are identified with death. Yet the value of the fire is keenly appreciated *because* of the energy of the elements opposed to it, which have their own kind of splendour and fatal fascination. This last quality is particularly evident in the account of the book the young Jane is reading in the first chapter, of which I have only quoted a small part, and which is given a prominence that is accountable only in terms of thematic suggestion. The situation of the heroine looking through a window which is a fragile barrier between domestic warmth and the raging elements is a recurrent one in *Jane Eyre*,[15] and in a curious way she longs to be out amidst the war of earthly elements, to engage with the forces of death. It is indeed her destiny to do so.

The section of the novel that deals with Lowood school is generally recognized as a brilliant piece of writing, based, as we know, on pain-

---

[15] Kathleen Tillotson has remarked on the recurrence of the window motif in *Jane Eyre*, in *Novels of the Eighteen Forties* (Oxford paperback edn., 1961), p. 300. Dorothy Van Ghent has explored the significance of windows in *Wuthering Heights* in *The English Novel: Form and Function* (Harper Torchbooks, New York, 1961), pp. 161–63.

fully personal experience. It, too, fits into the pattern I have been describing.

We set out cold, we arrived at church colder: during the morning service we became almost paralysed . . . How we longed for the light and heat of a blazing fire when we got back! But, to the little ones at least, this was denied: each hearth in the schoolroom was immediately surrounded by a double row of great girls, and behind them the younger children crouched in groups, wrapping their starved arms in their pinafores (VII).

In this context a great deal is made of the fire in Miss Temple's room, when she invites Jane and Helen Burns there for tea:

. . . her apartment . . . contained a good fire, and looked cheerful (VIII).
How pretty, to my eyes, did the china and bright teapot look, placed on the little round table near the fire! (ibid.).
Tea over and tray removed, she again summoned us to the fire (ibid.).
The refreshing meal, the brilliant fire, the presence and kindness of her beloved instructress, or, perhaps, more than all these, something in her [Helen's] own unique mind, had roused her powers within her. They woke, they kindled: first, they glowed in the bright tint of her cheek, which till this hour I had never seen but pale and bloodless, then they shone in the liquid lustre of her eyes . . . (ibid.).

In this chapter the emphasis is not so much on the physical comfort of fire, as on what it symbolizes in the way of kindness, friendship, acceptance. It is interesting, too, to note how Helen's awakening spirit is conveyed through metaphors of fire (*kindled, glowed, shone*), which seem an extension of the visible effects of firelight. Jane's second and most serious conversation with Helen took place while the latter was reading a book "by the dim glare of the embers" of a fire (VI).

There are many other occasions in which important interviews, significant moments of communication, are lit by fires. Jane's first two interviews with Rochester—in the drawing room and dining room of Thornfield—are so characterized (XIII and XIV). In the second of these scenes Jane takes in the appearance of her master as it is illuminated by the firelight, and when Rochester wishes to examine *her*, he stands with his back to the fire, a position which, he says " 'favours observation.' " The idea of firelight being a truth-yielding light is more elaborately exploited in the scene where Rochester, disguised as a gypsy, makes a covert declaration of his love under the pretence of telling Jane her fortune:

An extinguished candle stood on the table; she was bending over the fire, and seemed reading in a little black book, by the light of the blaze. . . . I stood on the rug and warmed my hands, which were rather cold with sitting at a distance from the drawing-room fire (XIX).

(Jane's distance from the fire in the drawing-room is an index of her underprivileged social standing at this point in the action.)

I knelt within half a yard of her. She stirred the fire, so that a ripple of light broke from the disturbed coal: the glare, however, as she sat, only threw her face into deeper shadow: mine, it illumined (ibid.).
"Kneel again on the rug."
"Don't keep me long; the fire scorches me."
I knelt. She did not stoop towards me, but only gazed, leaning back in her chair. She began muttering,—
"The flame flickers in the eye; the eye shines like dew; it looks soft and full of feeling . . . (ibid.).

The rest of this passage has already been quoted [see above, p. 111]. Rochester's reading of Jane's physiognomy is a truthful one; but it is the glancing light of the fire, illuminating a strong, masculine hand and an unmistakable ring, that gives Rochester's own game away.

It is surely significant that the scene of Rochester's proposal, in which Jane is the victim of a deception more serious and more successful than the gypsy charade, is illuminated not by firelight but by moonlight—traditionally associated with deception, mystery, and evil:

"Will you be mine? Say yes, quickly."
"Mr. Rochester, let me look at your face: turn to the moonlight."
"Why?"
"Because I want to read your countenance; turn."
"There: you will find it scarcely more legible than a crumpled, scratched page. Read on: only make haste, for I suffer."
His face was very much agitated and very much flushed, and there were strong workings in the features, and strange gleams in the eyes (XXIII).

The only fire in this scene is portentous, avenging fire: the wind rises, the chestnut tree writhes and groans, and is struck by lightning. This scene is richly Romantic, and particularly reminiscent of *Christabel*.[16]

[16] "But what had befallen the night? The moon was not yet set, and we were all in shadow: I could scarcely see my master's face, near as I was. And what ailed the chestnut tree? it writhed and groaned; while wind roared in the laurel walk, and came sweeping over us (XXIII).
Compare Coleridge's use of interrogatives to create an atmosphere of mystery and the supernatural:

"Is the night chilly and dark?
The night is chilly, but not dark."

"The night is chill, the forest bare;
Is it the wind that moaneth bleak?"

"And what can ail the mastiff bitch?"

The action of the first part of *Christabel,* of course, takes place in moonlight.

The chestnut tree, favourite Romantic image of organic life, is split in two, signifying, as has been often noted, the later separation of Jane and Rochester. The two halves are, however, still connected at the roots.

> The cloven halves were not broken from each other, for the firm base and strong roots kept them unsundered below; though community of vitality was destroyed—the sap could flow no more: their great boughs on each side were dead, and next winter's tempests would be sure to fell one or both to earth: as yet, however, they might be said to form one tree—a ruin, but an entire ruin.
>
> "You did right to hold fast to each other," I said: as if the monster-splinters were living things, and could hear me. "I think, scathed as you look, and charred and scorched, there must be a little sense of life in you yet; rising out of that adhesion at the faithful, honest roots: you will never have green leaves more—never more see birds making nests and singing idylls in your boughs; the time of pleasure and love is over with you: but you are not desolate: each of you has a comrade to sympathise with him in his decay" (XXV).

This passage plainly prefigures the eventual reunion of hero and heroine, but is touched by melancholy, hinting that when that re-union takes place Rochester will have been "charred and scorched" by the fire of Thornfield, and that beforehand life will have been as cruel to the separated Jane and Rochester as the winter tempests will be to the riven tree. Jane utters this soliloquy in Rochester's absence immediately prior to the wedding, during which period she has seen Rochester's wife. Her emotional restlessness in Rochester's absence is expressed through her response to weather, and her solicitude for Rochester in reference to fires:

> Then I repaired to the library to ascertain whether the fire was lit; for, though summer, I knew on such a gloomy evening, Mr. Rochester would like to see a cheerful hearth when he came in: yes, the fire had been kindled some time, and burnt well (XXV).
>
> "Well, I cannot return to the house," I thought; "I cannot sit by the fireside, while he is abroad in inclement weather" (ibid.).

Rochester returns and:

> When we were again alone, I stirred the fire, and then took a low seat at my master's knee (ibid.).

She tells him how uneasy she has been the previous night, repeating and elaborating the pathetic fallacy as she leads up to the apparition of Bertha:

> But, sir, as it grew dark, the wind rose: it blew yesterday evening, not as it blows now—wild and high—but "with a sullen moaning sound"

far more eerie. I wished you were at home, I came into this room, and the sight of the empty chair and fireless hearth chilled me (ibid.).

The pathetic fallacy takes on an independent metaphorical existence in the superb passage describing Jane's emotions after the marriage service has been interrupted and prevented by the revelation that Rochester is already married. Significantly it begins by establishing a contrast between Jane "ardent" (or burning) and Jane "cold."

> Jane Eyre, who had been an ardent expectant woman—almost a bride —was a cold, solitary girl again: her life was pale, her prospects were desolate. A Christmas frost had come at midsummer; a white December storm had whirld over June: ice glazed the ripe apples, drifts crushed the blowing roses; on hay field and cornfield lay a frozen shroud: lanes which last night blushed full of flowers, today were pathless with un- trodden snow; and the woods, which twelve hours since waved leafy and fragrant as groves between the tropics, now spread waste, wild and white as pine forests in wintry Norway (XXVI).

Jane's physical reaction to the shock is of the same kind:

> At first I did not know to what room he had borne me; all was cloudy to my glazed sight: presently I felt the reviving warmth of a fire, for, summer as it was, I had become icy cold in my chamber (XXVII).

These last three quotations illustrate very clearly the remarkable flexibility of the language of *Jane Eyre*: restricted to a relatively nar- row range of "objective correlatives"—wind, rain, snow, ice, warmth, fire—it moves from the quasi-metaphorical to the fully metaphorical to the literal without any sense of strain. The central passage, by its astonishing audacity of conceit, its elegiac rhythms, its fluent but controlled syntax—in short, by its verbal intensity on every level— conveys the response of a keen sensibility to an extreme emotional crisis. But this essentially poetic flight grows naturally out of the literal staples of the novel. The description takes its place beside other, literal descriptions, scarcely less vivid, of the effect of weather upon landscape, so that we are not conscious of any abrupt shift from fact to fantasy: the interior landscape of Jane's emotions is no less real than the landscape she looked out on as a child in Mrs. Reed's house, or the arctic landscape she read about in Bewick's *History of British Birds*—which last is, indeed, specifically recalled by the reference to "wintry Norway." The reverse is also true: in the third, literal pas- sage, phrases that are potentially clichés are recharged with expres- sive force by echoing the daring tropes of the previous passage. *"Icy cold"* does not seem a mechanical hyperbole after so vivid a meta- phorical evocation of cold, and *"glazed* sight" puns delicately on the sense of *glazed* as "frozen," applied to the "ripe apples" just before.

Jane's sufferings in her voluntary exile are brought home to the reader through the same pattern of reference. While she wanders aimlessly through the countryside, penniless and homeless, she is at the mercy of the elements, content while the sun shines, but wretched when the weather is inclement. She is in a sense reliving her childhood experience of physical and emotional deprivation. Stumbling through the dark rain near Moor House, she reaches the nadir of her life, and is tempted to succumb to the forces of cold death which have always haunted her imagination:[17]

> And I sank down where I stood, and hid my face against the ground. I lay still for a while: the night-wind swept over the hill and over me, and died moaning in the distance, the rain fell fast, wetting me afresh to the skin. Could I but have stiffened to the still frost—the friendly numbness of death—it might have pelted on: I should not have felt it; but my yet living flesh shuddered at its chilling influence. I rose ere long (XXVIII).

She rises to follow a last hope, a glimmering light which she fears may be an *"ignis fatuus,"* which is in fact a lamp burning in the window of Moor House. Standing in the pelting rain, Jane peers into a room poignantly redolent of the good life of domestic peace and warmth that has so far eluded her. It is the "window-situation" in reverse:

> I could see clearly a room with a sanded floor, clean scoured; a dresser of walnut, with pewter plates ranged in rows, reflecting the redness and radiance of a glowing peat-fire. . . . A group of more interest appeared near the hearth, sitting still amidst the rosy peace and warmth suffusing it (ibid.).

Foreseeably, a good deal of attention is paid to fires in the succeeding description of how Jane is received into the house and restored to health.

The momentous interview in which St. John Rivers reveals to Jane the truth of her origins and fortune has the kind of setting that we have by now learned to expect on such occasions:

> I had closed my shutter, laid a mat to the door to prevent the snow from blowing in under it, trimmed my fire, and after sitting nearly an hour on the hearth listening to the muffled fury of the tempest, I lit a candle, took down Marmion . . . (XXXIII).

The entrance of St. John, covered with snow, into this firelit room,

---

[17] Cf. Jane's paintings, the first of which depicts a sinking wreck and a drowned corpse, and the third a deathly head superimposed on an arctic scene, with "the pinnacle of an iceberg piercing the polar winter sky" (XIII). These pictures derive some of their imagery from Bewick's *History of British Birds.*

establishes the basic incompatibility of their characters in a way more elaborately exploited on the metaphorical level, as I shall show later. But it is in place here to note one of Jane's attempts to formulate her antipathy to St. John:

> I saw he was of the material from which nature hews her heroes— Christian and pagan—her law-givers, her statesmen, her conquerors: a steadfast bulwark for great interests to rest upon; but, at the fireside, too often a cold, cumbrous column, gloomy and out of place (XXXIV).

It is Rochester alone who still suggests to Jane the possibility of combining the domestic warmth of Moor House, and the warmth of masculine love which it so signally lacks. At length she sets out for Thornfield, and finds it "a blackened ruin" (XXXVI), its evil spirits exorcised by fire. Jane tracks down its master, himself purged, exorcised (or in Chase's terms, symbolically castrated) by the fire and his own heroic response to it.[18] " 'I am no better than the old lightning-struck chestnut-tree in Thornfield orchard' " he says (XXXV). They are reunited, as we have seen, beside a dying fire, which Jane revives.

The above account by no means exhausts the wealth of literal references to fire in *Jane Eyre*, but it does, I hope, establish the importance of fire as the core of a cluster of emotions and values in the novel. I now turn to the figurative references to fire. Figuratively, fire is generally associated with the inner life of passion and sensibility, and this, though highly valued, is seen as morally ambivalent. Images of fire are almost entirely restricted to Jane and Rochester. They recognize the fire within each other—it is what gives meaning and value to their relationship; but they also recognize (Rochester only tardily) the perils of this fiery spirit and the necessity of controlling it.

This is well illustrated by the metaphors of fire used to express Jane's essentially rebellious temperament, which makes it difficult for her to control her anger in the face of injustice. I have previously quoted a reference to Jane's "volcanic vehemence" [see above, p. 111]. On her deathbed Mrs. Reed tells Jane:

> "You have a very bad disposition and one to this day I feel it impossible to understand: how for nine years you could be patient and quiescent under any treatment, and in the tenth break out all fire and violence, I can never comprehend" (XXI).

Rochester admires this fiery spirit in her—" 'I have seen what a fire-spirit you can be when you are indignant' " (XXIV)—and so do we; but we are also made to understand the cost of expending this spirit,

---

[18] I.e., Rochester's unsuccessful attempt to save Bertha's life, described in Chapter XXXVI.

the inevitable transitoriness of anger, and of the satisfaction afforded by venting it. After her first outburst at Gateshead the young Jane, locked up in the Red Room

> grew by degress cold as a stone, and then my courage sank. My habitual mood of humiliation, self-doubt, forlorn depression, fell damp on the embers of my decaying ire (II).

(Note how the elements of earth and water—"cold as a stone," "fell damp"—are opposed to fire here; "ire" is almost a pun.) And after her second act of rebellion the same idea is expressed in an even more striking fire image:

> A ridge of lighted heath, alive, glancing, devouring, would have been a meet emblem of my mind when I accused and menaced Mrs. Reed: the same ridge, black and blasted after the flames are dead, would have represented as meetly my subsequent condition, when half an hour's silence and reflection had shown me the madness of my conduct and the dreariness of my hated and hating position (IV).

To control the emotional fluctuations of childhood, from vivid anger to vacant depression and despair, is a necessary condition of Jane's progress to maturity. That she does mature in this way is suggested by her thoughts on her return to Gateshead just before Mrs. Reed's death:

> I still felt as a wanderer on the face of the earth; but I experienced a firmer trust in myself and my own powers, and less withering dread of oppression. The gaping wound of my wrongs, too, was now quite healed; and the flame of resentment extinguished (XXI).

Many other aspects of Jane's character, besides her quick temper, are expressed through images of fire. She feeds her vague, romantic longings on "a tale my imagination created, and narrated continuously; quickened with all of incident, life, fire, feeling, that I desired and had not in my actual existence" (XII). Rochester, as he himself hints to Jane in the gypsy scene, offers the possibility of releasing this fire from the subjective dream world: " 'You are cold, because you are alone: no contact strikes the fire from you that is in you' " (XIX). He is the man to recognize and appreciate this fire

> ". . . to the clear eye and the eloquent tongue, to the soul made of fire, and the character that bends but does not break . . . I am ever tender and true" (XXIV).

for he has it within himself:

> Strange energy was in his voice; strange fire in his looks (XV). . . .
> "I am insane—quite insane: with my veins running fire . . ." (XXVII).

It is volcanic fire, which surges up and erupts at moments of crisis: " 'To live, for me, Jane, is to stand on a crater crust which may crack and spue fire any day' " (XX). At Mason's interruption of the wedding, "his face flushed—olive cheek, and hueless forehead received a glow, as from spreading, ascending heart-fire" (XXVI); and when Jane declares her intention of leaving him, "Up the blood rushed to his face; forth flashed the fire from his eyes" (XXVII).

Jane uses a remarkable volcanic image to express her changing emotional response to Rochester from fear to desire, made all the keener at this point in the story by envy of Miss Ingram, whom she believes to be Rochester's intended:

> And as for the vague something—was it a sinister or a sorrowful, a designing or a desponding expression?—that opened upon a careful observer, now and then, in his eye, and closed again before one could fathom the strange depth partially disclosed; that something which used to make me fear and shrink, as if I had been wandering amongst volcanic-looking hills, and had suddenly felt the ground quiver, and seen it gape: that something, I, at intervals, beheld still; and with throbbing heart, but not with palsied nerves. Instead of wishing to shun, I longed only to dare—to divine it; and I thought Miss Ingram happy, because one day she might look into the abyss at her leisure, explore its secrets and analyze their nature (XVIII).

The volcanic image is extraordinarily effective in conveying the awe that colours Jane's relationship with Rochester even after fear has been overcome by love: the sense of the danger as well as the exhilaration of exploring hidden, perhaps forbidden, daemonic, subterranean depths of the life of passion. When she wrestles, physically and spiritually, with Rochester after the prevention of the marriage, the agony of the conflict is again presented through powerful fire-imagery:

> I was experiencing an ordeal: a hand of fiery iron grasped my vitals. Terrible moment: full of struggle, blackness, burning (XXVII).
> He seemed to devour me with his flaming glance; physically, I felt, at the moment, powerless as stubble exposed to the draught and glow of a furnace—mentally, I still possessed my soul, and with it the certainty of ultimate safety (ibid.).

This latter quotation carries Biblical echoes, particularly of Isaiah:

> Therefore as the fire devoureth the stubble, and the flame consumeth the chaff, so their root shall be as rottenness, and their blossom shall go up as dust (Isaiah 5:25).
> Behold, they shall be as stubble; the fire shall burn them; they shall not deliver themselves from the power of the flame; there shall not be a coal to warm at, nor fire to sit before it (47:14).

To quote these passages is to realize at once how much the whole

system of elemental and natural imagery we have been exploring in
*Jane Eyre* owes to the language of the Old Testament.[19] The second
passage quoted, from the triumphant prophecy of God's judgment on
Babylon and Chaldea, has a special interest in that it counterposes
two kinds of fire—the avenging, consuming kind, and the domestic,
comforting kind—in a manner strangely parallel to Charlotte Brontë's.
The differences are, however, obvious and important. In the novelist's
image of stubble, the heat emanates from a source of passionate love,
not of vengeance, and the possibility of being consumed by it is as
seductive as it is terrifying.

*Jane Eyre* is remarkable for the way it asserts a moral code as rig-
orous and demanding as anything in the Old Testament in a universe
that is not theocentric but centred on the individual consciousness.
Explicit references to the orthodox idea of Hell-fire are few in *Jane
Eyre*, and generally irreverent. Consider for example Mr. Brocklehurst's catechism of the young Jane:

> "Do you know where the wicked go after death?"
> "They go to Hell," was my ready and orthodox answer.
> "And what is hell? Can you tell me that?"
> "A pit full of fire."
> "And should you like to fall into that pit, and to be burning there
> for ever?"
> "No sir."
> "What must you do to avoid it?"
> I deliberated a moment; my answer, when it did come, was objection-
> able: "I must keep in good health, and not die" (IV).

Towards the end of the book Jane recognizes a similar attempt to
frighten her into obedience by St. John Rivers. (He is reading from
Revelations):

> ". . . the fearful, the unbelieving, etc., shall have their part in the lake
> which burneth with fire and brimstone, which is the second death."
> Henceforth, I knew what fate St. John feared for me (XXXV).

But if the fear of Hell is considered an unworthy motive for virtue
in *Jane Eyre*, the ethical system actually proposed is very far from
enlightened self-interest or humanist altruism. The sanctions of Old

[19] Cf. Jane's descripion of her desolation when her marriage to Rochester is prevented, "I seemed to have laid me down in the dried-up bed of a great river; I
heard a flood loosened in remote mountains, and felt the torrent come," an image
which is explicitly connected with a quotation from the Sixty-ninth Psalm, "The
waters came into my soul, I sank in deep mire: I felt no standing; I came into deep
waters; the floods overflowed me" (XXVI). Charlotte Brontë's punctuation, especially
her use of colons and semi-colons, rather than full-stops, between grammatically
independent clauses, also seem to be modelled on the Old Testament in the
Authorised Version.

Testament morality—punishment by fire and water, destitution, exile, solitariness—are still very much in evidence on both the literal and metaphorical levels, but the symbolic art of the novel presents them as extensions of the individual consciousness. The relationship of Jane and Rochester appears to us not as something which, according to its lawfulness or unlawfulness, will bring punishment or reward from an external source, but as something which contains within itself extreme possibilities of fulfilment and destruction. For this reason Rochester's conventionally Christian expression of penitence at the end of the novel (XXXVII) strikes a discordant note.

One of the most fascinating examples of Charlotte Brontë's literary manipulation of the elements as objective correlatives for the inner life is her treatment of Jane's relationship with St. John Rivers. When Jane first comes to know Rivers, he is struggling against a love, which he feels to be weak, for Rosamund Oliver; and, noticing his response to Rosamund's presence, Jane attributes to him, for the first and last time, the fire of human passion:

> I saw his solemn eye melt with sudden fire, and flicker with resistless emotion. Flushed and kindled thus, he looked nearly as beautiful for a man as she for a woman (XXXI).

Rivers suppresses this passion because of his call to the missionary life, which Jane compares to a different kind of fire:

> He seemed to say [to Rosamund] . . . "I love you, and I know you prefer me. . . . If I offered my heart, I believe you would accept it. But that heart is already laid on a sacred altar: the fire is arranged round it. It will soon be no more than a sacrifice consumed" (XXXII).

It is to this kind of consuming, sacrificial fire that Rivers later summons Jane herself, believing he recognizes in her "a soul that revelled in the flame and excitement of sacrifice" (XXXIV). The temptation to yield is great for Jane, for her capacity for self-sacrifice and renunciation has been proved by her separation from Rochester. But St. John insists that, for the sake of propriety, she must accompany him to the mission fields as his wife, and this Jane finds utterly unacceptable. She finds it unacceptable because she cannot conceive of a relationship between a man and a woman which is not one of passionate communion and domestic intimacy. These qualities she has experienced with Rochester, but she could never experience them with Rivers. For on the domestic level he is "at the fireside a cold, cumbrous column, gloomy and out of place" (XXXIV), while emotionally he is a man of stone and ice.[20]

[20] In Chapter IV Mr. Brocklehurst, standing on the hearthrug, impresses the young Jane as a "stony stranger" and a "black pillar."

This basic incompatibility of Jane and Rivers, the incompatibility of fire with water and earth, is intimated in the scene already alluded to where he visits her little cottage in a snow-storm, bringing her the news of her inheritance and family history:

> . . . it was St. John Rivers, who, lifting the latch, came in out of the frozen hurricane—the howling darkness—and stood before me; the cloak that covered his tall figure all white as a glacier. . . . I had never seen that handsome-featured face of his look more like chiselled marble than it did just now; as he put aside his snow-wet hair from his forehead and let the firelight shine free on his pale brow and cheek as pale . . . (XXXIII).

The fireside, as usual, proves a propitious place for confidences and revelations, but Jane has to insist before Rivers makes his hints explicit. In their banter there is a significant play on "fire" and "ice":

> "But I apprised you that I was a hard man," said he: "difficult to persuade."
> "And I am a hard woman,—impossible to be put off."
> "And then," he pursued, "I am cold: no fervour infects me."
> "Whereas I am hot, and fire dissolves ice" (XXXIII).

In subsequent stages of their relationship Jane persistently returns to imagery of water and earth in forms suggestive of hardness, coldness, destructiveness—ice, rock, stone, torrents, avalanches—to express her physical and emotional alienation from Rivers.[21] Some of the images are casual and conventional:

> This silence damped me (XXXIV).
> . . . his reserve was again frozen over, and my frankness was congealed beneath it (ibid.).
> I fell under a freezing spell (ibid.).
> There are no such things as marble kisses or ice kisses, or I should say, my ecclesiastical cousin's salute belonged to one of these classes . . . (ibid.).
> "He is good and great, but severe; and, for me, cold as an iceberg" (XXXV).

But these virtually dead metaphors are revived by, and themselves prepare for, more daring tropes drawn from the same sources:

> "And you will not marry me? You adhere to that resolution?" Reader, do you know, as I do, what terror those cold people can put into the ice of their questions? How much of the fall of the avalanche is in their anger? of the breaking up of the frozen sea in their displeasure? (XXXV).

---

[21] Rochester, anticipating Jane's reaction to the news that he is married, says: " 'you will say,—"That man had nearly made me his mistress: I must be ice and rock to him"; and ice and rock you will accordingly become' " (XXVII).

There may be some significance in Rivers's name,[22] for imagery of cold, rushing water is persistently applied to him.

". . . he asks me to be his wife, and has no more of a husband's heart for me than that frowning giant of a rock, down which the stream is foaming in yonder gorge" (XXXIV).

I was tempted to cease struggling with him—to rush down the torrent of his will into the gulf of his existence, and there lose my own (XXXV).

The latter image is particularly interesting when compared to the volcanic image applied by Jane to Rochester in Chapter XVIII [see above, p. 127]. In both cases a relationship with a man is seen as process of going down into something, being swallowed up and consumed by something. In Rochester's case the something is fire, in the case of Rivers, water. Imagery of fire keeps pace with the earth and water imagery applied to Rivers:

. . . his wife—at his side always and always restrained, and always checked—forced to keep the fire of my nature continually low, to compel it to burn inwardly and never utter a cry, though the imprisoned flame consumed vital after vital—*this* would be unendurable (XXXIV).

To me, he was in reality become no longer flesh, but marble; his eye was a cold, bright, blue gem; his tongue a speaking instrument—nothing more.

All this was slow torture to me—refined, lingering torture. It kept up a slow fire of indignation, and a trembling trouble of grief, which harassed and crushed me altogether. I felt how—if I were his wife— this good man, pure as the deep sunless source, could soon kill me: without drawing from my veins a single drop of blood, or receiving on his own crystal conscience the faintest stain of crime (XXXV).

It is not surprising that Charlotte Brontë has often been compared to the author of *Women in Love*.[23] Dare one suggest that she manages her transitions from the literal to the visionary rather more successfully than Lawrence?

One of the few attempts to account for the effects of Charlotte Brontë's prose fiction in terms of its iterative and controlling symbolism is Robert B. Heilman's article "Charlotte Brontë, Reason and the Moon" [24] which I must take note of here. Heilman begins by de-

---

[22] The name of Helen Burns, the most sympathetic representative of Christianity in the novel, is nicely ambivalent, evoking both water and fire. (I am indebted to Mrs. Elsie Duncan-Jones for this suggestion.)

[23] See Cecil, op. cit., p. 114, and Allen, op. cit., p. 189. One thinks particularly of the characterization of Gerald Crich in *Women in Love*. "St. Mawr" is notable for its insistent fire-imagery, used to convey the marvellous yet frightening power and energy of the horse.

[24] Robert B. Heilman, "Charlotte Brontë, Reason and the Moon," *Nineteenth Century Fiction*, XIV (1960), pp. 283–302.

fining the conflict in Charlotte Brontë's work "between reason–judgment–common sense and feeling–imagination–intuition." He identifies
these two polarities with terms used by Mr. Robert Graves in *The
White Goddess*: "solar reason" and "lunar superstition," and says
that "If the movement in Charlotte Brontë's novels—the growth of
her protagonists—is towards something that we can call "daylight,"
the field of significant action is often the dark . . . whether by plan
or through an unconscious or semiconscious sense of forces at work
in the world, Charlotte tends to make the "White Goddess" a presid-
ing deity, if not over the novels as a whole, at least over moments of
crisis." [25] He proceeds to note the numerous references to the moon
in Charlotte Brontë's novels, particularly in *Jane Eyre*:

> in *Jane Eyre* the moon is an aesthetic staple, at times a scenic element
> inherently charming to the writer, at times almost a character; at its
> most interesting it reveals an author groping for a cosmic symbolization
> of reality, or towards a reality beyond the confines of everyday reality,
> toward an interplay of private consciousness and mysterious forces at
> work in the universe.[26]

This comment supports my argument that the visionary grows very
naturally out of the literal in Jane Eyre because the objective correlatives for the heroine's emotional life are susceptible of very varied
treatment. Heilman seems to me, however, to overestimate and oversimplify the authority given to the White Goddess in the novel, because he does not consider the moon in the context of a larger system
of elemental imagery and reference. While it is true that the two
quasi-supernatural interventions which help Jane to resolve a conflict
between conscience and instinct—the apparition of her mother's spirit
and the telepathic call from Rochester—are attended by moonlight,
the moon is not always so propitious, as Heilman admits. The first
reference to the moon in the novel is a description of a picture in Bewick's *History of British Birds* which depicts a "cold and ghastly moon
glancing through bars of cloud at a wreck just sinking" (I). The moon
presages Bertha's attempt on Mason's life (XX); Jane has a prophetic
dream of Thornfield gutted and ruined, bathed in moonlight (XXV);
Rochester, describing the crisis of his wretched married life in the
West Indies says that, on the night he determined to take his own
life, " 'the moon was setting in the waves, broad and red, like a hot
cannon-ball—she threw her last bloody glance over a world quivering
with the ferment of tempest. I was physically influenced by the atmosphere and scene' " (XXVII). Rochester describes this scene while re-

[25] Ibid., pp. 288–89.
[26] Ibid., p. 292.

lating the story of his life to Jane after the interruption of the wedding service. They are sitting beside a fire; beside a fire Jane always learns the truth. I have already suggested the implications of moonlight in the scene of Rochester's proposal.

One of the most puzzling references to the moon in *Jane Eyre,* which Heilman does not comment on, becomes fully explicable only in terms of the larger elemental context. I refer to the superficially arch and facetious scene in which Rochester teases his ward, Adèle, when she is accompanying him and Jane on a shopping expedition (to buy a trousseau). Adèle, catching a hint of Rochester's that she is to be sent away to school, asks if she is to go *"sans* mademoiselle." Rochester then tells Adèle of his forthcoming marriage in the following manner:

> "Yes," he replied, "absolutely *sans* mademoiselle; for I am to take mademoiselle to the moon, and there I shall seek a cave in one of the white valleys among the volcano-tops, and mademoiselle shall live with me there, and only me."
> "She will have nothing to eat: you will starve her," observed Adèle.
> "I shall gather manna for her morning and night: the plains and hill-sides in the moon are bleached with manna, Adèle."
> "She will want to warm herself; what will she do for a fire?"
> "Fire rises out of the lunar mountains: when she is cold, I'll carry her up to a peak and lay her down on the edge of a crater."

Rochester spins out of this fable at some length, but the allegory is already plain: the flight to the moon is Rochester's proposal of marriage, and Adèle, by rejecting with "genuine French scepticism" Rochester's fantasy, indicates that his offer of marriage is empty and deceitful. There is no fire on the moon, and no food: i.e. Jane's need for domestic happiness cannot be satisfied by the false marriage, although her more romantic longings might be, by the "volcanic" fire of passion.

The moon, then, has a multiple and ambivalent function in *Jane Eyre.* As a prominent feature of the natural world its variable aspect is exploited *via* the pathetic fallacy to reflect inner states of being; while its ancient, mythical associations and its prominence in Romantic poetry of the supernatural make it an appropriate feature of those scenes in the novel when, for good or ill, nonrational forces command the situation.

As Heilman observes, "the movement of the novel . . . is towards something we can call 'daylight.'" The sequence of night and day, day bringing relief from the trials and terrors of the night, is one of the basic rhythms of the book. But imagery of and reference to the sun is not quantitatively or qualitatively very striking in *Jane Eyre.* Generally such imagery and references are associated with the same values

as are associated with domestic fires—peace, tenderness, acceptance—
but they scarcely call attention to themselves by any freshness or orig-
inality. "Even for me life had its gleams of sunshine," observes Jane,
recording an act of kindness by Bessie (IV). Rochester's smile is "the
real sunshine of feeling" (XXII), and Jane hopes that if he marries
Blanche Ingram he will keep herself and Adèle "under the shelter of
his protection, and not quite exiled from the sunshine of his presence"
(XXII). " 'What is the matter?' " asks Rochester when she is disappointed by his refusal to let Adèle accompany them on the shopping
expedition, " 'All the sunshine is gone' " (XXIV). Of her life as a
schoolmistress Jane observes, "To live amidst general regard, though
it be but regard of working-people, is like 'sitting in sunshine, calm
and sweet'; serene inward feelings bud and bloom under the ray"
(XXXII). There is just one point in the novel where the sun is presented as *anti*-pathetic to Jane, and I believe that this is no trivial
exception. I refer to the explicit assertion that the climate of India,
where Rivers wishes to take Jane as his wife and fellow-missionary,
will be death to her. When Rivers makes the proposal Jane reflects:
"I feel mine is not the existence to be long protracted under an Indian
sun" (XXXIV), and her cousin Diana confirms this intuition:

> "Madness . . . you would not live three months there, I am certain.
> . . . You are much too pretty, as well as too good, to be grilled alive in
> Calcutta" (XXXV).

Tropical and exotic places invariably have pejorative associations
in *Jane Eyre*. Rochester's disastrous first marriage takes place in the
West Indies, and his misery reaches its climax in a tropical storm. A
"sweet wind from Europe" urges him to seek a solution to his problem
there (XXVII). In the capitals of Europe he searches for his "ideal
woman" who had to be "the antipodes of the Creole," and finds her
at last when "on a frosty winter afternoon, I rode in sight of Thornfield Hall" (ibid.). When he is prevented from marrying Jane, he tries
to persuade her to run away with him—to southern Europe: " 'You
shall go to a place I have in the south of France: a white-walled villa
on the shores of the Mediterranean' " (XXVII). Jane refuses and, later
in the novel, when she is vindicating this decision to herself, makes an
explicit connection between climate and the loss or preservation of
moral integrity:

> Which is better?—To have surrendered to temptation; listened to
> passion; made no painful effort—no struggle;—but to have sunk down
> in the silken snare; fallen asleep on the flowers covering it; wakened in
> a southern clime, amongst the luxuries of a pleasure villa: to have been
> now living in France, Mr. Rochester's mistress. . . . Whether it is bet-

ter, I ask, to be a slave in a fool's paradise at Marseilles—fevered with delusive bliss one hour—suffocating with the bitterest tears of remorse and shame the next—or to be a village-schoolmistress, free and honest, in a breezy mountain nook in the healthy heart of England? (XXXI).

This aspect of *Jane Eyre* is connected with its author's efforts to free her literary imagination from her juvenile work, in which the exotic, tropical environment of Angria provided an appropriate setting for an excessive indulgence in the gestures of Romanticism. That Charlotte Brontë recognized the need to disengage herself from the seductive but debilitating myth of Angria has been persuasively argued by Professor Kathleen Tillotson[27] who quotes from a fragment of the Charlotte Brontë papers, speculatively dated 1839, which is very much to my purpose here:

> I have now written a great many books and for a long time I have dwelt upon the same characters and scenes and subjects. . . . My readers have been habituated to one set of features . . . but we must change, for the eye is tired of the picture so oft recurring and so long familiar.
>
> Yet do not urge me too fast, reader; it is not easy to dismiss from my imagination the images which have filled it so long; they were my friends and intimate acquaintances, and I could with little labour describe to you the faces, the voices, the actions, of those who peopled my thoughts by day, and not seldom stole strangely into my dreams by night. When I depart from these I feel almost as if I stood on the threshold of a home and were bidding farewell to its inmates. When I strive to conjure up new images I feel as if I had got into a distant country where every face was unknown and the character of all the population an enigma which it would take much study to comprehend and much talent to expound. Still, I long to quit for a while that burning clime where we have sojourned too long—its skies flame—the glow of sunset is always upon it—the mind would cease from excitement and turn now to a cooler region where the dawn breaks grey and sober, and the coming day for a time at least is subdued by clouds.[28]

This is Charlotte Brontë's "farewell to Angria." The "cooler region" is the physical and moral landscape of her mature work, preeminently *Jane Eyre*. Her imagination responded deeply to the fascination of climatic extremes—the polar cold as well as the tropical heats—but her heroine works out her destiny in a temperate—though not idyllic—zone. Extremes of heat and cold are death to Jane, we are made to feel, and paradoxically in her last great crisis, St. John Rivers threatens her with both: physical death by heat and emotional death by cold.

[27] Kathleen Tillotson, *Novels of the Eighteen Forties* (Oxford paperback edition, 1961), pp. 269ff.
[28] Quoted by Tillotson, op. cit., pp. 272–73.

In the war of earthly elements, in preserving a precarious equilibrium between opposing forces, Jane Eyre finds the meaning of life. Day is welcomed because it follows night, calm because it follows storm. Fire is a source of warmth and light, but it is most keenly enjoyed when snow and rain beat on the windows.

# Charlotte Brontë, the Imagination, and *Villette*

## by Andrew D. Hook

That her creative gift, her imagination, by turning her away from the external, social world of duty and moral responsibility, might finally destroy her, was a possibility that never ceased to haunt Charlotte Brontë. The significance of her exchange of letters with Robert Southey lies in this fear. As is well known, at the end of December, 1836, Charlotte, only seventeen years old, wrote to Southey apparently asking for advice on her prospects in a literary career, enclosing some poems as examples of her work. Charlotte's letter does not survive, but Southey's reply does. Courteous and conscientious as it is, it nonetheless contains a note of warning: "The day dreams in which you habitually indulge are likely to induce a distempered state of mind. . . ." And Southey goes on to set up an opposition between a woman's "proper duties" and the world of literature. Miss Brontë is not advised to give up the exercise of her creative gift, but her exercise must be a careful one: "I only exhort you so to think of it, and so to use it, as to render it conducive to your own permanent good." The letter seems unquestionably to suggest the characteristic self-doubt of the nineteenth-century artist: a distrust of the imagination itself expressed in a sense of the latent opposition between the imaginative world of dream on the one hand, and the world and responsibility on the other. In her reply Charlotte appears to accept Southey's implied rebuke. She insists mildly on the conscientiousness with which she has fulfilled the duties consequent upon her position in life, but seems to agree with her correspondent on "the folly of neglecting real duties for the sake of imaginative pleasures." (Notice that the pleasures are "imaginative" rather than "imaginary.") In conclusion she trusts that she "shall never more feel ambitious to see [her] name in print." Even more interesting, perhaps, is Southey's second letter to Charlotte. On March 22, 1837, Southey wrote to express his pleasure at Charlotte's

"Charlotte Brontë, the Imagination, and *Villette*," by Andrew D. Hook. This essay is printed here for the first time.

137

reply to his initial letter, and took the opportunity to reiterate his point about the need for self-discipline and the avoidance of too much (imaginative) excitement. "It is," he wrote, "by God's mercy, in our power to attain a degree of self-government, which is essential to our own happiness, and contributes greatly to that of those around us. Take care of over-excitement, and endeavour to keep a quiet mind . . . , your moral and spiritual improvement will then keep pace with the culture of your intellectual powers." Here again there is surely a strong suggestion that Southey suspects that Charlotte's poems had expressed a state of "over-excitment" incompatible with "a quiet mind," and one which in his view involved an abandonment of that self-discipline essential to "moral and spiritual improvement." Charlotte had been warned again of the dangers inherent in the world of the creative imagination.[1]

But Charlotte Brontë was already committed to that world, dangerous or not. Since 1829 at least Charlotte had been engaged in spinning that "web of childhood" which Fannie Ratchford has done most, among modern scholars, to unravel. Even Mrs. Gaskell, however, the first biographer, testifies to the existence of "an immense amount of manuscript, in an inconceivably small space—tales, dramas, poems, romances written principally by Charlotte. . . ." [2] The vast quantity of this early material, describe it as "juvenilia" or not, and the incredible care and precision of its production, suggest both the abundant creativity of Charlotte's imaginative life and the kind of tenacity with which it was pursued. Even more relevant is the nature of the world that Charlotte created in the childhood legends of Angria. Here again Mrs. Gaskell tells us enough for obvious conclusions to be drawn, even if modern scholars had not made many of the originals available to us. The precocious world of Charlotte's childhood creation emerges as a world of high romance, exciting adventure, and violent passion, sometimes written in a manner that Mrs. Gaskell clearly found disturbing. On the character of Charlotte's "purely imaginative writing at this period," she comments, "while her description of any real occurrence is, as we have seen, homely, graphic, and forcible, when she gives way to her powers of creation her fancy and her language alike run riot, sometimes to the very borders of apparent delirium." [3] Like Southey, Mrs. Gaskell speaks here in the characteristic accent of her time: the worlds of reality and the imagination are in opposition; the creative power is something to which the artist "gives way"; and undisciplined, it carries him towards the condition of "delirium."

---

[1] For the full text of the letters quoted see Clement Shorter, *The Brontës' Life and Letters* (London, 1908) I:126–31.

[2] E. C. Gaskell, *The Life of Charlotte Brontë* (London: John Murray, 1924), p. 82.

[3] Gaskell, *The Life of Charlotte Brontë*, p. 89.

The existence of the great body of Angria material compels us to conclude that the tendency towards "day dreams" which Southey thought he recognized in Charlotte's poems—and which he felt it his duty to warn her away from—had been given uninhibited and continued expression in her writing up to this time. For many years of her childhood and adolescence Charlotte had been indulging, expanding, and elaborating an imaginative world of an intensely romantic kind; a world, too, which was a secret or buried one in terms of her actual existence in Haworth. But the episode of the Southey letters makes it clear, I believe, that as she approached maturity, Charlotte was coming increasingly to reflect that her creative life was endangering her commitment to values more mundane, but moral and responsible.

How then are we to understand Charlotte's decision to become a novelist? For Fannie Ratchford the answer is a simple one. She agrees that from the period of her return to Miss Wooler's school at Roe Head as a teacher (1835), when she was nineteen, Charlotte experienced a continuing inner struggle between the dictates of conscience and the appeal of the imaginative world of Angria. But, she argues, in the end Angria won and Charlotte continued to write. Unquestionably the passages Miss Ratchford quotes from Charlotte's Roe Head journal are moving and powerful in their expression of Charlotte's longing and regret for her private world of the imagination:

> Friday August 11th—All this day I have been in a dream, half-miserable, half-ecstatic,—miserable because I could not follow it out uninterruptedly, ecstatic because it showed almost in the vivid light of reality the ongoings of the infernal world.

Or again:

> And now once more on a dull Saturday afternoon I sit down to try to summon around me the dim shadows, not of coming events, but of incidents long departed, of feelings, of pleasures, whose exquisite relish I sometimes fear it will never be my lot again to taste. How few would believe that from sources purely imaginary such happiness could be derived! Pen cannot portray the deep interest of the scenes, of the continued train of events, I have witnessed in that little room with the low narrow bed and bare whitewashed walls twenty miles away. What a treasure is thought! What a privilege is reverie! I am thankful I have the power of solacing myself with the dream of creations whose reality I shall never behold. May I never lose that power, may I never feel it grow weaker. . . .[4]

Certainly such a passage as this offers an unequivocal endorsement of

[4] See F. E. Ratchford, *The Brontës' Web of Childhood* (New York; Columbia University Press, 1941), pp. 109, 107.

the gift of imagination. Yet to suggest that Charlotte simply carries
over that gift into the creation of her novels is to oversimplify her
position. The authenticity of feeling in the passage is beyond question.
But set it beside the following passage from *Shirley* (1849) and a
greater complexity, not to say bitterness, of tone is perfectly evident:

> . . . who cares for imagination? Who does not think it a rather dan-
> gerous, senseless attribute—akin to weakness—perhaps partaking of
> frenzy—a disease rather than a gift of the mind?
>     Probably all think it so, but those who possess—or fancy they possess
> —it. To hear them speak, you would believe that their hearts would
> be cold if that elixir did not flow about them; that their eyes would be
> dim if that flame did not refine their vision; that they would be lonely
> if this strange companion abandoned them. You would suppose that
> it imparted some glad hope to spring, some fine charm to summer, some
> tranquil joy to autumn, some consolation to winter, which you do not
> feel. An illusion of course; but the fanatics cling to their dream, and
> would not give it for gold.[5]

There is a clear shift of feeling here. The endorsement of imagination's power is still present, but now it is indirect, expressed defensively,
and so shielded from hostile criticism. The brave confidence of the
passage from the 1835 journal has disappeared. However important
the long apprenticeship of Angria may have been for Charlotte Brontë
the novelist; however far the novels may draw on Angrian material
and characters—and the debt is clearly a very large one—the novels
are nonetheless not of the same order as the Angrian stories. There
is a change between the two kinds of creative writing and the nature
of that change has to be recognized. In it lies the key to Charlotte's
decision to write for the public world.

Almost three years after the exchange of letters with Southey
Charlotte brought herself to bid farewell to the world of Angria. The
terms in which the conclusion of that farewell is expressed are of the
greatest interest:

> I long to quit for a while that burning clime where we have sojourned
> too long—its skies aflame—the glow of sunset is always upon it—the
> mind would cease from excitement and turn now to a cooler region
> where the dawn breaks grey and sober, and the coming day for a time at
> least is subdued by clouds.[6]

It is clear that Charlotte is not about to abandon writing completely;
it is a particular kind of writing that is being given up, the kind
devoted to the celebration of a world of romantic excitement and brilliant color. From the world suggested by "burning clime," "skies

---

[5] Charlotte Brontë, *Shirley*, The Shakespeare Head Brontë (Oxford, 1931), I:49.
[6] Ratchford, *The Brontës' Web of Childhood*, p. 149.

aflame," and "excitement," she is to turn to "a cooler region," "grey and sober." Charlotte is taking leave of uninhibited high romance. In so doing she is discovering a way of continuing to write. Daydream is to be rejected; the world of reality will take its place. The "demystification" of the self has begun; and one of its consequences will be a growing ambivalence of attitude towards the visionary world of the romantic imagination.

The farewell to Angria in her diary looks ahead of course to her declaration of intent in the preface to *The Professor,* the first of her novels to be written though the last to be published. In that preface she insists that the novel does not represent a first attempt at writing, "as the pen which wrote it had been previously worn a good deal in a practice of some years." Through this earlier work, she explains, she had got over "any such taste as I might once have had for ornamented and redundant composition" and had come to prefer "what was plain and homely." At the same time she had adopted "a set of principles on the subject of incident, etc."—which emerges as a commitment to a strict realism. Her hero, "as Adam's son" should "share Adam's doom, and drain throughout life a mixed and moderate cup of enjoyment." Ironically she had discovered that publishers did not share her preference for realism: "Men in business are usually thought to prefer the real; on trial the idea will be often found fallacious: a passionate preference for the wild, wonderful, and thrilling—the strange, startling, and harrowing—agitates divers souls that show a calm and sober surface." Given the qualities of the kind of writing that Charlotte has persuaded herself to abandon, the irony here is deep indeed.

In fact, the realism that Charlotte struggled to achieve in *The Professor* is oddly flawed in quality. The story of the Crimsworth brothers, and the enmity between them, is taken up only to be rather arbitrarily set aside in favour of the story of William Crimsworth in Brussels and his love affair with Frances Henri. No doubt there is much truth in the view that these two elements in the story reflect a hardly successful yoking together of material from the imaginary world of Angria and Charlotte Brontë's actual experiences at the Pensionnat Héger. Again, the dividing of Charlotte's own experience between Crimsworth and Frances has the effect of undermining the reality of both. Frances in particular is too ideal a figure quite to match the assertions of the novel's preface. But perhaps the fundamental weakness of the book is simply that Charlotte's self-disciplining control over her imagination is all too successful. The calm and sober surface of reality is too inadequately ruffled.

It is difficult not to feel that the release of Charlotte's powers that is apparent in *Jane Eyre* has much to do with the publishers' negative response to the grey and sober quality of *The Professor*. Not of course that *Jane Eyre* is simply to be seen as rejecting the kind of realism that the preface to *The Professor* lays claim to. Charlotte will never return to the untrammelled freedom of the world of Angria. There is much in *Jane Eyre* that is Gothic, romantic, extravagant; much that is dreamlike and visionary. But there is an equally strong awareness of the "plain and homely," of the realities of pain and suffering in the most ordinary contexts of life. *Jane Eyre*, however, marks a major advance on *The Professor* in that Charlotte Brontë now sees that the answer to the problem created by her sense of the latent opposition between the imagination and the social and moral duties of ordinary existence, the problem that had obsessed her since at least the period of the exchange of letters with Southey, lies not in choosing between them—not even if the choice is disguised simply as one between different literary modes—but in working the problem itself into the texture of her writing. Rather than try to solve her problems, Charlotte now chooses to articulate them. In that articulation lies the true realism of her art.

The pivotal conflict in *Jane Eyre* is never clearly defined as that between the appeal of imagination and the world of moral choices and decisions. Rather, more conventionally, it is portrayed as a clash between Reason and Passion. Passion comes to include all the possibilities of excitement, change, experience, even love, which the romantic imagination so intensely celebrates. As the conflict develops within Jane herself it is often given a strictly moral, or even religious, significance. It is as though, in allowing the world of imaginative indulgence and hope its human vitality and warmth, Charlotte felt compelled to circumscribe the debate within the categories of orthodox morality. So successful is she that on occasion the true meaning of the novel is in danger of being obscured or betrayed. In the matter of the key issue of Rochester's previous marriage, for example, we may choose to see Jane's dilemma as no more than that of the conventional Victorian heroine choosing between passionate but illicit love on the one hand, and duty and moral integrity on the other. While it is true that the text sometimes invites us to see the matter in this light, it is nonetheless not the true light. The real danger that threatens Jane is not that of becoming a fallen woman, but of allowing herself to be swept out of the world of moral responsibilities altogether into that other seductive world of high passion and romance that Charlotte herself had for so long imaginatively indulged.

The other major weakness that *Jane Eyre*, fine as it is, reveals, is that sections of its external action remain too much part of the world of high romance with which Jane herself is internally in conflict. Jane's marriage with Rochester at the end is no doubt intended to be

unromantic. But romantic nonetheless is what it is. Again, the final
episodes of the novel avoid rather than confront the issues that have
been centrally raised. Maimed and blinded, Rochester is no longer
any kind of threat to Jane. The demands of duty and the instincts
of feeling and love now fortuitously coincide.

## II

*Villette* is Charlotte Brontë's last and most searching exploration
and analysis of the basic conflict that had troubled her so long. Only
now the implications and consequences of that conflict are seen as ex-
tending into further areas of human experience. The world of romantic
daydream, of visionary delight and hope, is as appealingly portrayed
as ever, but the rocks on which that world is wrecked are presented less
in terms of moral and religious negatives and more in terms of the
nature of reality itself. Such an extension of meaning is characteristic
of the book. In one sense, however, *Villette* represents a narrowing
of focus compared with *Jane Eyre*. Whereas in *Jane Eyre* the world
of romantic excitement is given partial externalization in character
and event, in *Villette* its existence is almost wholly internalized within
the mind of the novel's protagonist, Lucy Snowe. Such a development
is perhaps the only one through which the world of romance can be
properly assimilated into a novel committed to an essential realism.

With its action so largely internalized, *Villette* is above all a psychological novel: its drama is the drama of a consciousness. Whose
consciousness is indicated by the novel's narrative method? That it is
told in the first person by Lucy Snowe is a clear suggestion of its
subject; a failure to recognize this is the source of most of the common
objections to the book. If Lucy Snowe is to be seen for much of the
story as no more than a rather colorless onlooker who serves as narrator, then it is true that large sections of the novel are scarcely
relevant; and it is equally true that about half way through interest is
switched from one set of characters to a new set. But Charlotte Brontë
makes Lucy Snowe narrator precisely to draw attention formally and
dramatically to her centrality. This is true no matter what personal
qualities, dull or interesting, prim or passionate, her telling of the
story reveals. Character and event are important in *Villette* only in
relation to Lucy Snowe's response, as first-person narrator, to them.
Just as much as in a novel by James it is the story of the story that
really matters. It is through the central recording consciousness of
Lucy that the coherence of *Villette* is achieved.

If character and event in *Villette* are subordinate to the consciousness that renders these, then the nature of that consciousness comes

very much into question. We have Charlotte Brontë's own word for it
that Lucy's name is of symbolic value. The comment is a familiar one.
"A cold name she must have . . . for she has about her an external
coldness." [7] Notice that the coldness is carefully defined as "external"
only. Of course some characters in the novel never see beyond externals.
Dr. John, for example, never learns to see Lucy as anything other
than quiet, retiring, self-effacing; for him she is "quiet Lucy Snowe,"
his "inoffensive shadow"; she suffers from "overgravity in tastes and
manner—want of colour in character and costume." [8] M. de Bassohm-
pierre, Lucy feels, sees her as "the essence of the sedate and discreet,"
"the pink and pattern of governess-correctness" (II:64). For Ginevra
Fanshawe she is unfeeling throughout. Of course the impression suggested by these descriptions is one which Lucy in a sense consciously
creates; her colorless exterior is a symbol of an internal stance that
she struggles to maintain. She describes herself as "tame and still by
habit" (I:42). When the Bretton household is disturbed by Polly's
grief at the departure of her father, "I, Lucy Snowe, was calm" (I:22).
In fact Lucy seems to be fully conscious of the implications of her
name. After a night of turmoil, occasioned by her recognition that
Mme. Beck is suspicious of her relationship with Dr. John, she reports
that "next day I was again Lucy Snowe" (I:148).

But that Lucy should be so disturbed as a result of her awareness of
Mme. Beck's suspicions points to the side of her nature that is opposed
to the colorless calm of her exterior. Lucy's inner life is as active,
variable, passionate and feeling as her external is passive. The "repose
of her nature," disturbed by Mme. Beck, if it exists at all, is the consequence of strict inner discipline. It is a condition that has to be
struggled towards, and once attained is irresolutely defended. That she
does feel, and sometimes with passionate intensity, Lucy occasionally
admits: "I had feelings: passive as I lived, little as I spoke, cold as I
looked, when I thought of past days I *could* feel . . ." (I:134). This
acknowledgement by Lucy of her capacity to feel comes quite soon
after her arrival at the Pensionnat of Mme. Beck and clearly hints at
a discontent with the superficial calm of her existence there. The re-
appearance of Dr. John has no doubt contributed to her disturbed
state. That she is disturbed is made very clear:

> At that time, I well remember whatever could excite—certain accidents of
> the weather, for instance, were almost dreaded by me, because they woke
> the being I was always lulling, and stirred up a craving cry I could not
> satisfy (I:134).

[7] Shorter, *The Brontës, Life and Letters*, II:286.
[8] Charlotte Brontë, *Villette*, The Shakespeare Head Brontë (Oxford, 1931), II:84,
105. All subsequent page references are to this edition.

The ensuing thunderstorm lifts Lucy to a pitch of intense emotional excitement. For a moment the wildness of the storm releases all her pent-up desires to escape from the nugatory present. But the romantic intensity of this is quickly "knocked on the head" in the following paragraph, and a kind of calm restored. The price of that calm is suggested by the Jael and Sisera reference which Charlotte Brontë uses to define it. "Unlike Sisera," the feelings in question "did not die: they were but transiently stunned, and at intervals would turn on the nail with a rebellious wrench; then did the temples bleed, and the brain thrill to its core" (I:135). The almost masochistic physical immediacy of this is disturbing. But it leaves no room for doubting the vivid, emotional, passionate quality of Lucy Snowe's inner nature.

The division within Lucy Snowe suggested by her external coldness and her inner anguish implies two quite different stances towards life. What these are an examination of the opening episodes of *Villette* will help to clarify. The story opens in a house in Bretton's "calm old streets" (I:139). The house is an asylum of peace and tranquillity. "The large peaceful rooms, the well-arranged furniture, the clear wide windows, the balcony outside, looking down on a fine antique street, where Sundays and holidays seemed always to abide—so quiet was its atmosphere, so clean its pavement—these things pleased me well" (I:1). Despite its lack of incident, Lucy Snowe is very much at home in this world: "The charm of variety there was not, nor the excitement of incident; but I liked peace so well, and sought stimulus so little, that when the latter came I almost felt it a disturbance, and wished rather it had still held aloof" (I:2). The Brettons, in whose house Lucy is living, match the equitableness of their environment. Graham Bretton's inheritance from his mother includes "her spirits of that tone and equality which are better than a fortune to the possessor" (I:2). Such spirits are the guarantee of a life of comparative peace, even if they deprive their possessor of both the heights and depths of feeling. Into this Sunday world of the Brettons, all calm and peace and quiet, comes the fantastic, elfin figure of Polly. In strong contrast to the Brettons, Polly is quintessentially feeling and imagination. Her devotion to her father in the first place, and subsequently to Graham Bretton, is powerful and tenacious. But the very strength and intensity of her feelings make her exquisitely vulnerable. So much so that Lucy Snowe fears for her amid "the shocks and repulses, the humiliations and desolations" which she believes to be part of the "battle with this life" (I:38). Polly then is a small example for Lucy, a sketch of the dangers which are bound up with the life of feeling.

Lucy's own stay in the calm world of Bretton proves to be only temporary. (Soon even the Brettons are to learn that such tranquillity and ease are short-lived.) After leaving Bretton Lucy passes over the

next eight years of her life, though indicating that they were years in
which there was no return to the safe harbour of a Bretton. "I will
permit the reader," she says, "to picture me . . . as a bark slumbering
through halcyon weather, in a harbour still as glass—the steersman
stretched on the little deck, his face up to heaven, his eyes closed:
buried, if you will, in a long prayer" (I:39). Notice that the romantic
dream the reader is allowed is imaged very much as Bretton had been;
the suggestion is of a calm, still, comfortably uneventful existence,
perhaps even once again of a perennial Sunday. The "real" sea on
which Lucy sails in these years is, on the contrary, tempest-tossed.

The action of these opening chapters of the book, like so much of
the action that is to come, is a kind of extended metaphor. Through
it Charlotte Brontë establishes the two main poles of the novel's
movement. At once on the external level of Lucy's life, and, more
important, on the internal level of her mind and consciousness, the
major rhythm of *Villette* is that between calm and excitement, between quiet passivity and action, between engagement with life, despite
all its shocks and desolations, and retreat from life. The text of the
novel often offers and contrasts categories of experience of a more
definite and more limited kind: Reason and Feeling preeminently,
Reason and Imagination, Necessity and Hope, but all of these are
subsumed within the larger rhythms I have described. As is the case in
*Jane Eyre,* Charlotte's interpretive glosses often seem narrower than
the experience of the novel warrants.

On the level of external action *Villette's* major movements involve
Lucy's search for some haven of calm where she will be sheltered from
the suffering produced by the storms of experience. Driven by un-
explained necessities, she comes to London on her way to the continent.
At first she is fearful and confused. But the old inn in which she stays
provides her with temporary security sufficient to give her a momentary
sense of the pleasures of involvement in the busy life of the city
streets. After the stresses and strains of the channel crossing, and the
difficulties with which she has to contend on arrival, the Pensionnat
of Mme. Beck again appears as a kind of retreat, a place of safety and
security. (Later we are frequently reminded of the way in which
the school is insulated from the busy life of the great city around it:
"Quite near were wide streets brightly lit, teeming at this moment
with life . . ." (I:133). Finally, the security of the Pensionnat will
become that of a prison.) After Lucy's mental and physical breakdown, the house of the Bretton family into which she wakes is another temporary asylum where peace is briefly rediscovered. And finally
there is the house provided by M. Paul, overlooking the Eden-like
garden, where Lucy's school is to be set up, and where for one day

M. Paul and she are together. Each of these resting places is achieved after a period of intense inner strain and torment.

This large rhythm, however, of periods of difficulty and danger followed by intervals of comparative calm and tranquillity, is only a mirror of the novel's more essential internal movement, similarly a question of rising and falling rhythms of inner passivity and acceptance on the one hand, emotional excitement and turmoil on the other. Even when Lucy's external life is at its most uneventful, her inner life is never entirely quiescent. In her early days at the Pensionnat her impulse towards a quiet obscurity is for the moment satisfied, but even then she talks of her "two lives—the life of thought, and that of reality," and opposes "the strange necromantic joys of fancy" to "daily bread, hourly work, and a roof of shelter" (I:92–93). The possibility of conflict between Lucy's two lives, with their hint of the old opposition between Angria and the more immediate calls of duty, is clear enough. Such a conflict does of course occur and reoccur, though a clash between "thought" and "reality" is only one of several possible definitions of the conflict's nature and source. Rarely indeed does Lucy's internal life attain to the calm tranquillity she encourages herself to seek.

After the introductory account of the Bretton world, *Villette* pauses again before undertaking its central narrative of Lucy's experience. The Miss Marchmont episode both reinforces the implications of the initial Bretton experience, and suggests a stance to be adopted in light of these. Polly, a mere child, suffers because of the intensity of her feelings. Miss Marchmont's experience of the life of passionate feeling and hope is more mature, but the outcome is the same: suffering. For Lucy there is again the note of warning. But Miss Marchmont offers Lucy a further lesson: the lesson of suffering accepted and endured. As Jane Eyre believes she should emulate Helen Burns, so Lucy Snowe tries always to learn Miss Marchmont's lesson. Miss Marchmont's is the stance towards experience that Lucy admires and which she sometimes believes herself to have achieved.

In both these opening episodes, then, Lucy finds a temporary retreat, a shelter from the challenges and risks of life, where she can indulge the "cold" side of her nature, the impulse to remain only the uninvolved observer of life. Both episodes contain suggestions about the nature of the world outside and the dangers that follow from engagement with it. The larger rhythm of the novel involves movements from and towards the calm tranquillity of the Bretton world and the passive stoicism of Miss Marchmont. What the reader recognises, as Lucy does not, is that in the first episode calmness, peace and tranquillity are polarized against sensibility, feeling, and imagination;

and that stoical endurance in the second is sustained only by the memory of a happiness achieved, however fleetingly. The cost of that calm tranquillity which Lucy seeks is apparently the complete rejection of the feelings and imagination which are part of her being; hence the inner anguish that belies the external coldness of her nature.

In the opening episodes of *Villette* Lucy Snowe's role is only that of observer. What she observes hints at the nature of the conflict she is soon to experience in her own person. But to understand that conflict more fully it is necessary to move on to her personal experience which is the novel's primary subject. The major rhythm I have identified develops through Lucy's relationships first with Dr. John, then with M. Paul. In other words it is the passion of love which challenges most seriously the calm repose of Lucy's nature. Harriet Martineau objected to what she felt to be *Villette's* preoccupation with the force of love in women's lives. But in the novel love is important, not as it were for its romantic self, but because it is the sharpest focus of feeling, excitement, and imagination. Such a definition gives love its significance, suggests its danger, and explains why it is inevitably Charlotte Brontë's prime subject.

Feeling, excitement, and imagination are all resisted by Lucy Snowe because, perhaps from her early experiences at Bretton and with Miss Marchmont, she believes she knows their dangers. Jane Eyre, we recall, struggled to check and subdue her feelings, usually in accordance with some moral or religious ideal. Lucy may not listen to the voices of feeling and hope, not so much because to do so is morally wrong, but because she believes that such voices direct her towards a painfully unrealizable world. With their promise of a life of excitement and fulfilment they are supremely appealing, but what they effect is only renewed awareness of a world permanently beyond reach: beyond reach, that is, of all except the favored few, such as Paulina, for whom life really is a romance. To combat these voices, Lucy calls on the power of reason. Reason tells her to abjure the world of the passional imagination; only thus may ultimate despair be avoided. Better surely to be a mere onlooker on life, colorless and obscure perhaps, but nonetheless preserving a calm, tranquil repose otherwise unattainable.

But Lucy's inner nature rebels against the conclusions of reason. And that rebellion is supported by Charlotte Brontë. In the first place, both Lucy and the reader are offered an example of the consequences for a human being of the denial of feeling. In the portrait of Madame Beck the dehumanizing effect of such a denial is clearly revealed. Lucy admires Madame Beck for her efficiency and her professional competence, but in the end she sees that Madame Beck is heartless. Her physiognomy is a reliable indicator of her personal qualities:

. . . her forehead was high but narrow; it expressed capacity and some benevolence, but no expanse; nor did her peaceful but watchful eye ever know the fire which is kindled in the heart or the softness which flows thence (I:86).

Madame Beck's benevolence is of a purely rational kind. She is entirely devoid of feelings of sympathy: ". . . to attempt to touch her heart was the surest way to rouse her antipathy, and to make of her a secret foe. It proved to her that she had no heart to be touched . . ." (I:89). Madame Beck's behavior in the rest of the novel will amount to no more than an active confirmation of the characteristics ascribed to her here.[9] Again, it is in the area of feeling that the inadequacy of Dr. John too is finally recognized. The cool equanimity that he normally possesses, the Bretton calm that he embodies, exists at the expense of at least the deepest experiences of human feeling. Recognizing this frees Lucy from his spell. On the occasion of their watching the performance of the actress Vashti Lucy comes to full understanding of the basic contrast between Dr. John and herself. Vashti's acting disturbs the deep foundations of Lucy's nature. Dr. John remains unmoved:

> Her agony did not pain him, her wild moan—worse than a shriek—
> did not much move him; her fury revolted him somewhat, but not to the
> point of horror. Cool young Briton! The pale cliffs of his own England
> do not look down on the tides of the channel more calmly than he watched
> the Pythian inspiration of that night (II:10).

There is much that is right about Dr. John's infatuation with the empty-headed, unfeeling Ginevra Fanshawe.

In their coolness towards the world of feeling, Madame Beck and Dr. John are merely expressing what is fundamental to their natures. Lucy Snowe's nature is alien to theirs; hence the disastrous consequences of her attempts to equal their cool dispassionateness in her

[9] The delineation of character by way of phrenology and physiognomy which occurs here is typical of Charlotte Brontë. In *Villette* both M. Paul and Lucy are skilled in these "sciences." M. Paul reads Lucy's character on the night of her arrival at the Pensionnat of Madame Beck. Later, on the occasion of the school play, it emerges that he had divined that, despite appearances, Lucy had great powers of imaginative self-expression. Robert A. Colby in his "Villette and the Life of the Mind," *P.M.L.A.* 75 (September, 1960) 415, argues that "on the whole phrenology plays a lesser part in the characterization of the personages of *Villette* than in that of the other three novels of Charlotte Brontë," and suggests that here character *analysis* replaces character *reading*. To me any such change in *Villette* seems no more than marginal. The interesting implications of a serious use of the ideas of phrenology and physiognomy remain: character for Charlotte Brontë is ultimately static; it does not develop. Dormant elements may be brought out by changed circumstances, but the essentials of character are fixed and unchanging.

own life. Lucy's attempt to discipline and restrain the emotional side
of her nature brings her at least once to total nervous and spiritual
breakdown. Alone in the Pensionnat in the late part of summer,
physically exhausted by the demands made on her by the cretin, a
child incapable of normal human feelings, whom she is looking after,
Lucy's external environment mirrors her internal condition. The impulse to hope, to imagine a life beyond that of drab duty, has been
repressed and denied to the extent that Lucy is destroying her truest
self. Hence the collapse that brings her in the end to the confessional.
The account of this breakdown contains some of the most brilliant
passages in the novel. They suggest most powerfully how the denied
and thwarted imagination takes control in dream and trance sequences
as soon as rational checks begin to give way:

> The solitude and the stillness of the long dormitory could not be borne
> any longer; the ghastly white beds were turning into spectres—the
> coronal of each became a death's head, huge and sun-bleached—dead
> dreams of an elder world and mightier race lay frozen in their wide
> gaping eyeholes (I:201).

The nightmare quality of such a passage is powerful evidence of the
degree of dislocation in Lucy's nervous state that unflinching self-
dedication to the calls of duty and responsibility produces. The hot,
arid Indian-summer days in which this episode in Lucy's experience
occurs are interrupted by fierce equinoctial storms: a fitting image of
the manner in which Lucy's attempt to accept an existence devoid of
any kind of visionary hope or excitement is overwhelmed by an erup-
tion of uncontrollable feelings from the repressed and thwarted side
of her nature.

If these powerful sequences suggest Charlotte Brontë's unqualified
recognition of the dangers that result from total rejection of the world
of feeling and imagination, contrasting scenes suggest the dangers on
the other side of the unchecked indulgence of feeling. Juxtaposing
these scenes will serve once again to clarify the fundamental conflicts
that are explored in the subject-matter and form of *Villette*. What Lucy
Snowe understands as the dangers implicit in the unchecked indulgence
of feeling and the imagination emerges after her performance in the
play directed by M. Paul. M. Paul's reading of her skull is proved
correct. When Lucy allows herself to get inside the role assigned to
her she discovers that play she can, even as M. Paul had insisted. But
in the cool light of day she rejects her triumph in terms that are highly
significant:

> Yet the next day when I thought it over, I quite disapproved of these
> amateur performances. . . . A keen relish for dramatic expression had
> revealed itself as part of my nature; to cherish and exercise this new-

found faculty might gift me with a world of delight, but it would not
do for a mere looker-on at life; the strength and longing must be put
by . . . (I:176).

Through Lucy's acting "a world of delight" is brought within her
grasp. But that world is rejected as inappropriate to "a mere looker-on
at life." There is a suggestion here of how closely related Charlotte
Brontë saw the world of imaginative reality, as she understood it, and
the actual world of social and moral responsibility. The imaginative
world of acting is not to be easily set aside from the concerns of the
actual. The imaginative world is a feeling world above all; it draws
on and acts upon the passionate side of experience; and the feelings it
indulges and releases—feelings of hope, expectancy, fulfilment—are
as dangerously real as those produced by any other stimulus. Rejecting
her acting, Lucy is struggling to master her own passionate nature, to
choke off a mode of *self-expression* which if encouraged would be
self-indulgent.

This reading of Lucy's rejection of her own acting is reinforced
subsequently by her account of her response to the great actress Vashti.
Lucy's account of Vashti's performance is so impassioned as to be
almost incoherent. But the telling confusion is that between the role
Vashti is playing and the actress herself. Is it to her performance or
to the actress that Lucy responds with such burning intensity? The
point is that Charlotte Brontë blurs any such distinction. It is the
passion that Vashti both supremely embodies and superbly projects
that concerns her. The passion that Lucy witnesses is so overwhelmingly
real that it challenges the orthodoxies of conventional morality. Lucy
is possessed by Vashti's passion, but not swept away. Her response is
deep and full; but self-control survives. "Hate and Murder and Madness
incarnate, (Vashti) stood," she tells us.

It was a marvellous sight; a mighty revelation.
It was a spectacle low, horrible, immoral (II:7).

The ambivalence in Charlotte Brontë's response to the world of the
romantic imagination could not be more surely pointed. In Vashti's
performance, as experienced by Lucy Snowe, art and morality are
openly pitted against each other. For Lucy and for Charlotte Brontë
it is a crucial moment of truth.

But the episode is not complete at this point. One uncomfortable
truth is followed by another. The evening ends with powerful confirmation of the dangers that are the consequence of the unchecked
indulgence of passionate feeling. The fiery passion of the stage is
translated into the rumor of actual fire in the theatre. Immediately
the audience becomes a struggling, jostling, mindless mob. It is only
Dr. John's cool self-control that saves the day. The moral is clear and

it is taken to heart by Lucy Snowe. Where Jane Eyre runs away from her feelings, Lucy tries to preserve self-control by stifling hers. The burying of Dr. John's letters is both literal and symbolic.

What these various episodes in Lucy's experience after her arrival in the Pensionnat of Madame Beck suggest is an enlargement and development of hints contained in the opening chapters of the novel. If the price of the calm repose of nature is the total denial of the experience of feeling, then the paying of the price produces a kind of death, a self-denial that in a normally sensible person leads to physical and spiritual collapse. Uninhibited indulgence of feeling, on the other hand, produces an equally destructive moral anarchy: the self becomes the prisoner of forces which both encourage the distortion of reality and threaten to deprive it of its proper freedom. Lucy Snowe's fate is to become aware in her own experience of both these dangers; to feel the threat of both within herself. For most of the novel she is struggling with one or the other of them. What she has to learn is that there is no salvation to be found either in repression and self-denial or in visionary, romantic yearnings. There is no answer to be found either in the ultimately self-destructive role of the mere onlooker on life or in Dr. John. Above all Lucy needs to come to terms with both sides of her nature. Hence the importance of M. Paul. With M. Paul she is finally able to be wholly herself, because his nature is like her own. "You are patient, and I am choleric; "M. Paul says, "you are quiet and pale, and I am tanned and fiery; you are a strict Protestant, and I am a sort of lay Jesuit: but we are alike—there is affinity" (II:148). M. Paul goes on to develop his sense of the likeness between them, and he is right to do so. The affinity is there, and it is the source of the mutual self-understanding which distinguishes their relationship from that between Lucy and Dr. John, M. de Bassohm-pierre, Madame Beck and the rest, and which finally brings them together.

Lucy's love for M. Paul provides such resolution as *Villette* offers for the broadly moral and psychological conflicts it explores. But the fact that these conflicts are clarified by (for example) acting scenes reminds us again of the complex relationship that Charlotte Brontë recognized between the worlds of moral choice and the aesthetic imagination. The sense in which the imagination has become a moral issue in *Villette* is hinted at by Lucy's behavior over her role in M. Paul's play. She agrees to play the part, but she refuses to "dress up" for it. She will not disguise what she really is. This is in small Charlotte Brontë's mode of writing in *Villette*. The disguise of romance is abandoned in favor of a basic realism. Hence the retreat in *Villette* from the more Gothic elements of plot and character in *Jane Eyre*. The trappings of the world of romance persist in the later novel in the legend of the nun, and the use made of it by Ginevra and de Hamal. But the point is the sham/deceitful quality of such romantic stuff; it deceives but does not seriously challenge the rational world. (One may nonetheless isolate one of the novel's weaknesses here. Undeniably too much attention is paid to the nun, the mysterious *billet-doux*, the shadowy figures in the garden walk. The explanation is to be found in the use of the first person narrative. As James argued, the danger of such a narrative mode is its "fluency" in the longer piece. What we are interested in is not the mysteriously romantic events themselves, but Lucy's reaction to them. How will she cope with these extraordinary manifestations? But as narrator she has to tell us what the events are, their circumstances, and the rest. At such points Lucy's roles as narrator and protagonist conflict.)

The world of romance, then, as it appears in the external action of *Villette* is a factitious one, appropriate to certain characters whose grasp of reality is limited, but something nonetheless to be seen through and rejected. The episodes involving the nun interestingly also involve aspects of Lucy's self-delusion.[10] The nun appears in the attic where Lucy is reading one of Dr. John's letters; she appears again in the attic, where Lucy had been locked by M. Paul to learn her part in the play, when Lucy is about to leave with Dr. John to see Vashti at the theatre; the episode of the burial of the letters at the base of the tree where the nun is supposed to have been entombed is also associated with the appearance of the mysterious figure. And last of all, there is the confusion of the legendary nun with the dead Justine Marie—against whom, for no obvious reason, M. Paul warns Lucy— along with Lucy's mistake about the relationship between M. Paul and the living Justine Marie. All of these episodes involve either errors of judgement or unrealizable visionary hopes and dreams; and all are associated with moments of high romantic mystery and sensation. The linking of romance with delusion in some form is insisted on.

The same argument may be used in relation to the concluding section of the novel, which has often been attacked as inferior to the rest. In the account of the efforts made to keep M. Paul and Lucy apart there is clearly a large admixture of the Gothic in both character and event. But again one may recognize an association between a more Gothic vision of the nature of reality, and the falsity and deviousness of those who manipulate that reality. It is as if here, for Charlotte Brontë, the worlds of Roman Catholicism and Gothic romance become organically related as subject-matter and style. The aesthetic sleight-of-

---

[10] For an excellent account of the significance of the supernatural in *Villette* see E. D. H. Johnson, " 'Daring the Dread Glance': Charlotte Brontë's Treatment of the Supernatural in *Villette*," *Nineteenth Century Fiction*, xx (March, 1966), 325–36.

hand of the one becomes perhaps the moral jesuiticalness of the other. Whatever the nature of their external action, the final chapters of *Villette* do nothing to undermine the realism of the portrait of Lucy Snowe. "Cloud" is the climax of the novel and in this chapter Lucy's inner conflicts are partially resolved. Driven by an overwhelming need to act rather than merely to be acted upon; a need to fight back against an imposed passivity; a need to assert her individuality and her freedom, Lucy finds herself escaping out of the prison of the sleeping school into the fast-flowing current of life in Villette on festival night. Responding to the promptings of her deepest nature, Lucy denies the rational self that is constantly advising that security and calm and the avoidance of active suffering are to be discovered in the passive role of the mere onlooker at life. The strictest self-control is yielding in the face of pressures whose source is passionate feeling and an awakened imagination. However far the reader may respect such a development, Charlotte Brontë's own feelings clearly remain ambivalent. Lucy's behavior is explained away as the consequence of a drug administered to her by her enemies. This it is that is responsible for her irrational, impulsive behavior. More important, however, is the fact that the drug is explicitly identified as a surrogate for the imagination. The drug, we learn, had produced the opposite of its intended effect:

> Instead of stupor, came excitement. I became alive to new thought—to reverie peculiar in colouring. A gathering call ran among the faculties, their bugles sang, their trumpets rang an untimely summons. Imagination was roused from her rest, and she came forth impetuous and venturous (II:255).

It was Imagination that lured Lucy to leave "the glimmering gloom, the narrow limits, the oppressive heat of the dormitory," and "follow her forth into dew, coolness, and glory" (II:255). Imagination speaks here in such rhetorically suspect terms that one is tempted to believe that Charlotte intended an aesthetic reflexion of Lucy's drugged state. Certainly much of Lucy's account of her experiences that night beautifully suggests the twilight world between dream or nightmare and vision. Nevertheless, it is more probable that Lucy's excited condition is an accurate reflexion, as Charlotte Brontë sees it, of that produced by imagination's power. In other words the "drug" has a moral, rather than aesthetic, significance. It allows Charlotte to continue to suggest the moral uncertainty she felt about the status of the imagination. And the grounds of that uncertainty are further suggested by the errors of judgment, the overheated fancies that Lucy falls victim to in her "distempered state" (as Southey would have called it). Yet the release from the prison of the self that Lucy experiences remains for her fundamentally necessary and right. Only thus, through the imagination, whatever its perils, may she enter the world of feeling where the truth about herself is to be discovered.

In *Villette,* just as in *Jane Eyre,* Charlotte Brontë sets high value on individual independence and freedom. Both Jane Eyre and Lucy Snowe have a healthy sense of their own worth, and many of their trials arise from their need to assert and preserve their individuality. Even the necessity of rational self-control may be understood in these terms. Subjection to passionate feeling involves the temporary loss of individual identity. But what Lucy discovers in this closing section of the book is that freedom is not to be defined only as a negative preservation of individual independence, and is not to be achieved at the expense of feeling and the imagination.[11]

Obedient to the forces that have sent her out into the festive life of Villette, Lucy is made to recognize her commitment to a love "furnace—tried by pain." The mistake over M. Paul's relationship with Justine Marie may strike the reader as a meretricious device to hold his interest. But it is Lucy who is deceived rather than the reader; and the self-deception is central to her understanding of her own position. The notion that M. Paul is to marry someone else is almost welcome to her. Such an outcome, she imagines, will put an end to the feelings that have meant "hourly torment," disturbing the calm repose of her nature. Once again, as it were, she will be Lucy Snowe. The truth, she believes, has set her free: "Truth stripped away Falsehood, and Flattery, and Expectancy, and here I stand—free" (II:278–79). But the degree of self-delusion in this is immediately made obvious: "Nothing remained now but to take my freedom to my chamber, to carry it with me to my bed and see what I could make of it" (II:279). For Lucy there is in fact to be no return to the kind of freedom that is obtained at the expense of feeling. The "drug" that

---

[11] It is worth noting that a concern for the independent rights and privileges of others may lead to morally teasing problems for the novelist himself. The nature of his own relationship with his characters comes into question. An episode in *Villette* suggests that Charlotte Brontë had become aware of this difficulty. In an exchange with M. Paul, Lucy makes it clear that she cannot accept his secret observation of her life, however well-intentioned it may be. M. Paul at the lattice window with his spy-glass is an image that Lucy finds deeply disturbing:

> Monsieur, I tell you every glance you cast from that lattice is a wrong done to the best part of your own nature. To study the human heart thus, is to banquet secretly and sacrilegiously on Eve's apples (II:146).

Lucy implies that M. Paul's behavior is a result of his Catholic background, but it is probable that the passage articulates a fear of Charlotte Brontë's own. That the novelist may violate the sanctity of the human heart is a possibility that disturbs her just as it disturbs other nineteenth-century novelists both English and American. Hence perhaps her preference for the first-person narrative form. Self-revelation involves no encroaching on the inner freedom and privacy of others.

has directed Lucy's behavior on the night of the fête may have distorted reality, but an awakened imagination has also made her recognize the truth. Lucy is now at last allowed the freedom to feel, intensely, urgently, and in the closing pages of the novel that freedom, with M. Paul, is fleetingly enjoyed. Fleetingly, that is, in the real world of duties accepted and of suffering endured; in the world of romance, perhaps, the end is a different one. In either case the value of that freedom remains.

# The Other Emily

## by Denis Donoghue

Emily Brontë's poems were first published in *Poems by Currer, Ellis, and Acton Bell* (1846). When the second edition of *Wuthering Heights* was issued in 1850, in a volume which also contained *Agnes Grey* and a selection of poems by Emily and Anne, Charlotte Brontë added a biographical notice of the two sisters. Of Emily's poems she wrote:

> One day, in the autumn of 1845, I accidentally lighted on a MS. volume of verse in my sister Emily's handwriting. Of course, I was not surprised, knowing that she could and did write verse: I looked it over, and something more than surprise seized me,—a deep conviction that these were not common effusions, nor at all like the poetry women generally write. I thought them condensed and terse, vigorous and genuine. To my ear, they had also a peculiar music—wild, melancholy, and elevating.

Some of the poems were written as early as 1834, when Emily Brontë was sixteen. Between that date and 1846, she wrote about 200 poems, most of them short pieces, and some fragments. In February, 1844, she transcribed a selection of verses into two notebooks: one contained thirty-one poems, autobiographical lyrics; the other, forty-four poems from the Gondal saga, a childhood legend propounded by Emily and Anne. Charlotte speaks of one volume, but the first printed poems come variously from both sources, the personal poems as well as the Gondal pieces; no distinction is announced. This has caused some confusion. A reader who comes upon "The Night is Darkening Round Me" in, say, W. H. Auden's anthology, *Nineteenth Century Minor Poets,* is likely to read it as a personal lyric, unless he happens to know that it is a dramatic lyric spoken by the guilty Augusta in the Gondal saga. The paralysis of will which is represented in the poem is Augusta's, not Emily Brontë's. Again, "Heavy Hangs the Raindrop" does not express the relation between Emily Brontë and Nature; it marks a moment in the relation between the imprisoned Arthur of Exina and R.C., the little fair-haired girl who loves him.

"The Other Emily," by Denis Donoghue. This essay is printed here for the first time.

In fact, most of Emily Brontë's poems, and several of her most celebrated pieces, are Gondal poems.[1] We are to think of a mythical island in the North Pacific, divided into several hostile kingdoms. Julius Brenzaida, Prince of Angora in Northern Gondal, is loved by Rosina, Princess of Alcona in the south. He conquers the kingdom of Almedore, and sacks the city of Zalona. Then he secretly marries Geraldine Sidonia, daughter of a conquered family. Soon, however, he leaves her, possibly to return to Rosina. Geraldine has a child, Augusta Geraldine Almeda, and she decides to bring the infant to Julius. But on the voyage the ship is wrecked, and Geraldine is drowned. The child is saved and brought to Julius, who arranges to have her reared in the mountains of Angora. Julius then marries Rosina. A child is born to them, a beautiful boy. Julius captures the city of Tyndarum. Shortly after, he betrays Gerald of Exina, and casts him into prison along with Gerald's son Arthur. But a rebellion is raised against Julius, and he is murdered. (Rosina mourns him in the famous threnody, "Cold in the Earth, and the Deep Snow piled above Thee.") By now, Augusta has grown up. The second part of the saga is largely concerned with her passionate intrigues. Her first lover is Alexander of Elbe, but he is already married. When a daughter is born to them, Rosina and Alexander decide that she must be killed, since Alexander's royal rights would be forfeit if the existence of an illegitimate child were known. Augusta abandons the child in the snow. When Alexander's wife dies, he marries Augusta, but soon after, he dies, and Augusta is imprisoned.

Released after some years, Augusta returns to Alcona. Fernando De Samara falls in love with her, but she quickly forgets him. He is thrown into the prison caves of Gaaldine, but escapes, and kills himself in despair. Augusta falls in love with Geraldine's brother, Alfred Sidonia, lord of Aspin Castle. She becomes his wife, but he soon dies. Augusta herself is murdered by Douglas, one of Julius's murderers. The saga ends with the marriage of Henry, Rosina's son, to Alfred's fair-haired daughter, at Aspin Castle.

The personal poems issue directly from Emily Brontë's experience; many of them testify to her isolation, her sense of decay and mutability, the melancholy to which Charlotte referred, Emily's "dark

[1] The contexts of the poems are clarified in *Emily Jane Brontë: Gondal Poems*, ed. Helen Brown and Joan Mott (Oxford: Basil Blackwell for the Shakespeare Press, 1938); *The Complete Poems of Emily Jane Brontë*, ed. C. W. Hatfield (New York: Columbia University Press, 1941); and *The Complete Poems of Emily Brontë*, ed. Philip Henderson (London: The Folio Society, 1951). The Gondal saga is reconstructed in Laura L. Hinkley, *The Brontës: Charlotte and Emily* (London: Hammond, 1947), pp. 273–82, from which the present synopsis is taken. Fannie E. Ratchford argues in her *Gondal's Queen* (Austin, Texas: University of Texas Press, 1955) that all of Emily Brontë's verse "falls within the Gondal context."

world," her dreams, visions, fancies, or Branwell's tragedy. A few poems are direct invocations of her Muse, sometimes called Imagination as opposed to "stern Reason," the admonishing voice of daylight and law. These are moorland poems, in the sense that they praise the visionary power by which the bleakness of the moors is transformed and enriched. "My sister Emily loved the moors," Charlotte writes; but she has already remarked that in these relationships we receive but what we give. The moors do not provide the desired beauty from their own resources; rather, they provoke it in the perceiver, compelling the visionary power to invent it. "If she demand beauty to inspire her," Charlotte writes, "she must bring it inborn; these moors are too stern to yield any product so delicate." So that product must come from within. "The eye of the gazer," Charlotte says, "must *itself* brim with a 'purple light,' intense enough to perpetuate the brief flower-flush of August on the heather, or the rare sunset-smile of June; out of his heart must well the freshness, that in latter spring and early summer brightens the bracken, nurtures the moss, and cherishes the starry flowers that spangle for a few weeks the pasture of the moor-sheep." Finally, "unless that light and freshness are innate and self-sustained, the drear prospect of a Yorkshire moor will be found as barren of poetic as of agricultural interest." But to Emily Brontë's imagination, absence and bareness were just as provocative as presence. Her characteristic powers were innate and self-sustained; they did not delight in a given plenitude, if the gift seemed independent of her imagination.

We distinguish between these autobiographical poems and the Gondal poems, but we should not push them too far apart. Beneath the overt difference, there is continuity. Demonstrably, and in more than the obvious sense, every poem issues from a single imagination, bearing Emily Brontë's signature. Moving from *Wuthering Heights* to the Gondal saga and then to the autobiographical poems, we mark the obvious differences of genre, but we are also aware of a landscape of feeling, shared by all these works. The landscape is given in certain pervasive images, recurring figures, patterns, rhythms. Some of these are so distinctive that they assert themselves. When Emily Dickinson read Emily Brontë's poems, she found one stanza lodging in her mind; it struck her as somehow definitive, and she quoted it in several letters:

> Though Earth and Man were gone
> And Suns and Universes ceased to be
> And thou wert left alone,
> Every existence would exist in thee—

The first line should read: "Though earth and moon were gone"; but it hardly matters. What matters is a certain gesture. Emily Dickinson recognised it as Emily Brontë's particular sign; ostensibly, a syntax of excess, of hyperbole, but in the declared case not excess at all, since the feeling lives up to the declaration. It is a characteristic cadence, especially in the verve with which All is identified with One. The cadence is memorable in the poems, and it is one of the definitive tropes of *Wuthering Heights*; as in Chapter IX, where Catherine says of Heathcliff:

> If all else perished, and *he* remained, *I* should still continue to be; and if all else remained, and he were annihilated, the universe would turn to a mighty stranger: I should not seem a part of it.

It is typical of Emily Brontë's imagination that it runs to the extreme case, or to the extreme form of a common case, and that it is impatient with mediate things, relative or provisional moods. It is also typical of her imagination to define character by its extremity, and to make extremes meet. So Augusta, the fatal heroine of the Gondal saga, is a trial version of Cathy in *Wuthering Heights;* when we add Julius to that version, we see that Heathcliff is already in a measure defined. Emily Brontë did not possess, in any Shakespearean sense, a dramatic imagination. Her characters, in the novel as in the poems, are functions or projections, if not of herself, then of certain forces which belong to her as intimately as her desires. These forces are few, but each is definitive. Each is absolute. The novel and the poems are continuous in this respect, that they release these forces, at whatever cost to other forces which are ignored. Emily Brontë's limit is the outer limit of those forces which she releases, separately or in powerful conjunction. Her fictive world is not, indeed, complete. It is not, in the common sense, rich, diverse, plenary. Rather, it compels by the power of its limitation. Many images of life are absent, but we are forced to feel that they are absent because they have been rejected as irrelevant. Whatever beauty she needs, she invents, but her necessities are not of that order. Her deepest need is to make a clear space for her imagination; what she demands of space is that, for her sake, it be empty.

Indeed, her imagination is so exclusive that it discloses itself in a certain pattern, a plot. The plot is a fiction; it is not to be found in any single poem or in the novel, but in the configuration of the whole work. It suggests itself as an abstract or virtual fiction, compounded of a few typical figures and motifs. It is often said of Shakespeare's plays that they constitute a single work, a single poem. The remark is not fanciful. Emily Brontë's entire work constitutes a single poem, a single fiction. Its plot runs somewhat as follows. The story begins in childhood; the young spirit is in harmony with Nature, delighting in "the splashing of the surge,/The changing heaven, the breezy weather." "Laughing mirth's most joyous swell" is delightful for the same reason, the swell, the great sense of life as motion and action. Spirit conceives itself as action, and recognizes action in every natural appearance. Indeed, life itself is unified by this terminology, so that no gap is disclosed between consciousness and experience. But in the next period a change occurs. Natural events are felt to have changed their character. The terminology of action persists, but its characters and signs are altered. Breezes become storms, malignant because independent; change becomes decay. The splashing of the surge now denotes the violence and hostility of Nature, there is no kinship:

> O cold, cold is my heart!
> It will not, cannot rise;
> It feels no sympathy
> With those refulgent skies.

Everything is felt as external. Sometimes this feeling is embodied in imagery of imprisonment, severance, and burial. The spirit feels itself defeated by a "tyrant spell." "I hear my dungeon bars recoil." The hidden God has turned tyrant. In other moods, the feeling comes as a sense of guilt, either a categorical feeling of guilt as innate and original, or else guilt arising from a specific sin, perhaps a sinful passion. Both feelings now merge in an archetypal figure, to be discussed later in the present essay, the child lost in a forest. The child is lost, abandoned, either because of a Malicious God or because of an original sin. In the next period there is a corresponding desire for rest, release, silence, calm. The terminology of action is given up altogether, since it has proved itself fallacious. The pervasive images in this new period are quietist:

> How still, how happy! These are words
> That once would scarce agree together;

But now they agree together. In this condition the ideal imagery features the loss of definition and character; states once welcomed as separate and therefore rich are now dissolved. Sometimes the old images of rigor, ice, and snow, are melted; there is consolation in nullity, when all things are returned to an original, undifferentiated source. The earth itself is tolerable when bare and silent, but the only joy is in absence. Finally, there is a movement of feeling beyond earth and time; the things of earth and time are transcended, or retained only as shadows of themselves. The relative appearances offered to the senses are translated into their absolute equivalents, so that the appearances themselves may be discarded:

> But first a hush of peace, a soundless calm descends;
> The struggle of distress and fierce impatience ends;

Mute music soothes my breast—unuttered harmony
That I could never dream till earth was lost to me.
Then dawns the Invisible, the Unseen its truth reveals;
My outward sense is gone, my inward essence feels—

Death is the only good thing, after all; the spirit frees itself from the
heard melodies of time, since the divine malice resides in melody
itself. "O for the time when I shall sleep/Without identity." The
motto for this period is given in one of the poems: "I'm happiest when
most away." In another, the spirit speaks of the terror felt when, after
such happiness, the senses reassert themselves:

Oh dreadful is the check—intense the agony
When the ear begins to hear and the eye begins to see;
When the pulse begins to throb, the brain to think again;
The soul to feel the flesh and the flesh to feel the chain!

Yet I would lose no sting, would wish no torture less;
The more that anguish racks the earlier it will bless;
And robed in fires of Hell, or bright with heavenly shine,
If it but herald Death, the vision is divine!

The vision is divine; specifically, these transcendental desires are
addressed toward an angelic figure, variously called messenger, idol,
"visitant of air," "Strange Power." Sometimes the power is invoked as
God, sometimes it is identified with the creative power of the imagination. Under any name, its place is "the steadfast, changeless
shore," otherwise "Eternity" or "Immortality." One poem begins with
"Death" and ends with "Eternity," a characteristic sequence, but
Eternity here has nothing to do with the Christian hope of resurrec-
tion. The tone is different. The dominant feeling is deemed to be fulfilled in rest, calm, obliteration; as in those Renaissance manuals of
iconography in which Night is featured as a woman with black wings,
"in one, a sleeping white child to signify Sleep, in the other a black
one that seems asleep, and signifies Death." [2]

The only validity I would ascribe to this plot or *figura* is that of
forming a qualitative context for the fiction and poems of Emily
Brontë. It does not determine the local plots, the stories. Perhaps its
main use is to suggest the grand rhythm of the work as a whole within
which we hear the more specific rhythms of the individual poems and
the novel. But the matter may be brought further. The grand rhythm,
as I have described it, is one of the marks of an imagination intensely subjective. Indeed, Emily Brontë's imagination is remarkably

[2] Jean Seznec, *The Survival of the Pagan Gods,* trans. Barbara F. Sessions (New
York: Pantheon Books, 1953), p. 291.

true to the Romantic archetype which Georges Poulet describes in *Les métamorphoses du cercle:*

> Peut-être ne pourrait-on mieux définir, sinon le romantisme, au moins l'un des côtés les plus importants de celui-ci, qu'en disant qu'il est une prise de conscience du caractère fondamentalement subjectif de l'esprit. Le romantique est un être qui se découvre centre. Peu importe que le monde des objets soit hors de portée, il sait qu'au fond de lui-même il y a quelque chose d'inassimilable à un object, et qui est le moi-sujet, la partie de son moi la plus authentique, ou celle qu'il reconnait le plus volontiers pour sienne. Privé de la périphérie, le romantique va longuement se familiariser avec le moi, le centre.[3]

One way of describing the *figura* in Emily Brontë is to say that it marks the gradual discovery, on her part, that the periphery was lost, the world of objects a deceit. In her "first" moments she was herself part of the sustaining periphery; progressively, as the world of objects lost its consoling force, she discovered that her own imagination must occupy the creative center of whatever circle might be drawn. The result is that her characteristic poems do not explore the objective world; they do not even define or test a sense of the world as already formed. These poems act on the assumption that the world of objects is, indeed, given, but given as foreign and indifferent. To know the world in greater depth or in richer detail would not alter that new sense of its character, it would merely confirm it. Emily Brontë has already passed sentence upon the world. In "The Night Wind" and "Shall earth no more inspire thee?" the genius of Earth woos her, persuading her to return to his favor and protection. But the spirit answers that the music of Earth has no power over her; her feelings run in another course. Emily Brontë writes, in fact, as if a knowledge of the world were not in question; before speech begins, that knowledge is present. She writes as if, on that theme, there is nothing further to be said. A knowledge of the world is already her possession, and therefore her fate. What each poem proposes, therefore, is not so much to confirm her sense of the world; but rather to define the self in which that sense has been formed. Inevitably, her sense of the world comes to seem crucial because it is her nature, not because it bears upon such an object. The subject is the important member. Emily Brontë's romanticism is indeed her subjectivity, her sense of herself as center.

The more this sense was developed, the more inward it appeared. The inward essence is increasingly distinguished from the outward sense; it is, in several poems, the distinction between God and man. Whether the ostensible object of invocation is the imagination,

[3] Georges Poulet, *Le métamorphoses du cercle* (Paris: Librairie Plon, 1961), p. 136.

fancy, or the angelic messenger, it is, in fact, a function of Emily
Brontë's nature. Finally, the imagination must identify itself with
God, if the logic of the imagery is to prevail. The distinction between
God and man may persist as an interim rhetoric, but it cannot remain when the one center becomes All. At that moment the only
relevant circle is the new circle formed by the center which expands
itself, occupying ground laid waste for that purpose. The center begins to expand when "the world without" is sharply and critically
distinguished from "the world within." In "To Imagination" the
creative power within is invoked to "call a lovelier life from death/
And whisper with a voice divine/Of real worlds as bright as thine."
The principle is Coleridgean; the imagination as the secular version
of the divine power, the infinite I AM:

> O God within my breast,
> Almighty ever-present Deity!
> Life, that in me has rest,
> As I, Undying Life, have power in thee!

The theology itself is circular, as it must be when the only vivid
terms move about an ever-expanding center. In a poem to Imagination, Emily Brontë writes:

> And am I wrong, to worship where
> Faith cannot doubt, nor Hope despair,
> Since my own soul can grant my prayer?

It could hardly be a more explicit assertion. In this idiom poetry and
religion become one, faith and aesthetics become one. A new world
arises when the old world, discredited, is transcended. The old world
was based upon the primacy of object; the new world is based upon
the primacy of subject.

This goes some distance to explain why Emily Brontë's efforts to
establish a liaison between herself and the objective world were few,
and those few perfunctory. This child, lost in a forest, repudiates the
forest; a certain subjective hauteur is operative. Hélène Tuzet has
discussed this motif in *Le cosmos et l'imagination:*

> Un enfant perdu dans la forêt: ce thème qui a souvent, parfois mer-
> veilleusement, inspiré la fantaisie romantique est peut-être la meilleure
> image de l'homme dans le cosmos, tel que le voit cette même fantaisie.
> Le plaisir que goûte le Romantique à s'insérer dans l'Univers n'est plus
> celui de se sentir à sa place, mais bien de se sentir égaré. Il y a une
> volupté à ne *pas* embrasser l'ensemble, à ne pas comprendre, à s'avouer
> dépassé, débordé, à fermer des yeux éblouis ou épouvantés, à s'abandonner
> aux Puissances paternelles et terribles.[4]

[4] Hélène Tuzet, *Le cosmos et l'imagination* (Paris: Librairie José Corti, 1965), p. 121.

But this pleasure, this vertigo, is available only when the child-spirit feels that it may now invent a new world, emanating from the self as centre. The child does not then negotiate with the forest, since to deal with the world in those terms is to be compromised. The answer to loss is willful disengagement. Hence:

> Fall, leaves, fall; die, flowers, away;
> Lengthen night and shorten day;
> Every leaf speaks bliss to me
> Fluttering from the autumn tree.
> I shall smile when wreaths of snow
> Blossom where the rose should grow;
> I shall sing when night's decay
> Ushers in a drearier day.

The ultimate ideal, as we have seen, is to answer one rejection by another, the spirit transmuting everything into itself:

> When I am not and none beside—
> Nor earth nor sea nor cloudless sky—
> But only spirit wandering wide
> Through infinite immensity.

When we speak of the expansion of the center to fill the entire circle, we posit a continuous act of will. Nothing less will answer. If the objective world is maintained by God or by some other force, the subjective world is maintained only by the subject; the imagination, endlessly creative, sustained by that form of itself which is called the will. It is a commonplace that *Wuthering Heights* is a fiction remarkable for its representation of life in terms of will; indeed, the novel owes little to any other manifestation of human life. We make the point when we say, and it is again a commonplace, that Heathcliff and Cathy are more readily understandable as forms of energy than as characters; absolute because self-sustaining. Their identity, upon which Cathy insists, is the center, the vortex, from which the relevant forms of energy issue. It is in this sense that passion, in *Wuthering Heights,* is given as a natural force; natural and therefore immune to the moral considerations of men and women in the historical world. Heathcliff is a purer form of energy than Cathy; a point made in the novel by the multiplicity of considerations which are deemed irrelevant to him. Indeed, what gives the book its uncanny power is the verve with which so much of human life is set aside as irrelevant. Here again the continuity between Emily Brontë's imagination and Heathcliff as one of its characteristic projections is clear. Both are defined by the nature of their wills; in both, sublimity is egotistical.

There is a famous passage in Hazlitt's lecture on Shakespeare and

Milton, one of the *Lectures on the English Poets.* Hazlitt is speaking
of the "generic quality" of Shakespeare's mind, "its power of communication with all other minds—so that it contained a universe of
thought and feeling within itself, and had no one peculiar bias, or
exclusive excellence more than another." He goes on "He was the
least of an egotist that it was possible to be. He was nothing in himself; but he was all that others were, or that they could become."
Keats extended Hazlitt's description of the Shakespearean imagination, distinguishing it from the Wordsworthian or egotistical sublime.
"When I am in a room with People," he wrote to Richard Woodhouse
on October 27, 1818, "if I ever am free from speculating on creations
of my own brain, then not myself goes home to myself: but the identity of every one in the room begins to press upon me (so) that I am
in a very little time annihilated." It is the special mark of Emily
Brontë's imagination that it resists annihilation by maintaining itself
at the center of its circle. So her Gondal poems are not, in fact,
dramatic monologues: they are soliloquies, diverse only in their set-
tings. What is different, in each case, is the circumstance. The difference does not require a variation in the demonstrated character of
the world; but only in the feeling of the perceiver. To Emily Brontë,
even in the Gondal poems, soliloquy is a mode of introspection; the
circumstance provides the occasion, but it does not offer itself as the
object of consciousness. If we distinguish between the Gondal poems
and the personal poems, the distinction should admit the consideration that, at a certain level of description, the local differences tend
to disappear. It is not necessary to push the argument. Hazlitt rebuked certain contemporary poets for trying to "reduce poetry to a
mere effusion of natural sensibility"; surrounding the meanest objects
"with the morbid feelings and devouring egotism of the writers' own
minds." In Emily Brontë's imagination there is, indeed, a trace of the
morbid, but she does not parade her sensibility: she is concerned
with sensibility only as a form of the will. She takes no pride in the
expression of will; the will is supreme because innate and categorical.

　　Her imagination, that is to say, does not allow the identity of an
object to assert itself in her presence. The ideal moment, for that
imagination, is when the plenary objects of the world are either
hidden or transcended. Emily Brontë is a lunar poet, if we distinguish
between poets lunar and solar. The solar poet delights in the mani-
fold richness of objects. The lunar poet waits until night, when objects lose their force, the earth withdraws, and the imagination proceeds to fill the empty space between itself and the stars. Rochelle's
muse in "The Prisoner" is the same as Emily Brontë's in the poem
"Stars":

O Stars and Dreams and Gentle Night;
O Night and Stars return!
And hide me from the hostile light
That does not warm, but burn—

That drains the blood of suffering men;
Drinks tears, instead of dew:
Let me sleep through his blinding reign,
And only wake with you! [5]

It is the same in kind and hardly different in degree. This justifies the association and marks the continuity of the feeling engaged.

But our account is too general if it does not specify the choice poems and observe them. Henry James complained, in "The Lesson of Balzac," that the romantic tradition associated with the Brontës had virtually prevented any critical attention to their works. The image of "their dreary, their tragic history, their loneliness and poverty of life" stood as a force "independent of any one of their applied faculties." That image, he maintained, had supplanted the works themselves, had offered itself more insistently than *Jane Eyre* or *Wuthering Heights*; so that the question of the Brontës "has scarce indeed been accepted as belonging to literature at all." Literature, he argued, is "an objective, a projected result; it is life that is the unconscious, the agitated, the struggling, floundering cause." The case is somewhat different now, but there is always, and preeminently in the consideration of Emily Brontë, a disposition to allow the causes to speak for the results. Indeed, the best claim we can reasonably make for the paradigm, the *figura* as we have called it, in Emily Brontë's poems is that it mediates between cause and result, between the original agitation and the resultant forms. The paradigm is not merely agitation; but it is not yet form. It is a mediating fiction, no more. Its chief merit may be that it recalls the agitation and foresees its probable forms.

A reasonable showing, among the 200 poems, would include these, listed in no particular order but with an implication of weight and representative merit: "Sacred watcher, wave thy bells"; "Fall, leaves, fall"; "A little while, a little while"; "How still, how happy"; "The night is darkening round me"; "If grief for grief can touch thee"; " 'Tis Moonlight"; "Aye, there it is"; "In Summer's Mellow Midnight"; "I See Around Me Tombstones Grey"; "The Day is Done"; "How

---

[5] Fannie E. Ratchford (*Gondal's Queen,* p. 87) argues that this poem is to be read as part of the Gondal saga; interpreting it as A.G.A.'s apostrophe to Julius. This seems to me a strained reading. It is probably better to take the poem as a personal lyric.

Clear She Shines"; "Well Hast Thou Spoken"; "The Linnet in the
Rocky Dells"; "When Weary with the Long Day's Care"; "O Thy
Bright Eyes"; "Enough of Thought, Philosopher"; "Cold in the
Earth"; "Death, that Struck when I was Most Confiding"; "Heavy
Hangs the Raindrop"; "How Beautiful the Earth is Still"; "Often
Rebuked"; "In the Dungeon Crypts"; "Silent is the House"; "No
Coward Soul." One of these will help to show some of Emily Brontë's
"applied faculties":

> Aye, there it is! It wakes to-night
> Sweet thoughts that will not die
> And feeling's fires flash all as bright
> As in the years gone by!
>
> And I can tell by thine altered cheek
> And by thy kindled gaze
> And by the word thou scarce dost speak,
> How wildly fancy plays.
>
> Yes I could swear that glorious wind
> Has swept the world aside,
> Has dashed its memory from thy mind
> Like foam-bells from the tide—
>
> And thou art now a spirit pouring
> Thy presence into all—
> The essence of the Tempest's roaring
> And of the Tempest's fall—
>
> A universal influence
> From Thine own influence free—
> A principle of life intense
> Lost to mortality.
>
> Thus truly when that breast is cold
> Thy prisoned soul shall rise,
> The dungeon mingle with the mould—
> The captive with the skies.

The motif is characteristically Romantic. The wind is invoked as
the natural force of action, the Aeolian lyre, the "correspondent
breeze," life itself as motion and spirit. Spirit is universal, wind is
the form it takes, and the form of the poem is the process by which,
from first word to last, every objective image is transformed into
spirit. This interchange of state is the motive of the poem. The wind,
waking sweet thoughts and feelings in the recipient, begins the process of changing him into its own terms. The first signs of change

are the "altered cheek," the "kindled gaze," of the second stanza. In the second stage of transformation the terms of earth and time are dissolved, "the world" and its memory. The change is complete when the recipient is entirely spirit. At that stage wind and recipient are one, alike in function and power: "And thou art now a spirit pouring/Thy presence into all"; like the original wind itself. Appropriately, existence is purified to essence, while essence retains, like the wind, its proper terminology of action; "The essence of the Tempest's roaring/And of the Tempest's fall." In the next stanza the terms are moral rather than philosophical. Just as the recipient's existence was purified, transformed into its proper essence, so now his finite "influence" is transformed into that "universal influence" which is spirit in its moral idiom. "From Thine own influence free"; free, as prefiguring the freedom from mortality invoked in the next lines. "A principle of life intense"; intense, since principles and absolutes do not obliterate the manifestations they transform, in this case manifestations of force and power. The last stanza is a vision of the future, the transformation complete, soul released to the skies. This is more than freedom, as commonly understood, since it enforces the victory of a subjective terminology upon every alien power.

The poem is, then, a ritual, designed to break the chains of time, place, and body. Most of the work, so far as the language goes, is done by the verbs; most assertively in the third stanza, where the "glorious wind/Has swept the world aside,/Has dashed its memory from thy mind." "Glorious" is not a mere counter, given that the wind's achievement is martial and heroic. But in fact all the verbs are verbs of transformation, changing every state into its spiritual equivalent: wakes, flash, plays, swept aside, dashed, rise, mingle. The verbs testify to a formative principle of change and are themselves, preeminently, the vehicles of that change. The nouns are, for the most part, the great subjective terms; feeling, fancy, memory, mind, spirit, presence, influence, soul, principle, essence; with their descriptive cousins—fire, wind, cheek, gaze, breast, thought. The adjectives are those of human and natural relations, with a supporting air of extremity and change; sweet, bright, wild, kindled, glorious, intense. But in saying that the main work is done by the verbs we should also remark that the essential movement of feeling is a stanzaic movement; where each stanza is a lyric moment, sustained and effected by the action of the verbs, for the most part, up to that point. Within each stanza there is little change; rather, a change is registered, defined in the stanza. The plot of the poem, if the term is permissible, is a sequence of lyric moments, each stanza marking a certain stage in the large cadence of feeling. The process is subjective, but only because the relevant transformation is personal, an act of will. Nature does not, in this case, enforce itself: it is invoked in that character. The movement of feeling arises from within the soul of the speaker; the transformation is effected by calling upon a natural force already hospitable to such changes. This explains the typical grammar of the poem. Emily Brontë begins with the indicative, "Aye, there it is"; simple because true. But gradually she uses indicatives as if they were imperatives; or rather, a poet with less confidence in the transforming power of will and the subjective idiom generally would be obliged to use imperatives where Emily Brontë uses indicatives. "And thou art now a spirit" means "Be thou now a spirit," but it is unnecessary to change to the imperative mood, since the indicative already has the air of an assumption. "Already with thee!" is Keat's equivalent in the "Ode to a Nightingale." The point to make, indeed, is that Emily Brontë's poem is doing the traditional work of metaphor, but in slow motion, and by degrees. The process of metaphor is the process of transformation, metamorphosis. Metaphor acts suddenly, in a flash; the poem achieves a metaphorical object, but slowly, earning the right to do so as it moves along, stanza by stanza.

## II

But a critical difficulty persists. We have reached the stage of describing Emily Brontë's poems as soliloquies; but if they are soliloquies, they cannot be dramatic lyrics, Gondal monologues. So, according to the logic, the Gondal saga is irrelevant, at best a romantic smoke screen. I hope to show that the contradiction is more apparent than real, but it must be faced, perhaps along the following lines.

It is clear that Emily Brontë's imagination found in Gondal sustenance not available in the daily life of Haworth. Gondal was an invented kingdom, neither England in general nor Haworth in particular; that it was the joint invention of Emily and Anne increased its distinction, giving the invention a note of conspiracy. It made, for the two sisters, a "world elsewhere"; that world is the source of the "peculiar music" which Charlotte heard in Emily's poems. Gondal was a fiction, not necessarily better than historical fact in every respect but certainly better in respect of freedom. To Emily it offered a world in which she could play roles far more diverse than those available to her at Haworth. The roles she chose to play are now male, now female, now adult, now child; but, more important, the roles are played in an aboriginal world. We are to think of Gondal as a place not yet marked out by conventions, laws, morals, society. These forces have not yet arrived; to Emily Brontë, so much the better. The only laws are those of passion and will: punishment is primitive, but natural. Gondal is anthropological, Haworth is historical. Like *Wuthering Heights* it proposes a mode of life which exists, powerful and intransigent, beneath the accretions of manners, morals, and society. That Emily Brontë's imagination needed such a world can hardly be disputed.

But the creation of Gondal did not really extend her imagination: it fulfilled the needs of that imagination without changing its nature or composition. Emily Brontë could not suppress herself in favor of her invented characters, could not, or would not. The characters, once invented, are allowed to move and live in Gondal, but they are still extreme functions of Emily Brontë's own personality. She does not release them; she endows them not with free will, but with her own will in diverse forms. When they speak, therefore, what we hear is a kind of ventriloquism. There is no precise word for this, as far as I know. "Dramatic monologue" will not do, because this proposes a strict separation of speaker and poet. "Soliloquy" will not do, because this implies a speaker communing with her own feelings. The word we need is somewhere between these two phrases; but where, precisely, and what word?

Perhaps we can approach it by noting a certain sequence. We call that imagination "Shakespearean" which delights in registering modes of feeling not its own. We may call another kind of imagination "Yeatsian" if it has a particular flair for registering modes of feeling related to its own by contrast and opposition: we have in mind, for this description, Yeats's account of the imagination as operating in terms of mask, role-playing, anti-self, and so forth. *A Vision* and "Ego Dominus Tuus" are the theoretical occasions. There is also, for a third stage, the imagination which we may call "Proustian": thinking of a remark by Roland Barthes in *Le Degré Zéro de l'Écriture* that "a character of Proust materializes into the opacity of a particular language, and it is really at this level that his whole historical situation . . . is integrated and ordered." Finally, there is an imagination which we call "Eliotic," which delights in secreting "characters" from materials entirely verbal, the characters therefore being merely virtual or ostensible. Thus Hugh Kenner has observed in *The Invisible Poet* that "J. Alfred Prufrock is a name plus a Voice: he isn't a 'character' cut out of the rest of the universe and equipped with a history and a little necessary context, like the speaker of a Browning monologue." So there are several identifiable positions between the two extremes, soliloquy and drama; more, indeed, than the standard critical terminology encourages us to recognize. Josiah Royce has shown, in his *Lectures on Modern Idealism,* that it was characteristic of nineteenth-century idealists to develop by way of dialectics, truth being a process in the grappling of opposites. Arnold speaks, in his Preface to the 1853 edition of his *Poems*, of "the dialogue of the mind with itself" as constituting the modern element in literature. But Emily Brontë does not commit herself to these procedures. The relation between her and, say, Augusta in the Gondal poems is not Shakespearean; Emily does not suppress herself for Augusta's sake. On the contrary, Augusta is established only in the sense that Emily's imagination secretes her; her fictive existence depends upon Emily's will and is, indeed, an extreme version of that will. Yeats speaks somewhere of "the will trying to do the work of the imagination": his tone is sharp in rebuke. In Emily Brontë's Gondal poems the will restrains the act of the imagination, sets an outer limit beyond which the imagination, in the creation of characters, may not go. In detail, the same limit is marked by the opacity of the language; the Proustian comparison need not be forced.

# Chronology of Important Dates

1816     Charlotte born.

1817     Branwell born.

1818     Emily born.

1820     Anne born.

           Family moves to the parsonage at Haworth, nine miles from Bradford in Yorkshire.

1821     Mrs. Brontë dies. Household managed by Miss Branwell, the elder sister.

1824     Charlotte and Emily go to Cowan's Bridge school (the "Lowood" of *Jane Eyre*).

1829     Charlotte and Branwell begin their Angrian stories and "magazines."

1831     Charlotte goes to Miss Wooler's school at Roehead (the source of much of the material in *Shirley*).

1831     Emily and Anne begin the Gondal saga. (The creation of an imaginary world like Angria, which they wrote about for the rest of their lives. Only the poems are extant.)

1835     Charlotte goes to Miss Wooler's school as a governess, taking Emily (and later Anne) with her as a pupil.

1842     With the aim of establishing their own school at Haworth, Charlotte and Emily go to learn foreign languages at M. Héger's school in Brussels (the source of material for *The Professor* and *Villette*).

1844     Charlotte finally returns to Haworth.

1846     Under the names Currer, Ellis, and Acton Bell, the Brontës produce, at their own expense, their first volume of poems. Two copies were sold.

1847     (August) Charlotte's *Jane Eyre* accepted and published within three months by Smith, Elder & Co. An immediate success.

(December) Emily's *Wuthering Heights* and Anne's *Agnes Grey* published. Poorly received.

1848        Anne's *Tenant of Wildfell Hall* published.

Branwell dies.

Emily dies.

1849        Charlotte's *Shirley* published.

Charlotte meets Thackeray, to whom she dedicated *Jane Eyre*.

Anne dies.

1851        Charlotte meets Harriett Martineau. Visits the Great Exhibition.

1853        Her *Villette* published.

Meets Mrs. Gaskell, her future biographer.

1854        Marries Arthur Nicholls, her father's curate.

1855        Charlotte dies. Buried in Haworth churchyard with Emily and Anne.

1857        Charlotte's *The Professor* published posthumously.

Mrs. Gaskell's *Life of Charlotte Brontë* published.

# Notes on the Editor and Contributors

IAN GREGOR, Professor of Modern English Literature in the University of Kent, Canterbury, is editor of a critical edition of Matthew Arnold's *Culture & Anarchy* and author (with Brian Nicholas) of *The Moral & The Story* and (with Mark Kinkead-Weekes) of *William Golding: A Critical Study*.

RICHARD CHASE is the author of *The American Novel and Its Tradition, Emily Dickinson,* and *Walt Whitman Reconsidered.* He has edited numerous collections of fiction by American authors, as well as anthologies of folk tales and songs.

DENIS DONOGHUE is Professor of Modern English and American Literature in University College, Dublin. He is the author of *The Third Voice, Connoisseurs of Chaos, The Ordinary World,* and *Jonathan Swift: A Critical Introduction.*

PHILIP DREW, Senior Lecturer in English in the University of Glasgow, is author of *The Poetry of Browning: A Critical Introduction* and editor of *Robert Browning: A Collection of Critical Essays.*

JOHN HAGAN is Professor of English at Harpur College of the State University of New York at Binghamton.

ROBERT B. HEILMAN, Professor and Chairman of the Department of English at the University of Washington, is the author of *American in English Fiction, 1760–1800, This Great State: Image and Structure in King Lear,* and *Magic in the Web: Action and Language in Othello* and is the editor of several collections of drama and fiction.

ANDREW HOOK is Lecturer in English and American Literature, at the University of Edinburgh.

MARK KINKEAD-WEEKES is Senior Lecturer in English, University of Kent, Canterbury. He is the author (with Ian Gregor) of *William Golding: A Critical Study* and editor of *Twentieth Century Interpretations of The Rainbow.*

DAVID LODGE, Lecturer in English at the University of Birmingham, is the author of *The Language of Fiction,* as well as three novels: *The Cinemagoers, Ginger, You're Barmy,* and *The British Museum is Falling Down.*

ROBERT C. McKIBBEN, formerly of the University of New Hampshire, is the author of "The Image of the Book in *Wuthering Heights.*"

C. P. SANGER, a Chancery lawyer, first published his essay under the initials C.P.S. in 1926.

175

# Selected Bibliography

The most comprehensive edition available at present is the *Shakespeare Head Brontë*, edited by T. J. Wise and J. A. Symington, 19 volumes (Oxford, 1931–38). The most complete edition of Emily Brontë's poems is that edited by C. W. Hatfield (New York and London, 1941).

There is in preparation a definitive edition of the Brontë novels. The first volume is The Clarendon Edition (eds. Ian and Jane Jack) has appeared— *Jane Eyre* (eds. Jane Jack and Margaret Smith (Oxford, 1969).

## Life and Letters

Gaskell, E. C. *The Life of Charlotte Brontë*. 1857. A classic study, reprinted several times.

Gérin, Winifred. *Charlotte Brontë: The Evolution of Genius*. Oxford, 1967.

Hanson, L. and Hanson, E. M. *The Four Brontës*. London, 1949.

Lane, M. *The Brontë Story: A Reconsideration of Mrs. Gaskell's Life of Charlotte Brontë*. London, 1948.

Spark, Muriel, ed. *The Brontë Letters*. London, 1954.

## Juvenilia

Ratchford, Fannie. *The Brontës' Web of Childhood*. New York, 1941.

———. *Gondal's Queen*. Austin, Texas and Edinburgh, 1955.

## Criticism

Critical essays on *Wuthering Heights* in particular have now assumed the proportions of a heavy industry. What follows is a very select list of the writing that has been done, chiefly during the last twenty years. It excludes the essays contained in the present collection.

Abbreviations: *NCF—Nineteenth Century Fiction; PMLA—Publication of the Modern Language Association*.

Allott, Miriam. "The Rejection of Heathcliff?" *Essays in Criticism* VIII (1958).

Buchen, Irving H. "Emily Brontë and the Metaphysics of Childhood and Love." *NCF* XXII (1967).

Buckley, Vincent. "Passion and Control in *Wuthering Heights.*" *The Southern Review* I (1964).

Cecil, David. *Early Victorian Novelists.* London, 1934.

Craik, W. A. *The Brontë Novels.* London, 1968.

Cooper-Willis, I. "The Authorship of Wuthering Heights." *The Trollopian* II (1947).

Ewbank, Inga-Stina. *"Their Proper Sphere: A Study of the Brontë Sisters as Early Victorian Female Novelists."* Harvard and London, 1966.

Fike, Francis. "Bitter Herbs & Wholesome Medicines: Love as Theological Affirmation in *Wuthering Heights.*" *NCF* XXIII (1968).

Ford, Boris. "Wuthering Heights." *Scrutiny* VII (1939).  ....  ..  ..

Fraser, John. "The Name of Action: Nelly Dean and *Wuthering Heights.*" *NCF* XX (1966).

Goodridge, Frank. *Emily Brontë: Wuthering Heights.* London, 1964.

Gose, Elliot B. *"Wuthering Heights:* The Heath & The Hearth." *NCF* XXI (1966).

Hafley, James. "The Villain in *Wuthering Heights.*" *NCF* XIII (1958).

Heilman, R. B. "Charlotte Brontë, Reason and the Moon." *NCF* XIV (1960).

Kettle, Arnold. *"Wuthering Heights."* In *Introduction to the English Novel,* vol. I. London, 1950.

Klingopulos, G. D. *"Wuthering Heights."* *Scrutiny* XIV (1947).

Johnson, E. D. H. "Daring the Dread Glance: Charlotte Brontë's Treatment of the Supernatural in *Villette.*" *NCF* XX (1966).

Jordan, John E. "The Ironic Vision of Emily Brontë." *NCF* XX (1965).

Langman, F. H. *"Wuthering Heights."* *Essays in Criticism* XV (1965).

Leavis, F. R. and Q. D. *Lectures in America.* London, 1969.

Martin, R. B. *The Accents of Persuasion: Charlotte Brontë's Novels.* New York and London, 1966.

Mathison, John K. "Nelly Dean and The Power of *Wuthering Heights.*" *NCF* XI (1956).

Moser, Thomas. "What is the matter with Emily Jane? Conflicting Impulses in *Wuthering Heights.*" *NCF* XVII (1962).

Scargill, M. H. "All Passion Spent: A Revaluation of *Jane Eyre.*" *University of Toronto Quarterly* XIX (1950).

Shannon, Edgar. "The Present Tense in *Jane Eyre.*" *NCF* X (1955).

Thompson, Wade. "Infanticide and Sadism in *Wuthering Heights.*" *PMLA* LXXVIII (1963).

Tillotson, Kathleen. *Novels of the 1840's.* Oxford, 1954.

Traversi, Derek. *"Wuthering Heights after a Hundred Years."* *Dublin Review* CCXLV (1949).

Turnell, Martin. *"Wuthering Heights."* *Dublin Review* CCVI (1940).

Visick, Mary. *The Genesis of "Wuthering Heights."* Hong Kong and London, 1958.

Watson, Melvin R. "Form and Substance in the Brontë Novels." In *From Austen to Conrad,* edited by R. C. Rathburn and M. Steinmann, Jr. Minneapolis, 1958.

# TWENTIETH CENTURY VIEWS

## British Authors

(Continued on next page)

13975